Daughter of

GLORIAVALE

MY LIFE IN A RELIGIOUS CULT

LILIA TARAWA

ALLEN&UNWIN

SYDNEY•MELBOURNE•AUCKLAND•LONDON

First published in 2017

Allen & Unwin
Level 3, 228 Queen Street
Auckland 1010, New Zealand
Phone: (64 9) 377 3800

Email: info@allenandunwin.com
Web: www.allenandunwin.co.nz

83 Alexander Street
Crows Nest NSW 2065, Australia
Phone: (61 2) 8425 0100

A catalogue record for this book is available
from the National Library of New Zealand

ISBN 978 1 760631 49 9

Internal design by Anna Egan-Reid
Set in 11.5/18 pt Berling
Printed and bound in Australia by Griffin Press

10 9 8 7 6 5 4 3

CONTENTS

Foreword

I have written dystopian fiction, but Lilia Tarawa, the grand-daughter of Hopeful Christian, has lived the reality of it. I'm not the only one who finds it astonishing that an enclosed cult such as Gloriavale can survive and flourish in New Zealand in the twenty-first century, but thrive it does and thanks to the many documentaries, we've been able to see inside the cult—to some extent.

The secretive nature of the community leads to speculation. What's it really like there? Are people as happy as they appear to be? Why are those who've left turned away when they try to visit family still in Gloriavale? The documentaries tended to throw up more questions than Hopeful Christian and the Gloriavale hierarchy would permit them to answer. Probably the most-asked question has been how a convicted sexual offender can continue to lead his community. Lilia grew up believing her grandfather had been imprisoned by the evil world that was trying to destroy the church. During the course of writing her story, she discovered much she hadn't known about Hopeful Christian, the Star of God.

It's very satisfying to learn how the unusual names came about, and why people are happy to give their new babies names such as Dutiful, Meekness, Constant or Ardent. It's enlightening, too, to see how Lilia felt about the uniform she had to wear.

Why do people stay in an environment where every aspect of their lives is under the strict and rigid control of the leaders? What keeps them there? We're only too aware of the dark side of Gloriavale, but as Lilia's story shows this is also a loving, supportive and fun-loving community. It's a great place to live ... if you don't question the men. Here, Lilia speaks openly about the tension she suffered between what she knew in her heart to be right and what she saw happening around her.

How do people leave? How do ex-residents cope in the outside world when they've never handled money, caught a bus or bought their own clothes? What do they now believe about God, about Hopeful's preaching?

Lilia Tarawa is a strong, intelligent and beautiful young woman who's been able to forge her own identity despite the best efforts of her grandfather to make her into a meek and submissive Godly woman who accepted his every utterance without question.

It's been a privilege to mentor Lilia as she's been writing the story of her most unusual life.

Kia kaha, Lilia.

Fleur Beale
September 2017

ONE

Chaos

For I am come to set a man at variance against his father, and the daughter against her mother, and the daughter in law against her mother in law.

—THE BIBLE (KING JAMES VERSION), MATTHEW 10:35

There was nothing special about the mealtime to indicate it would end in chaos. As always, our community of more than 500 was sitting in our family groups at the long tables in the big dining room, chatting to each other as we ate. I was five years old, so I don't remember particular details but there was always lots of laughter and good-natured teasing between family and friends. Grandad Neville hadn't yet picked up the microphone to start preaching.

Wham! The main door was flung open, a man shouted and

1

immediately all the adults leaped to their feet in a headlong rush for the door. Others who couldn't get through the crush turned to tear back through the dining room and get out through the kitchen.

What was happening?

Somebody tugged my sleeve. It was my almost-twin, my cousin Bethany. 'What's happening, Lil? Why are people angry?'

We huddled together, terrified. Why were our men throwing a blanket over my aunt Prayer and her little daughter Cherish? Why were they carrying them away?

The crush of people swept Bethany and me up in a forest of legs and long skirts until I found myself outside on the lot in front of the building, mixed up in the shouting, yelling crowd. I'd lost Bethany.

What was going on? I had to find out. It was too scary not knowing. I wriggled under arms and around legs, pushing my way to the front, while the shouting raged above me.

There was a car parked in the middle of the lot. I didn't recognise it or the blond-haired man beside it. He wore strange clothes and he looked fierce and furious. He was shouting at the leaders, arguing with them. I'd never heard anyone so angry ever before. A whole bunch of our men pressed in around him, and I couldn't see anything, but the shouting grew louder. Then it looked like the Gloriavale men were swarming over the man and I heard the thump when they threw him to the ground. I cowered back against somebody's legs. I didn't want to be here any longer.

'Stop!' I heard a woman scream. 'Stop it right now!'

I clutched my throat in terror.

Mum! She threw herself into the fray, trying to break up the fight. *Don't hurt her. Don't hurt her.*

'That's enough!' she screamed. 'This isn't right.'

I was crying and so scared. Women weren't allowed to shout at men. Women weren't allowed to tell men what to do. But they took notice of my mother. They stepped back from the stranger. Some of them looked shocked and one or two of them seemed ashamed of themselves. I let my hands drop from my throat. Mum was so brave. Gloriavale women never set themselves against the actions of any man. I prayed she wouldn't be punished.

The blond man jumped up on his car. I slapped my hands over my ears. His voice was too loud and I couldn't shut it out. 'I've come to see my daughter! You've been hiding her here without my knowledge. I'm her father and it's my right to see her!'

My aunt Lani came running, Bethany clinging to her. She scooped me up and hurried us away, repeating over and over, 'Don't worry. It's OK, you're safe, don't worry.'

Lani wouldn't tell us who the man was. She said she didn't know what he was talking about—hiding his wife and daughter! What a thing to say.

Bethany and I looked at each other. It was plain Lani did know, just like it was clear the leaders had ordered the adults not to talk about the blond man or his accusations.

I learned later that he was my mother's brother Phil Cooper and he'd run away from Gloriavale before I was born. Not only that, but he'd abducted his children and snuck back a few weeks later to kidnap his wife.

Gloriavale told us that Phil was a wicked sinner. He'd come to Gloriavale that day determined to see his youngest daughter,

Cherish. She was my younger cousin and we played together all the time. I had so many photos of her and Bethany and me.

We'd had a television crew in the community filming a documentary about us and it was them who had broken the news to Phil that he had a two-year-old daughter called Cherish. My aunt Sandy had been pregnant with Cherish when she gave up the world and her other six children to return to Gloriavale for the sake of their souls. She conspired with the church leaders to keep the pregnancy and birth a secret. Sandy called herself Prayer and gave Cherish the surname of Darling, not Cooper like her father.

When I was older, Mum told me Phil had become furious when he heard the news. He had another child? A little daughter? Neville had no right to keep her away from him. He came roaring into Gloriavale determined to see Cherish, but the leaders hid her from him.

~

Phil was one of the sixteen children born to my grandparents Neville and Gloria Cooper, with fifteen living to adulthood. When I was growing up, seven of them were Gloriavale members and I grew up surrounded by about 50 first cousins and many more second cousins.

Grandad Neville had firm ideas about contraception. 'We in Gloriavale don't murder our unborn children. We don't flush our children down the toilet,' he would say. 'You kids who are number three or later, if your family lived on the outside, you wouldn't have been born.'

Contraception was murder and forbidden. Abortion wasn't

mentioned except as a sin committed by those in the evil outside world.

I knew nothing of the world outside Gloriavale's gates, but I supposed I must have had just as many cousins growing up in the outside world too, but they were living worldly lives and when they died they'd be consumed in the fires of hell. If I ever did think about them, it was with deep pity.

We were well acquainted with the concept of hell. We knew all about the fiery pits of brimstone awaiting sinners and we shuddered at images of the Devil raking burning bodies with claw-like forks.

The leader and founder of Gloriavale was my grandfather, the controversial Neville Cooper. I loved him dearly when I was little and wrote 'letters' to him when he was in prison. *Dear Grandad, I love you and I miss you. Please come home. Love from Lilia.*

I didn't know why he was in prison, but was later told that the world was trying to persecute him and our church.

TWO

Genesis

Go ye into the world and preach the gospel to
every creature.

—THE BIBLE (KING JAMES VERSION), MARK 16:15

Neville Cooper began life in Australia. He married my gentle,
sweet-natured grandmother Gloria when she was just sixteen
and didn't have a chance of ever standing up to her charismatic,
forceful husband. But she loved him and submitted to his will,
so from what I can tell it was a happy marriage.

Neville was a born-again Christian evangelist and he preached
the Word of God to church communities throughout Australia.
Unfortunately for him and his family, the pastors of each church
he associated himself with weren't submissive and compliant the
way Gloria was, and there'd inevitably be a mighty splitting and

parting of the ways. My grandfather would then find another church in a different area only to repeat the pattern. Eventually the Cooper family ended up in northern Queensland, where Neville finally found a way to bring the Word of God, as preached by Neville Cooper, to the common people.

He called his mission The Voice of Deliverance, and modelled it on similar principles to those of the North American evangelist Billy Graham, who preached the message of eternal life in heaven for the saved and everlasting punishment in hell for sinners. The foundational belief was that all men everywhere were lost and faced the judgement of God. Only the virgin-blood sacrifice of Jesus by way of his crucifixion could cover their sin and grant access to heaven if they became converted Christians and were baptised in His name.

Neville's strength of purpose and charisma attracted others to him and his cause. People believed in him and his message and were keen to help. A farmer donated a Fairchild aircraft to the mission and Neville was on his way. As an ex-airforce pilot, he was now able to extend his evangelical outreach to even more isolated parts of Australia. He became known as the 'Flying Evangelist', drawing hundreds of people from all over the isolated countryside to his sermons.

Back at home, Gloria birthed baby after baby, and coped uncomplainingly with Neville's regular absences, which often lasted months at a time. She was the epitome of a biblical New Testament wife who lived in submission to her husband and walked with a meek and quiet spirit.

When she was pregnant with my mother, her tenth child, she accompanied Neville and two Australian Aboriginal missionaries on a flight from Maryborough to Coolangatta. Disaster struck. About 190 kilometres north of Brisbane, over rugged and heavily timbered country, the plane developed engine trouble and at 1000 feet above ground it cut out all together.

Neville cut the switches to prevent fire. 'Pray, John Dalton. Pray for our lives!'

John burst into prayer, but it was in another language that not even he understood. It was like a scene from the Book of Acts and there was no panic in the cabin.

The Fairchild hit the treetops. The wings ripped off first, then the tail tore away, leaving only the fuselage with the four passengers inside. The cabin hurtled forward, ramming trees as it went, and hit the ground at terrifying speed, almost 100 kilometres per hour. When the pilot's door swung open, Neville climbed out, petrol pouring over him. The others, miraculously all alive, scrambled quickly out of the cabin.

John Dalton had suffered a broken neck, but the other three were relatively unscathed apart from nasty bruising. It was unbelievable. Neville, ever the opportunist, reached into the wreckage, pulled out his 8-mm colour movie camera and shot 40 feet of film capturing the whole story.

For three nights, they survived in wild country infested with snakes, mosquitoes and sandflies. Their only sustenance was a bag of mangoes they'd recovered from the wreckage and water from a nearby hole. Neville tore strips of calico from the skin of the plane and used them to spell HELP in an adjacent clearing.

No help arrived, so my grandfather, in typical fashion, took their survival into his own hands. He was in pain because the crash had damaged one of his kidneys, but he had God on his side. The first thing to do was get across the nearby saltwater Kauri Creek.

He dismantled the 25-gallon petrol tank from the aircraft, tied it to his body with a piece of rope from the wreckage and launched himself into the strong current. It was no good. He couldn't make the crossing.

Plan B: The next day Gloria unravelled a blue jumper she'd been making and knitted it into a rope. They tied it to the piece of real rope and Neville dived again into the swift current. This time he had the rope around his waist, while the party on the bank held the other end. He was three-quarters of the way across when the rope broke. He kept swimming for his life and eventually dragged his exhausted body up the opposite bank.

He found a fisherman who, unsurprisingly, could barely believe the story this soaked, insane-looking man told him, but agreed to return to the crash site and collect helpers on the way.

The rescuers declared the survival to be a Christmas Day miracle. The area policeman, Constable Rackemann, said, 'It was a miracle that anyone survived the crash. The aircraft was literally ripped to shreds and scattered over an area 200 yards [180 metres] across.'

On Wednesday 29 December 1965, Brisbane's *Telegraph News Pictorial* published a photo of the crash site under the headline: 'The Miracle: Four Survived This Plane Crash'.

Neville and his passengers attested that it 'was only God that [had] delivered them from certain death'.

Five months later Gloria gave birth to my mother and called her Miracle in honour of the incredible survival.

THREE

A life in common

I will share all my life and possessions with every member of this Church and Community, holding all things in common with them and caring for all their needs as well as I care for my own.

—*WHAT WE BELIEVE*,* 'THE COMMITMENT', P. 24

Grandad Neville never encouraged monetary offerings at his sermons or events, relying solely on faith in God to provide for his family's earthly needs. He supported his family by taking any job available in the periods between his evangelical missions. If he didn't know how to do something, he soon learned. He was,

---

* *What We Believe* is Gloriavale's doctrine, including how to interpret the Bible.

at various times, a panel beater, a baker and a mechanic.

The family lived in a caravan that Neville built from scratch. He was the one who sewed all the dresses for his five eldest daughters and he taught Gloria how to make clothing for the rest of the children. Sometimes the family would receive donations of money from Christian supporters, which were a massive help and confirmed for Neville that God would indeed provide.

He travelled to New Zealand on a gospel revival campaign, and the local churches celebrated the arrival of a spiritual leader who taught practical Christian advice rather than complicated religious theories. Neville's fresh perspective and down-to-earth sermons wrought new flame into limp church cultures. He was one of New Zealand's most popular and successful evangelists of the time.

The churches clamoured to have him speak. Congregations needed spiritual revival, counselling in their marriages and advice for rearing their children. At this stage, Neville gave wholesome guidance for practical Christian living, transforming many families' lives for the better.

He returned to Australia to collect his wife and children and they emigrated to New Zealand. After eighteen months of travelling up and down the length of the country, the family came to rest in Rangiora, near Christchurch, where Neville helped set up the local New Life Church. It was never going to work, though, because the incumbent pastor didn't accept all my grandfather's ideas. The old pattern repeated itself and Neville moved away to establish his own church. The difference this time was that he took half the congregation with him. They became known as The Christian Church at Springbank.

One morning Neville saw a couple pushing their baby to church in the rain while another family arrived in two expensive cars. The sight compelled him to preach about an equal, sharing Christian life based on Christ's principles of love and unselfish charity towards others.

'Why don't we sell our expensive cars, buy a bunch of cheap cars, fix them up and distribute them to families in need?' he suggested.

The church responded enthusiastically to the idea. They sold the unnecessary road bling and spent the money on bargains at a car auction. Neville's mechanical skills came in handy for restorations and the first vehicle was soon roadworthy.

On Sunday they wrapped the car in shiny black plastic, topped it with a gigantic bow and presented it to the couple Neville had seen walking in the rain. 'For us? For free?' They burst into tears of gratitude.

It was a time of excitement, happiness and joy for the church. It was Christ's teachings of love made practical—'He that hath two give to him that hath none'—and it was the birth of a new-era Christian community.

My grandfather's next step was to teach the congregation about total unselfishness and faith in God to provide. For one month, no one purchased anything for themselves. Instead, each family was assigned to care for another church family's needs, including groceries, rent, power and whatever else. No one knew who was caring for them. People went to their assignee's home to restock the cupboards and search out bills that needed to be paid. This fostered a culture of giving and equality, leading to people holding possessions in common pools rather than personal ownership. The church leaders started to purchase groceries in bulk to save money, but how could they distribute the food equally? Neville's son-in-law Tony Bellette invented a point system to apportion food equally between men, women and children. It worked perfectly.

Two of Neville's daughters married brothers from the Harrison family, well-to-do farm owners. The brothers inherited a farm at Cust which they donated to the church, which built a school centre and church complex on the property. The church set up thriving businesses—plumbing, drainlaying, gasfitting, aircraft engineering, motor mechanics, waterbed manufacturing and cabinetry. They farmed pigs and sheep and grew crops. They were astute businessmen and very hard workers.

The point system was used to divvy up wages and profits from the church businesses, but soon the church was providing everything a family could need, so people no longer needed their own money and wages were no longer paid out. Eventually people shut down their personal bank accounts and relied solely on distributions from the church to survive. Since the community was working together as a team, there was never anyone in need or poverty.

I'd been told stories of the church's history up to this point, but once I began writing about my life in Gloriavale I discovered that certain pieces of the puzzle were missing. I found myself needing—and wanting—to find out how a church that was truly Christian and loving in the beginning could have evolved into the one I knew, which was often far from loving, kind or forgiving. I wondered why people on the outside of Gloriavale hated my grandfather so much and I began to wonder, too, if the story that the leaders had told us to explain why Grandad had gone to prison was correct.

I began to search deeper.

~

I learned that not all the church members were on board with this new way of common living. Each radical change saw the culling of those who wanted to retain independence from the church, including some of my aunts and uncles. In the end, only those who, like my parents, fully believed in Neville's godliness remained.

Neville preached that people should wear modest clothing as taught in the Bible. Clothes were not to be tight, closefitting or revealing. They were to be simple and godly, not vain, costly or startling in style. He defined modest as meaning women would cover themselves in dresses to the ankle, wrist and neck. Men would wear full-length trousers and shirts with long sleeves.

Jewellery and make-up were vain, ungodly and forbidden. Christians, especially women, were to 'adorn themselves in modest apparel, with shamefacedness and sobriety; not with broided hair, or gold, or pearls, or costly array.' (1 Timothy 2:9)

Nobody wore a wedding ring—Neville told us that the giving and receiving of rings had been adopted from ancient pagan rituals and that such practices would defile the Church of God. He told us that a marriage bond was formed by two things: a man and a woman's vows to each other and the sexual act of cleaving together as one flesh. After that, a husband and wife were mated for life and only death could break the bond.

Christmas, Easter, birthdays—we didn't celebrate any of them because no day should be observed above another. Whenever Grandad preached about it, I'd imagine Second Day getting its nose out of joint if we had a party on Fifth Day. However, we just accepted it. It was all we knew, so anything different was weird and wrong.

I don't remember the people wearing anything other than the blue uniforms, but they hadn't always dressed that way. Before, when people wore clothes of their own choosing, there was a lot of vanity and competition between women. Neville heard about the Hutterite and Amish communities in America, who wore plain, matching uniforms. Great idea! He designed a dark navy dress for all the women to wear. At first, the women of Springbank didn't take to their new garb too well. They felt their rights to choose pretty colours or garments that suited their body type were being taken away. However, they knew they must submit to the will of God and give up their prideful vanity.

More rules began to appear, and after a few years all the females from toddlers upwards wore long blue dresses and all the males wore long dark-blue trousers and light-blue shirts.

When my mother was pregnant with me, Grandma Gloria began experiencing raging headaches. Tests revealed a massive brain tumour. Neville was grief-stricken and barely able to cope with the reality of losing his faithful wife. During this time my mother was his biggest supporter and paced the hospital corridors with him as Gloria went under the knife.

Sadly, Gloria lived only two short months before going to be with the Lord. When she was buried, those of her children who were not a part of the church weren't permitted to go to the funeral. Mum's brother Michael, who suffered from a mental health issue, was unable to contain his grief and committed suicide.

I've seen video footage of my grandmother and listened to countless church members telling stories about her unselfish and caring nature. She was held in extremely high regard, adored by all. Not a single person spoke ill of her. My mother and my aunt Patience have the same loving and gentle nature as she did, as well as the inner strength Gloria was famous for.

~

The Christian Church at Springbank outgrew the space available at Cust. It was time for growth and they searched for a place with more land to settle and farm. What a relief when they discovered a remote dairy farm in Haupiri Valley, on the West Coast. The valley held the promise of new adventures and opportunity.

They purchased the property and soon acquired another one just across the Haupiri River. The second farm across the river was called Glenhopeful.

The church buzzed with excitement. A new home!

The first lot of pioneers set course and trekked into the rugged valley to explore their brand-new land. Haupiri Valley was breathtaking, a picture of West Coast wildness that sprawled for miles on end. The lake sparkled like polished glass and mist steamed off the foothills into the Southern Alps. Icy rivers cut down from the mountains through the forests and pastures. It was the land of promise. God's people were home.

The men travelled from Cust to build hostels for the faithful, and in 1999 the first hostel was ready for occupation. Neville called his church Gloriavale in honour of my deceased grandmother. Shortly after, he made good on the Bible teaching 'It is not good for man to be alone' by choosing a new wife: an elderly widow called Anna.

Brick by brick, a mighty church began to rise from the land. Massive sheds were erected and transformed into housing until the four large hostels could be constructed. When residents moved into the hostels, the sheds were repurposed into service sheds for business offices and manufacturing and engineering workshops. They planted a main centre for communal gatherings and feasts, designing it to serve a host of needs. It housed a commercially equipped kitchen, large mess hall, school rooms, preschool and office spaces. The men constructed a long shed on the back of the centre and fitted it with a commercial-grade laundry, a large boiler and various living spaces.

Gloriavale became an economic powerhouse on the West Coast. As well as the two large dairy farms, they founded a number of enterprises, including a sphagnum-moss export business, Discoveries in Gardening. My father was the business manager and had to travel for long periods overseas to market the products. We also had a farmed-deer business exporting velvet and producing venison. Any part of the carcass that wasn't used got sent to the pet-food manufacturing plant or was rendered down to fertilise the pastures. Nothing should go to waste.

When I was young, the church had an airline called West Coast Air, but it didn't prosper. Now they have the only helicopter-servicing business on the Coast.

The farm properties run up into the foothills of the Southern Alps—the mountain peak closest to us was called Mt Brian

O'Lynn. The closeness to bush and wilderness was a gift to such an enterprising group of men. They saw an opportunity to establish a world-class adventure-hunting business catering to wealthy overseas clients. Gloriavale land offered a variety of game—wild boar, ram, goat and game birds. They helicoptered their guests into the Alps to shoot mountain tahr and chamois. The Haupiri River was rich with fish, and Gloriavale added that to the package. They bred trophy red deer and established one of the best huntable herds of Asian water buffalo available in New Zealand. They built luxurious lodges in the valley to accommodate their guests and called their venture Wilderness Quest NZ.

We women looked after the guests by cleaning and preparing the lodges for each group. The women would prep the food in the lodge kitchen and stay to cook the meal if that's what the client wanted. The lodge food was always much better, tastier and more varied than we ever got to eat.

From the moment I saw the first hunting photos, I wanted to go too, but such a fun, challenging and exciting adventure belonged to the men's realm; it was only the men who got to go out in the hills to act as guides for the clients. The photos looked far more interesting that anything in the domestic realm. I thought I'd be better at it than a lot of the men, but I didn't even bother asking to go.

My grandfather was an inventor who encouraged innovation among his male followers. The Gloriavale men were adept at inventing or adapting machinery to serve the needs of the community's businesses. Right from the earliest days of his church, Neville had strictly defined the roles of men and women. Men are the head of the home and provide for the family. Women are to be keepers at home. Woe betide you if you want to step outside of your God-determined role. If you're a woman and you do rebelliously want a broader life than being a domestic worker in one of the four teams of women, then you have to be cunning to organise this for yourself. I was able to manoeuvre my way into doing the computer graphic-design work for the businesses and so reduced the time I had to spend doing the drudgery of domestic work.

I don't have many early memories of my grandfather, but I do remember driving to Christchurch to visit him in prison. The clearest memory I have of that visit is of going to a dairy where I was allowed to buy chocolate—a total luxury for a Gloriavale child.

I was about five and I'd just learned to write. I sent Grandad Neville simple letters telling him how much I missed him and couldn't wait for him to return home. I didn't understand why he wasn't with us. Why had the bad men taken him away and locked him up?

It wasn't until I was older that I learned that Grandad Neville had been jailed on three charges of indecent sexual assault towards ex-Gloriavale members aged twelve to nineteen years old at the time.

I had a difficult time coming to terms with the accusations against my grandfather. Surely they couldn't be true? I realised a part of me didn't want to face the hard truth of his wrongdoing and I broke down when I understood the extent of it.

What I do know is that Neville Cooper is a man of extremes. His attitude to sex and what was appropriate to share with his own sixteen children while they were growing up was extremely Victorian. They were punished if they mentioned anything to do with it. My mother repeated a joke she'd heard and didn't fully understand. She got a hiding for it, but no explanation as to why it was wrong. She told me that at one time she went into her parents' bedroom during the afternoon and they were both in bed, under the covers. She thought nothing of it because her mother often rested in the afternoons. When Grandad Neville came out of the bedroom to spank her she was completely bewildered.

When Neville's daughters began to marry, it became clear that their upbringing had left them woefully unprepared for the realities of the sexual aspects of marriage. In Neville's usual manner, he decided to fix the problem, but, as was also typical, he took it on himself to do so and again went to the extreme.

The hippie counter-culture craze had by this time swept the globe. Following the end of what became known as the 'Summer of Love' in San Francisco, about 750,000 North Americans had migrated into more than 10,000 intentional communes with similarities to the Gloriavale Christian Community.

Neville felt that the hippie movement, with its emphasis on sexual freedom, had something to offer—provided that the sex was between married couples. He began to hold married couples' meetings, where he lectured on the topic of sex. He told his followers, 'We need to loosen up sexually and be more open-minded about it. Don't be afraid to talk about sex and teach your children about it.' He began preaching that it didn't matter if children saw their parents having sex. 'Better they learn about sex from their parents than from their peers,' he reasoned. It was the parents' responsibility to properly prepare their children for marriage. As part of the new regime, couples were encouraged to be in the spa pool naked and have their children there with them.

He was still strict with unmarried people. Open talk about sexuality among singles would only lead them to fornication, but the whole change in attitude had taken a sharp detour from complete suppression of sexual awareness to the absolute opposite. It seemed the changes happened overnight and the sudden turn shocked Neville's children.

My own parents realised things were going too far and kept out of it. When friends began telling them of things that had happened, they were horrified. It was a dreadful situation for them, because disagreeing with Neville always resulted in public humiliation and being shouted at for hours in a Men's Meeting. They'd also become terrified they would go to hell for rebellious thoughts against the man God had appointed as their church leader.

The only consolation for my parents was being able to talk confidentially to a brother and sister of my mother's who were also in the community.

Neville was always lifted up as a man of God, and people believed he could do no wrong. Any actions he took were justified by good motivation. I was upset when I heard that he hadn't apologised to the victims at court or acknowledged the error of his actions.

Things came to crisis point for the outside family when his second wife, Anna, died and Neville again remarried. They discovered that their twice-widowed, 69-year-old father had married a girl of seventeen. They were horrified. It was time to try to do something about what was happening in the community regarding sexual practices. Several of them, including my uncle Phil, filed eleven complaints of sexual misconduct against Neville. The police raided the community and arrested him. This encouraged more ex-members to come forward with their stories.

It was a hideous time for my mother. She was called as a witness for Neville to prove he wasn't a sexual predator, and thus would not have committed the crimes he was accused of. She told everything she knew, careful to share the whole story about why her father had sexualised the community. When Neville was found guilty of ten of the charges, she was traumatised by the idea that perhaps, in her efforts to exonerate him, she may have instead confirmed the charges. Neville was still, in her eyes, God's messenger and the parent she must be obedient to.

He appealed the conviction and after a second trial in December 1995 was found guilty on three charges and sentenced to five years' imprisonment. He was released on bail after eleven months. Miracle went to the parole-board meeting to vouch for him to remain free. She didn't believe he was a paedophile; he didn't go around preying on young children. Everything he'd done, although it had been so wrong, had been done with the intention of helping those church members who relied on his guidance in their homes.

The moment the charges were made against him, the leaders worked swiftly to shape the story that would be accepted by the shocked and shaken Gloriavale community. 'This is persecution of the church,' they said. 'Neville is a martyr for the faith.' They said outsiders were seeking to destroy the community's way of life by attacking our leader and telling foul lies about him.

The allegations actually strengthened the church members' dedication to Neville and his imprisonment didn't stop him from leading his community. He wrote lengthy letters of instruction for his fellow leaders to read out to the people. The leadership group travelled to the prison each week to consult with him so that he kept abreast of everything that happened in the community. He was 'lifted up' as a faithful man of God the entire time he was inside, and held in awe by his followers.

It took my mother years to come to terms with her father's misconduct because she loved and respected him. The hardest pill to swallow was the fact that so many of the teachings the church members followed came from Neville, a proclaimed man of God. How could a man of God commit the sinful acts that he was being accused of? It wasn't possible.

My parents went to extreme lengths to separate themselves from sexual deviancies within the church and neither they nor any of us children ever suffered any sort of sexual abuse from Neville. Mum and Dad refrained from attending the private 'going out for tea' evenings in the community spa hut, where couples were rumoured to make love in the same room while covered by a blanket. 'People sensed we wouldn't tolerate it,' Mum remembers. 'We kept our guard up.'

Mum believes her mother must have struggled with what Neville was doing. Gloria loved him but all through their married life she'd learned not to question his actions because she'd be forcefully told she had no right to do so. Neville's refusal to accept he could ever be wrong or sinful meant that he had no compunction about involving himself in people's private relationships where he had no right to be.

Things in Gloriavale changed after the trials. The highly sexualised atmosphere became much more mainstream. The leaders were forced to be more cautious and careful with their teachings. When my family left in 2009, partition walls were being built in the family rooms to separate the children's quarters from those of their parents. Each family shared one room as living quarters, so, even before this, parents had been given greater privacy by a curtain being set up around their bed.

Sex was still openly talked about, but the prevailing attitude was healthier than it had been in previous years.

FOUR

Pioneering baby

Christian parents should bring up their children
to believe and obey the Lord Jesus Christ and to
follow in the way of the Church.

—WHAT WE BELIEVE, P. 70

I grew up in Gloriavale in a loving family. I was so lucky. My
parents, Miracle and Perry Tarawa, had a girl and a boy first. As
is typical of me, always so particular, I arrived exactly on my
due date—the Twenty-fourth Day of the Tenth month in 1990
at 2.30 am on the Fourth Morning, weighing just 3500 grams
(7 pounds 10 ounces). Mum said my arrival was a gift from God
and comforted her after she had suffered the grief of Gloria's
death just months before.

I got called the 'pioneering baby' because I was six weeks old when the young people first visited the new land at Gloriavale. My parents took me with them and Dad strapped me on his back to cross raging rivers with me, his little darling. I was so friendly and I loved having people around me. The young people would zip me up in their coats to keep me warm, and take me with them to see the calves or out to chop ragwort or see the horses.

Gloriavale's way of living fosters very close and loving relationships between families, and we were especially close to the family of Mum's brother, Mark, and his wife, Lani. Lani birthed Bethany just after I was born, and we two grew up side by side. Our mothers would often sit together and chat while breastfeeding us, with Bethany and I reaching out to clutch each other's chubby fists as we nursed. If Bethany was having a bath on the porch, I would invariably discover her and climb into the water, shoes and all. People joked that we were the brown and white twins because she was pale in comparison to my tanned skin.

Mark and Lani's family lived in the neighbouring room to ours on every hostel floor that we moved to, and we regularly shared family holidays and outings with them. Their kids were more like our siblings than cousins, we were so close. The older girls, Joanna and Serena, were like my big sisters.

I loved spending hours out on the farm. My older brother, Sam, would take me out riding on his white horse. I'd cling for dear life to his back, ecstatically yelping with joy and terror as we cantered through the pastures, jumping logs.

Sara, my eldest sister, was always wild and was a boundary-pusher. Whereas I worried ceaselessly about doing things right in the eyes of the church, she didn't seem to. She liked things her way and wasn't afraid to be curious. She always had this cheeky, mischievous grin on her face when she was up to something.

Sam adored her and followed her everywhere. He had the same wild spirit as his older sister, but he was kinder and more gentle. He would pat my cheeks and call me 'Lily'.

My brother Victor was just younger than me and he was the peacemaker during family squabbles. He was adventurous like we all were but had a way of bringing calm when stubborn natures clashed.

Mum had a loving and close relationship with Mark, her brother. They trusted each other and were able to confide in each other. Both held positions of great responsibility in Gloriavale. Mum was appointed House Mother and managed the women's realm—the domestic organisation of the 500-strong community. She was responsible for all aspects of Gloriavale's household duties and budgeting, and Mark managed the men's realm of all the commercial workings. They were answerable only to Grandad Neville and were trusted to make good decisions for the church.

My dad was away a lot when I was growing up because his first duty was to serve the church as business manager for Discoveries in Gardening. He was an appointed Servant (a leader) and sat on the board of approximately twenty Shepherds and Servants, Gloriavale's ring of men who tended to the Sheep (the flock of followers).

One night when I was six years old and it seemed to me that he'd been away forever, I was there begging to talk to him when he rang home. 'Can I talk to Dad? Please, can I?'

Mum finished her conversation and handed the phone to me.

'Hey, Dad.'

'Hello, Lil. How are you?' His distant voice echoed down the line.

'Where are you now, Dad? Are you still in Japan?' Japan sounded too amazing to be real.

I heard his laugh come all the way down the phone line. 'No, Lil, I'm in Saudi Arabia now.'

I only had a hazy idea of where that might be, but I thought if I could jump through the phone it would be a long way to where he was.

Trips like the one he was on were common for extended periods of time—even up to six months—to handle Discoveries in Gardening's new and existing international client relationships.

'When are you coming home, Daddy? I miss you.'

'Miss you too, Lil. I'm not sure when I'll get home. It depends on how long our work takes us,' Dad said.

I felt sad. We never knew when he would return. 'OK. Love you.' I gave the phone back to Mum.

It turned out we didn't have to wait so very long this time— only another month.

∿

When I woke on the day he was due home, I yawned, then sat up with a start. Dad was coming home today! I was excited. It would be so good to see him. Concentrating on schoolwork was going to be a challenge and I knew I wouldn't be able to sit still. What time would he be here? Would he look different? A frightening thought crossed my mind. Had I forgotten what he looked like?

All day, I kept expecting him to appear, but it was late afternoon with the last class of the day in session when Mum walked in the classroom door. After a brief word to the primary-school teacher Rose Standtrue she came to me and whispered, 'Pack up your books. Dad's home.'

At last! I was ecstatic and almost jumped out of my seat for joy.

We hurried to our room and I burst in the door. 'Dad!' I couldn't stop smiling as I gave him a big bear hug. He felt warm and strong. 'Did you bring me anything?'

Having Dad back from a trip was always exciting because he would bring souvenirs, trinkets and amazing toys—things we never normally saw in Gloriavale.

'This is for you.' He handed me a small cardboard box. What was it?

I ripped off the tape and opened the lid. Oh my goodness! Inside was a beautiful oval trinket box painted in a rich red gloss with gold-and-green embossed highlights.

'It's from China,' he told me.

I looked up at him, the wonder of the beautiful box blowing my mind. 'Dad, this is the most beautiful thing I've ever seen. I love it and I love you.'

He ruffled my hair and I knew he was pleased he'd made me happy.

The stories of my father's travels and experiences in the outside world made me heady. 'In Japan, they don't cook food before it's served to the table,' he told me. 'Instead, each place is set with a hot plate and a boiling pot of water. The food is all sliced up thinly, including the meat, and then everyone cooks their own food, right at the table.'

Wow. That was the coolest thing I'd ever heard.

Dad told us how the temperature in Saudi Arabia was so hot it could melt the paint on cars, and he showed us pictures of beautiful hotels with gigantic water fountains that cars could drive around. I looked at the photos with longing. The strangely clothed people and compelling culture mesmerised me. He had much more freedom than I would ever experience, and he had access to cash reserves to fund the trips that would never be available to me. These countries were so different from our life in Gloriavale. What would it be like to visit them?

I'd probably never know.

Gloriavale was my home for life.

FIVE

Who am I now?

Names should not just be pretty sounds with no
apparent meaning, nor should they be names taken
in honour of worldly relatives or film stars.

—WHAT WE BELIEVE, P. 95

In the early days of the community, a new campaign swept
through the church. We kids hated campaigns, because they
always meant sitting for hours at the tea table while Grandad
Neville preached about the newest revelation God had sent him
from heaven. The word would spread throughout the church,
entering every nook and cranny, permeating each household with
the news: 'Neville Cooper has undergone an epiphany.'

This one was about our names.

'When Jesus called the disciples to follow him, he gave them

31

new names to represent a new purpose in life. When God called Abram to become the father of many nations he changed his name to Abraham,' Neville told us. 'A person's name sends an important message about who he is. We need to choose names that inspire our Christian walk.'

Thus a dramatic revival flooded through the flock of followers. People shed the names given to them at birth and took new ones. Stan Bellette became Steady Standtrue; Alastair Barrett became Fervent Stedfast; and my grandfather Neville Cooper became Hopeful Christian.

For each resident who feverishly endorsed the campaign, there were also individuals who resisted the change. I was so thankful my parents, Perry and Miracle Tarawa, resisted. Their common sense meant they interpreted the Bible figuratively rather than literally and took Neville's teaching with a 'grain of salt'. They often stood in mute rebellion against radical evangelical changes and so began to get a reputation for not being as spiritual as they should be.

Neville, now known as Grandad Hopeful, approached my father to admonish him for his lack of submission. 'Why haven't you changed your name? You are the only ones who haven't done it. You're committing the sin of pride by wanting worldly names.'

One by one, members had submitted their will to Hopeful's radical campaign, and reluctantly Perry told Miracle, 'We have to change our names.'

Grudgingly she complied.

When Dad told us our surname would not be Tarawa any more, I was confused. Who was I now?

'You will be Lilia Just from now on,' he told me.

Lilia Just—my new name.

Even though my father had changed our surname, he kept his given name of Perry; since he held a position of such importance, no one dared question the decision.

My parents were also extremely artful in their naming of us. They gave us names that could be justifiably thought of as Christian or Biblical, to suit Gloriavale's standards, yet wouldn't be considered bizarre by outsiders. Sara was the name of a bible woman, and Samuel was the name of an Old Testament prophet. Victor meant 'conqueror', and I was named after a character in *The Ten Commandments* movie starring Charlton Heston, which was a Gloriavale favourite and shown many times on film nights.

'Your name is Hebrew for lily,' Mum whispered to me. 'You are a flower.'

That year Miracle gave birth to another baby girl. She had the same complexion as me and large, gorgeous brown eyes that lit up with joy when she giggled. I was so excited to have a little sister. My parents joined the names Gloria and Ana together. When my sister's birth was registered we each legally changed our surname from Tarawa to Just. I patted my little sister's head, kissed her fat wee cheeks and brushed her soft dark hair into a mohawk. 'Gloriana Just,' I cooed. We were going to be good friends.

Less than a year later, my aunt Patience birthed her first child. Patience was Neville's youngest daughter and my favourite aunt of all. She had the same blonde hair as Miracle and, like my mother, she was loving. We nicknamed her Patie, which was bad because it showed rebellion against our new Christian names, but we managed to get away with it. Patie was like a second mother to me. 'Take your elbows off the table. It's not ladylike,' she'd scold me.

'I don't want to be a lady,' I'd argue, but I always did as she said because I loved her.

Gloriavale's customs ensured that girls learn all aspects of womanly life and so I was called up to her room when she had just birthed her first child. 'You can cut the cord, Lil,' said an exhausted but elated Patie.

Taking the scissors with both hands, I snipped the umbilical cord neatly between the clamps. My new cousin, Trusty Disciple, had joined the world. I was seven years old and this was my introduction to the women's world of childbirth.

SIX

We don't want women like you

The women should at all times be in subjection to the men, and this they show outwardly, particularly when they pray, by covering their heads with a simple scarf.

—*WHAT WE BELIEVE*, P. 88

Later that week, Dad called Family Time in our family room. This was a period of thirty minutes to an hour set aside in the evening for us to commune as a family, and for Mum and Dad to teach us anything the church decided it was important for us to learn. We would also spend time in prayer. This time we were going over our half-yearly school reports prior to them being read out to the community at dinner. Dad would growl at my sister and brother when their teachers had written bad things in theirs. Sara and Sam were often out of order and rebellious, so they got in trouble a lot.

Usually, I dreaded Family Time and having to sit still for ages, but tonight I was excited. I'd received my first-ever school report! It was so exciting but also scary, because it was hugely important to get a good report. Tomorrow, Grandad would read all the reports, including mine, at the main meal table for the whole community to hear. If the report was good, the child would be praised in front of everybody. If the report was bad, then the child's reputation would be beaten down and battered until that child was obedient. I'd prayed and asked God to give me a good report, and I'd worked extra hard to do what was right.

Mum was walking to our family quarters when I ran up to tug her dress. 'Hey, Mummy, will we read my report tonight?'

She smiled and patted my cheek. 'Yes!'

Dad called us in from where we'd been playing in the big communal lounge on our hostel floor. I hurried into our family room to sit with my siblings on the beds while my parents sat on the end of their bed.

'Right, kids, your mum and I have been given your school reports.' He opened the first piece of folded white A4 paper with my sister's name printed boldly across the front. '*Sara often mucks around in class and leads people in the wrong direction.*'

I snickered at my sister, who looked humiliated. She was *so* naughty.

At last it was my turn. Dad opened my report and raised his eyebrows, as he scanned the page. I could barely sit still. *What did it say? Was it good?* He handed the report to my mother.

'Can I see?' I begged.

I opened it and scanned the first page with the academic scores. Subjects were listed in column one, then there were two more columns—one for Effort and one for Achievement. My eyes ran down the list: *A Maths, A+ English, A Social Studies, B++ Science.* These were good marks!

I turned to the next page where my teacher had rated my character:

Takes care of own and others' property: Always.

Respectful towards authority: Sometimes.

Willing to participate in community work: Always.

It was a good report.

'Lilia, this is so good,' Mum said. 'I'm so, so pleased with you. This is an awesome report to be read out to the community.'

I beamed from ear to ear. It felt good to make my parents proud.

The next evening, we gathered at the meal table. I could see the pile of reports sitting near the microphone at Grandad Hopeful's place. I felt nervous, but really proud that I had a good one. After the meals had been served and the women had come in from the kitchen to eat, Grandad Hopeful began to read through the pile. Eventually he opened mine.

Be humble. Don't be lifted up in pride, I reminded myself, as he began going through my academic marks and attitude scores, reading them out one by one.

Grandad Hopeful reached the teacher's summary section: '*Lilia demonstrates leadership skills which, if steered in the right direction, will be useful for when she gets older—*'

His voice stopped.

I looked up. Why had he stopped reading?

He looked at me, his face stern.

I was scared.

Frowning, Grandad Hopeful turned to the throngs of listeners and began to preach. 'This is not good. It is not godly that we teach our girls it's OK for them to be bossy. Women are to be meek and quiet. This is a terrible report.'

I froze and looked at Mum wide-eyed. *But* she *told me it was good!* Mum looked completely shocked.

'Rose Standtrue!' Grandad Hopeful addressed the second-grade teacher who'd written the report. 'This behaviour is not something that we want to be encouraging in our young girls. We don't want them to be leaders. We want them to submit to the men. Otherwise they turn out to be bossy, and that's not a trait that should be seen in girls. This sounds like the Women's Liberation Movement, where women want to be in the place of men. It's ungodly.'

I dropped my head and stared down at a crease in the plastic table cover.

Mum's face had gone bright red.

I was completely devastated. I couldn't believe this was happening. I felt sick and so embarrassed. I wanted to cry.

Grandad Hopeful's voice continued, 'The Women's Liberation Movement was started in 1968 by Simone de Beauvoir, when women decided they didn't want to be women any more. They wanted to be manly. Why would women want to be men? They cut their hair short and they look ugly. Do you want to look like these women, Lilia?' he spat.

My heart was slamming against my chest and the world around me had faded. All I could see was a small tear in the tablecloth. I clung to it like my life depended on it. I could feel air being sucked into my nostrils. Somehow I was breathing, but I felt like vomiting.

Hopeful shook his finger. 'Women are meant to be in submission to the man. Women's Lib is a sign of them wanting to take over from the men. Eve was the one who sinned and ate the fruit from the Tree of Life. God made Adam first, and then he made Eve from his rib. She was made as a helpmeet for Adam. God made woman to serve man. Now women want to wear zippers in the front of their trousers like a man. It's an abomination for women to wear men's clothing.'

Doubt started to creep into my mind. *What if he's right? What if I am rebellious and need to repent?*

'Perry and Miracle, it's your responsibility to teach your daughter submission, and reports like this are not what we want to be encouraging in the school. Our single women are to be meek and quiet with downcast eyes. We don't want women like this.'

I felt so small and there was nowhere to hide. I blinked rapidly and started to count my breaths as Grandad Hopeful preached upon the ungodliness of girls displaying leadership abilities. 'One . . . two . . . three . . .' all the way to ten, then I'd start at one again. After some time, the words of his forceful preaching stopped scalding me. I realised we were bowing our heads to give thanks and dinner was over. I glanced up at the clock. An hour of preaching had passed.

I stayed sitting at the table, waiting for the dining room to clear out. There were only a few people loitering when I picked up a pile of dirty plates and made my way to the kitchen.

Hosanna was running the racks of dirty plates through the commercial dishwasher.

I kept my head down as I did my task of scraping the leftovers, then stacked the plates into the dish racks.

I felt a tap on my shoulder. 'Hey, Lil, are you OK?' Patie had followed me into the kitchen. I nodded my head and bit my lip. 'Don't worry about what Grandad Hopeful says,' she said in a low voice, popping her arm around my shoulders. 'You did an awesome job and you're going to make a great team leader one day.'

I took a trembling breath. 'But why did he make it sound like I was bad? I tried really hard to get a good report.'

She sighed. 'Sometimes Grandad can be a bit harsh. It's just what he's like. Keep your chin up and don't let it get you down.'

I shrugged. 'Well, if it's God's will, then I have to accept it. The leaders know best. I have to submit my will to the church.'

She patted me on the head and smiled lovingly at me. 'C'mon, let's go find the other kids.'

SEVEN

Becoming a woman

Once a godly young woman's monthly menstrual
periods had begun, she was able to marry.

—*WHAT WE BELIEVE*, P. 65

Like all Gloriavale girls, I began participating in the work of the
women's world when I was six or seven. We'd be allowed to help
with setting the tables by carrying the sauce, salt and pepper out
to the dining room. When the meal was over, we helped clear up,
taking dirty dishes to the kitchen and scraping them in readiness
for the dishwasher. It didn't take too many months before those
tasks palled. However, there were others I really enjoyed. We
were taught practical life skills from a young age, and I was a
skilful cook, seamstress and knitter by the time I was ten.

Our class would learn these skills together and we were always trained by one of the older women. I enjoyed learning each craft but some duties were much more fun than others. I would much rather spin wool than clean toilets.

Each day, school finished at 3 pm and we girls would head immediately to join our work teams and help the women with whichever community duty they were rostered for.

One day, when I was ten, I was impatient for school to finish because I was rostered on with the team doing spinning. But first we had to get through lunch and afternoon lessons.

Weeeooooowwww the lunchtime siren blared across the valley, slicing through the crisp West Coast air and piercing the silent classroom.

I looked up at our high-school principal, Faithful Pilgrim, who sat at his desk writing busily in his notebook. The room was deathly silent for a long moment while we waited for him to finish. Eventually, he peered down his long nose at the eager faces and announced, 'Lunchtime. Everyone, put your books away and head to the kitchen. See me for your meal tickets first.'

Lively chatter spread like wildfire around the room. Books and desks slammed shut as we jumped out of our seats. The classroom whirled into action and I snatched up my maths theory and exercise book. I slid my pencil case in my desk, careful not to slam my hands, as the heavy wooden lid fell shut. I was proud of that case. I'd sewed its dark-blue cylinder from a velvet fabric lined with waxed-cotton lining and painted a white orca on the front.

My cousin Promise Overcomer was by the lockers. I hurried to catch up with her. 'Hey, wanna walk to lunch together?'

Promise nodded. 'Yup, sure. We have to get our meal tickets first, though.'

Promise was the oldest in Grade 10, the same class I was in. She was thirteen with medium tan-coloured skin courtesy of our Māori heritage. She had the same thick, shiny hair falling to her waist as I did, but her face was sprinkled with freckles thanks to her Dutch lineage on her father, Pilgrim's, side.

We made our way to the queue in front of the double doors leading into the massive communal dining area. Faithful waited at the front of the queue to hand out our meal tickets. The small green slip fitted neatly in my hand and I turned it over to read the inscription on the back: *If any should not work, neither should he eat. II Thessalonians 3:10.*

Looking at Promise, I rolled my eyes. The compulsory meal tickets were so over the top. I shoved it deep into the side pocket of my ankle-length uniform. There'd been a couple of misbehaviours during class and we knew that a few of the boys would not be eating lunch today.

We joined the line of kids at the servery. When our turn came, we handed our meal tickets to Prayer, who was on duty, and then we were permitted to get our lunches, which consisted of a cup of soup, sandwiches and a piece of fruit. Our two classmates who had been naughty got nothing—no ticket meant no lunch. They had to sit in the classroom with the rest of us eating our lunch around them.

～

Three o'clock arrived. We girls hurried to join our work team in the Service Shed. This building housed the woodwork shop, costume storage room, electricians' service room and a couple of spaces that were used for miscellaneous tasks and activities. Only a few minutes after we got there, the boys delivered big cardboard banana boxes packed with the freshly shorn wool we would spin into knitting yarn.

I reached in to grab an armful of raw wool that looked a little cleaner than the rest. 'Use these carders, girls,' my aunt Grace Ben-Canaan said, handing me and my cousin Bethany the spiked tools.

I knelt on the ground and lined up a couple of handfuls of wool, holding one end firmly in place to start carding it. I began to brush the wool: *Brssk, brssk*. The thin steel spikes on the carder caught the fibres of the wool, brushing out the dirt and dung till the handful of dirty wool became a clean, airy ball of fluff.

'Ouch!' The carder raked over my knuckles, ripping into the skin. I grabbed a homemade handkerchief from my pocket to stop the bleeding.

Grace frowned at me. 'Look what you've done,' she scolded. 'Quickly, wrap it up. We're about to start spinning and you need to bear your burden.'

I ran to the bathroom and watched the cold water turn bright red as I rinsed my hand under the tap. Wrapping the handkerchief tightly in place, I ran back and gathered up the armful of wool I'd prepped.

There were four single-treadle spinning-wheels available. I used my favourite of the bunch: an old, dark-stained wood machine that ran more smoothly than the rest and produced a more even thread. Selecting a spool from the box of empties, I set it between the maidens and flyer, then hooked the starter thread to pull it through the yarn guides. The drive-band tension felt right.

I loved spinning. I liked knowing how to do this ancient craft and do it well. I was proud of my skill. I enjoyed building a rhythmic momentum to feed the wool smoothly into the hungry machine. It was a gentle, meditative activity, but it also gave us the chance to gossip and form close relationships with the girls we worked with. Gladness started singing, then the rest of us joined.

The love of God is greater far
Than tongue or pen can ever tell
It goes beyond the highest star
And reaches to the lowest hell.

'Psst!' My cousin Bethany leaned over to me. 'Did you hear who's getting married?'

I widened my eyes and shook my head, while Blessing Helpful looked up, her eyes wide too.

'I'm not supposed to tell anyone.' Bethany giggled. 'But there's going to be an announcement tonight, so don't be late for dinner! Plus, you don't want to be forced to apologise in front of everyone for being tardy.'

I rolled my eyes in disgust. I hated the new rule that anyone who was late to the meal table had to stand up and publicly apologise in front of the entire community for tardiness.

'I won't be,' I assured her and started to spin even faster, while we chatted about Purity's new baby, the latest arrival in our community. All the time I wondered who was going to be married. Which of the young women next in line for an arranged marriage would it be? Who would be chosen to be her husband?

My hands worked automatically, and soon I had ten fat bobbins of wool ready for plying. After that they would be knitted, washed and dyed.

I checked the time on my watch. Seven minutes till dinner! I'd have to hurry or I really *would* be late. The thought of standing up in front of everyone to apologise for tardiness made me shudder.

I lived on the second floor of the First Hostel. It stood alongside a one-storey embankment that had been excavated to build the housing units. I ran up the side of the hill and raced on to the fenced walkway that bridged the gap from the embankment to the main entrance of my floor. Families were already headed to the Main Building for teatime and I dodged around them. Time was running out fast.

Mum emerged from the main entrance with my little brother just as I reached the glass door. 'Lilia!' she exclaimed. 'Aren't you rostered on Serving?'

'Yes, I'm trying to hurry,' I gasped, flinging the door open.

'Hurry up or you'll be late!' she called after me, as I disappeared past the bathroom and into the lounge. I ran down the long communal lounge. Our family's room was on the left rear corner of the hostel and was a 12-metre rectangle, with Mum and Dad's king-size waterbed at one end and two bunks fitted along the opposite end. Another bunk stretched horizontally through the middle with a full-length curtain that could divide the room in two for privacy. My clothes hung in the built-in wardrobe beside my parents' bed: five blue uniforms, three white aprons and a few jackets and cardigans. Seizing an apron, I flung it over my head, then ran to the drawer of my bottom bunk bed.

Where is it, where is it? I rummaged through my belongings. *There!* I grabbed the white cap from the back of the drawer, tugged the knotted scarf off my head and jumped up to stand in front of our tiny mirror. The cap was designed for working in the kitchen, as it held all of a woman's hair like a net. Twisting my long hair into a bun, I slipped the cap over my hair, then pulled it forward to a few centimetres from my forehead.

I slipped a couple of bobby pins on to each side to hold it in place, slammed the drawers shut and headed back out the front of the hostel to race across the dirt to the Main Kitchen.

Made it! I stepped through the glass door and collected myself. Seventy woman scurried about, all dressed in long dark-blue frocks exactly like mine. Each woman wore a white apron gathered on to a sash that tied around the waist in a neat bow at the back. Either a white cap or a triangular white scarf covered each of our heads. I made my way through the hustle and bustle down to the far end.

The kitchen was 35 metres long by 10 metres wide, and boasted heavy commercial equipment capable of processing the masses of food necessary for the 530 Gloriavale members. A three-mixer bread-making station stood at the head of the kitchen, followed by a line-up of various food-production machines organised in neat rows down the middle of the long room. These included a wood oven, electric oven, gas stations, commercial deep-fryers, four-compartment steamer cabinets, 100-litre steam kettles, 1-metre-square frying-pans and more.

Two food-serving stations were set up for dinner service: one at the top end of the kitchen, which served the adult meals, and one down the far end, which served the primary school and preschool meals. I positioned myself with seven other girls at the servery bench, with utensils ready to plate up the dinner food.

'Hey, where've you been?' Integrity Hopeful asked. She was two grades above me and we were firm friends.

'Finishing the spinning,' I murmured as I stood beside her at the server.

'Just as well you're not late,' she whispered. 'You know what happens to the late ones.'

I nodded. 'Well, I'm here now. Are we ready to serve?'

'We're just waiting on the mashed potato.'

As though she'd heard us, Mary Pilgrim appeared, wheeling a 60-litre mixing bowl of hot mashed potato. We lifted the heavy bowl off the trolley, using heat-protective mitts, and carefully tipped the steaming mix into the serving bowl.

'Thanks,' said Integrity, smiling at her. 'OK, girls, let's get going.'

The serving station kicked into gear, with the first girl taking a plate and serving up a spoonful of mashed spud, then passing it to the next girl, who dished out casserole. Next was steamed carrots, and after that green beans, then finally the plate passed to the first girl standing in the queue at the end of the station. She was charged with running the plate out to the dining tables. The station churned out plate after plate of food: mash, casserole, carrots, beans . . . mash, casserole, carrots, beans . . . Over and over, like a well-oiled manufacturing machine consisting of human parts.

Forty minutes later, food service was over and the serving girls were each issued with a plate of food. I collected mine, and Bethany and I made our way out through the double doors to find our families at the meal table.

The mess hall was about 40 metres long with six 10-metre tables running along the length of it. Heading to Grandad Hopeful's table, I took a seat next to Victor. The dining room hummed with chitchat from hundreds of voices as the Gloriavale families communed and broke bread together.

'Right, everyone, quieten down. Everyone, stop talking.'

Grandad Hopeful's voice came over the sound system.

I sat up straighter. The marriage announcement! Which of the three girls would it be? I hoped she would get a good man to be her husband. Then I had to stifle a gasp because Loyal was getting to his feet. *Loyal? Really?*

'Excuse me, everyone. I have something I'd like to tell you.' He looked so awkward, standing there at his family place, clutching the microphone. 'I've been searching for a wife and I believe the Lord has chosen one for me and her name is Joanna.'

Oh my God. Joanna? I turned to look at my cousin, who I considered a sister, just along the table from us. Joanna stood up. She was the sweetest, kindest and most loving of all Mark and Lani's children, whereas Loyal was such an abrupt, rough and humourless guy. Why on earth would God choose her to marry him? I glanced at Mum. She was scowling, and I knew she wasn't happy about it at all.

Everyone cheered, clapped and whistled as we did for every happy announcement. Everyone that is, except for Mum.

There were more weddings in the year that followed. I turned twelve and felt unworthy as my friends all started getting their periods. Why wasn't I, too, becoming a woman? What was wrong with me? I'd never be allowed to get married if Grandad Hopeful ever found out I wasn't a proper woman.

He preached that once we got our periods we were ready for marriage, and the only reason we couldn't become wives and mothers when nature decreed was because the law of the land interfered with peoples' rights and said sixteen was the right age. No wonder my friends were excited when they discovered they would be able to bear children, because that was the purpose of our lives.

One day I went into the bathroom, shut the door, squeezed my eyes shut and prayed my heart out. 'Please, God, can you let me get my period? I promise to serve you and if you give me my period I'll never be grumpy or cranky when I get it. I'll just take it without complaining.'

When it finally arrived, I was so excited. I ran to Mum. 'Mum! I'm a woman now!'

I felt that I could at last be accepted as a real woman of Gloriavale, a woman who could bear children for her husband.

EIGHT

The wedding

Man is the image and glory of God but the woman
is the image and glory of the man, she being made
for him and not him for her.

—*WHAT WE BELIEVE*, P. 61

The normal courtship period was about two weeks from when
the announcement was made. Those two weeks were frenzied
and super busy as we prepared for the wedding. As part of the
preparation, Joanna went to the sewing room to be measured
for the sexy lace and satin nighties, camisoles and panties which
were made for every bride. It was pretty special because single
girls weren't allowed to wear sexy underwear. After all, it's not
like they had a husband to impress.

Joanna's wedding dress was exactly the same design as our

uniform dresses but it was pink, not blue. Her head covering was trimmed with lace instead of piping. So beautiful.

The couple spent regular time with each other during courtship, always chaperoned by an elderly couple who would instruct them in preparation for married life. A founding principle was that older women were required to teach the younger ones details of lovemaking so that they were able to bring deep satisfaction to their husbands and build a strong marriage.

We were taught that, according to the Bible, the age we should be ready for marriage is defined by sexual development. If a young man had a strong sexual desire for his virgin and a young woman had 'flowered' or begun her menstrual cycle, then they should be of the mental maturity also to be married. New Zealand law decreed that a youth must be sixteen years of age before marriage so Gloriavale had to adhere to that.

On the wedding day, we all dressed in our best and gathered in the hall. The couple made a grand entrance together and took the seats of honour at the front. On the wall above them was a scripture: *What therefore God hath joined together, let not man put asunder.*

The scripture disturbed me. Was this really God's decision for them to be married? After all, Joanna didn't even want to be with Loyal. I shut out the rebellious thoughts. 'Sometimes the Lord's will isn't the same as our own,' I reasoned. Certainly God had revealed his message to Grandad Hopeful and it was therefore the right way.

Weddings, regardless of whether you agreed with them or not, were always a time of warmth and celebration with the community giving the young couple affirmation, encouragement, songs and scriptural advice. We called this 'edification', and we were taught to diligently 'edify' our brothers and sisters in Christ.

To Gloriavale, marriage is a lifetime commitment sanctioned by God. There is no such thing as divorce. Once a couple are bound to each other through marriage vows and sexual intercourse they become one flesh and should no longer live in selfish independence.

Joanna and Loyal stood and faced each other to make their vows before God and the church. They held hands—the first time in their entire lives they had touched each other.

Grandad Hopeful preached his usual sermon, including something along the lines of: 'The world, in their sinful hearts, have turned from God and accepted divorce and remarriage of divorced persons, which is adultery. Women should reverence and submit to their husbands, calling them "Lord" as did Sarah of the Old Testament days. Husbands should love, nourish and cherish their wives as well as providing for them and bearing responsibility in family life. The virginity of both the man and woman is to be presented as a gift to each other on the wedding day.'

First, Joanna spoke the Commitment marriage vow written and required by the church, which I remember being: 'I willingly submit myself to you and will call you lord. My body is yours.'

I winced. *Yuck.*

Loyal's response had to be, 'I promise to look after our children and lead our family in righteousness. If I ever turn from the church you are not required to submit to me any longer. My commitment is to God and the church first and secondly to you. I will never look upon another woman in lust.'

I thought it was pretty lucky for 'another woman' because she certainly wouldn't be pleased to receive lusty ogling from him.

After they'd made the vows required by the church, they spoke the vows they'd made up themselves. Joanna promised to submit herself to him and to make their home a place of harmony and love.

I had a lot of respect for the way she quietly bent her will to the dictates of the church. Each of us girls had been taught that when it came our turn to marry we must accept our fate with joy. God directly influenced the will of the leaders so to oppose their decisions meant turning your back on God. I, too, would willingly marry whomever God chose for me.

It was now time for The Kiss. This was the action which would seal their wedding vows in front of the whole community. It was their first kiss ever. As always at every wedding this one was full on—lips, tongues and hands went everywhere. The young couple had been encouraged to take no shame in their desire for each other.

I wanted to retch, it was so squirm-making. Eeew!

Loyal was grabbing her bum—gross. How could Joanna look so calm after a make-out session like that? But she managed to and even looked truly happy when everybody streamed up to greet and congratulate them.

The next part of the ritual was Grandad Hopeful leading them outside and driving them to the separate Gloriavale House away from the main community. A bed was prepared for them and it was where they must consummate their marriage with the sex act. They were not fully man and wife until this was done.

An hour later, Hopeful brought them back to where we all waited in the main dining hall. As soon as somebody heard the sound of the approaching vehicle, the word flew around—*Listen! They're coming! They're almost here!*

There was the usual air of high excitement as Joanna and Loyal walked in on the main stage and down the ramp into the dining room. The entire community clapped and hooted, welcoming them and congratulating them for now truly becoming one flesh. Joanna was no longer a virgin. In Grandad Hopeful's words, the seal she'd been keeping for her husband was broken.

It was inevitable that when the leaders found a husband for me I would be married in similar fashion to Loyal and Joanna. I found it gross to think about the reality of going to a bedroom to have sex with my husband for the first time then returning and having everyone know exactly what we'd done. But virgin coupling of a husband and wife was how the marriage bond was sealed. It was a necessary act and I was accustomed to how Gloriavale celebrated it openly.

We looked forward to the wedding feasts because they were always a good spread. Everything was special—food, decorations, cutlery. The food was nicer than what we usually had. The men would butcher a pig to roast and we'd be served kumara, peas, apple sauce, noodles, packets of lollies and sparkling apple juice. It was such a treat compared to the bland food we usually ate.

There was lots of laughter and tears of joy. We performed dances, songs, skits, speeches and comedy items for the couple. The kids loved it and went crazy on sugar highs. That night we played soccer, volley ball and skating, finishing up with watching a movie. It was truly a joyful celebration of the couple's union and spoke volumes about the loving church community surrounding our families.

I knew Mum was still very upset about the arranged marriage and I prayed Joanna would be able to find happiness with her husband. As was required of every woman in the church she would do her utmost to fulfil her wifely duties and submit to her husband. Even against her own will she would give herself in love to him and any children the Lord blessed them with.

NINE

A woman's duty

It is not the women's place to be the 'breadwinners' or income earners.

—*WHAT WE BELIEVE*, P. 71

The primary duty above all others for the women was to look after and serve the men. Grandad Hopeful wouldn't allow any deviation from his edict. Men often worked late on the farm and would come in after we'd eaten dinner. We always served up their meals but by the time they got in, their food would have gone cold.

Grandad discovered a few of them going into the kitchen to heat up their meals in the microwave. He hit the roof. 'If any man comes in from work, I want to see you women jump up and heat his meal for him and serve it to him.'

It didn't matter that she was probably busy putting her several young children to bed.

We didn't question the leaders' rules about our role in life, not openly anyway, and it did make for a very smooth running of the daily life of the community. We each knew what our programme was for every day, all designed to keep the whole engine functioning. I think that Mum must have often found it stressful to care for her own family when she had to always ensure that the machinery of the domestic realm kept ticking away like it should.

The machinery, consisting entirely of human female parts, was organised down to the smallest task. All the women were rostered on to four teams with a four-day cycle of duties. There was the washing, the cleaning, the cooking and the food preparation. Each team had two women who would lead it; a primary and a secondary. Outside of the four teams a number of women were rostered to school and preschool teaching or assigned to the sewing room.

Mum oversaw the entire organising of it. As House Mother, even men held great respect for her authority—although it probably didn't hurt that she was beautiful and had long blonde hair, porcelain skin and a gorgeous figure.

The appointed team leader allocated the tasks for the women in their team. Each day, she would write her team's duties in her notebook and the girls would arrive, check the book and go to their assigned tasks.

Some tasks had to be started much earlier than others so within the respective teams there were the adult women who would take turns to get up at 3 or 4 am—or whatever time the task required. Washing duty wasn't a load of fun. We had to get up at 4 am to run the cycles of churning washing through the commercial laundromat.

Cooking duty wasn't much better, but the start times were staggered. The first woman would get up at 3 am to begin the bread-making. She would weigh up the flour, add the yeast, oil and salt and set the dough to rise.

At 5.30, when the dough had risen and was ready for kneading, five girls would arrive.

At 6 am the rest of the team would arrive in the kitchen, check their various tasks and get to work preparing breakfast and other food for the day. Breakfast typically consisted of porridge and toast. The porridge was made by milling wheat, which the community bought by the tonne for our bread, porridge and baking.

The milled wheat was then cooked in a steam kettle with water till al dente. Milk was added and rolled oats to thicken the porridge and lastly the women would flavour it with salt and sugar.

Each morning our farmers delivered a truckload of fresh milk to the cooler, so we had milk with every meal. Other drinks at breakfast could be a health drink made by combining vitamin C, apple vinegar and honey. Hot drinks were made by mixing cocoa, carob powder, sugar and water into a thick paste. We heated 10-litre pots of milk on the wood stove and then mixed in the paste. Breakfast started at 7.30 and the girls who were on serving used stainless steel jugs to carry porridge and drinks out to the tables to serve to each person.

While we were still at school the earliest we had to start work was 6.30 am but this changed as soon as we left.

It was cleaning duty that I hated with a passion. I was about fifteen with my formal schooling finished when I had to start early shifts. It would still be dark as I slipped out of bed and climbed carefully down the bunk ladder so the creaky rungs wouldn't wake my family. I'd grope around in the dark to find my clothes then it was out to the shared bathroom where I'd brush my hair and don the cap.

The bathroom was quiet and it was a relief to get some private time. The cramped rooms of the hostel allowed little privacy, and everyone lived on top of each other. And, anyway, we weren't entitled to privacy or personal belongings—those types of luxuries had to be sacrificed for true Christian living. For the most part, we respected each other's personal space, but there were no locks on bedroom or bathroom doors.

On our hostel floor, there were four bathrooms (five toilets and four showers) to service all fourteen families on the floor. Hopeful Christian's room had its own ensuite with a spa bath (which was used for birthing), a toilet, a laundry tub and storage cabinets. The overseeing leader on each floor had a similar set-up.

Across from the spa room there was a bathroom that had a bath, toilet and shower all in the one room. Through a partition was a laundry tub and changing area for babies. This toilet was accessible for wheelchairs.

Each hostel floor was an exact replica of the others, except for the attic floor which was divided into large areas and used for picnics, games nights, family going-out-for-tea nights or activities like Sixth Day team games.

Sixth Days were special both for meals and activities. Meals were often different from what we usually ate and we'd have luxuries such as eggs, pikelets or Bircher muesli for breakfast. For dinner, we would have a treat like spaghetti and meatballs or fried rice then after dinner three of the four family teams, men included, would pitch in to clean up.

The fourth team was granted a night off cleaning so they would start a game like soccer or volleyball that everyone else would join in until the leaders called us up for the Sixth Night cinema experience. We'd take our places on the chairs placed in rows upstairs in the Main Building to watch a movie my father had carefully censored to cut out any swearing, sex scenes or content inconsistent with Gloriavale's beliefs and way of life.

There would be an intermission at half-time and each family would have supper of something sweet like doughnuts, biscuits and milkshakes.

It was a bonus for Sara, Sam and me that our dad was in charge of editing the movies because he had a full editing suite set up in our family bedroom, and I often had the opportunity to see more worldly movies than others did. When our family went on vacation Dad would take us to Video Ezy in Greymouth to help him select new movies for the community.

My siblings and I often stole un-edited movies out of his stash to watch in secret.

~

I was jumping with joy. At last vacation time had arrived! (We were forbidden to use the word 'holiday' because it is an adaptation of 'holy day' and that would be blasphemy.) Finally the vacation announcement had been made—each family was granted one week off work.

At Family Time that night, my siblings and I chatted noisily about what fun adventures we'd have. We couldn't wait to escape the humdrum of ordinary life. It had been two years since our last family vacation and it would be another two until our next one. We were determined to make the most of it.

We could only choose vacation activities that were within the parameters of Gloriavale's stipulations, but we were glad for any bit of freedom. We decided to hike Mt Brian O'Lynn, trek horses across the valley, pitch tents under the stars and pack the canoes with things for a lakeside barbeque. On top of that we intended to binge watch movies from the community stash.

I desperately hoped our family would be allowed to stay at Glenhopeful House. It was on the furthest side of Haupiri River, whereas the other holiday house was just a few paddocks away from the main commune complex. At Glenhopeful we'd have so much more privacy.

In typical fashion I appointed myself organiser of the event (under Mum's supervision) and I planned extravagant menus for it. I could already taste the yummy treats that we would stuff our bellies with—sweet slices, biscuits, dried fruits, fizzy drinks—it would be an epic binge. However, there were boundaries which we had to keep within.

When the time arrived I was ecstatic to discover that we were indeed headed to Glenhopeful House. Hallelujah! I threw my bags in the van and within fifteen minutes we'd arrived. The large homestead was nestled into the hilltop with full-length windows that overlooked the farm. Our paradise for one week.

In the background, the younger children were arguing about which bedroom was theirs. I helped Mum unpack then went to find them playing outside.

'Higher, Lil, higher!' Asher shouted, as I gave the swing a hard shove. Grinning, I paused to catch my breath then straightened. *That's odd.* I squinted. *What a strange thing.* I could see a tiny white structure perched on the edge of the bushline. It was about the size of a garden shed or hut, and quite a distance from Glenhopeful House. What was it for?

After dinner that evening I wanted to explore the hills and take a closer look at the hut. It bothered me. I stuffed my feet into gumboots and unlatched the paddock gate. Mud sucked at my boots as I trudged up the slope towards the bushline.

Glenhopeful House looked small in the distance when I reached the hut. The door was shut and wouldn't budge when I tried to open it. Feeling nervous, I pushed the door with my shoulder and it flew open. The hut was empty. To my right stood an unmade single bed. On the bench lay some utensils and a plate . . . a dirty plate. I froze. Someone was living here. *Creeaakk.* I stopped breathing. I backed away from the open door I'd just entered. My heart pounded.

'Hey!' A small head popped through the door.

'Victor!' I exclaimed. 'You gave me the biggest fright!'

'What are you doing?' he asked.

'Nothing. We need to leave. Come on.' I banged the door shut behind us. We raced back across the paddocks and arrived breathless at Glenhopeful House.

I didn't mention the hut to my parents. If they knew I'd been snooping around I might get in trouble, but for the next couple of weeks I kept wondering about it. Who was living in the hut? And why?

TEN

Outsiders

It is entirely against the will of Christ for any
Christian to persevere in any belief or practice
which he knows is contrary to that which is
followed in the Church.

—*WHAT WE BELIEVE*, PP. 47–8

I was ten when Peter Hoover's family first arrived in Gloriavale.
It was a mealtime and there was a strange family sitting between
Grandad Hopeful's family and ours. They wore very immodest
clothing. The entire family wore short-sleeved tops, which was
a very worldly thing to do. The father wore a shirt with long
pants held up by braces. He had a beard. This fascinated me
because men in Gloriavale weren't allowed to grow facial hair.
If a young man avoided shaving for a few days he'd get called

worldly, unkempt and unruly.

The man's wife wore a small white headscarf over her hair and a coloured smock that fell over her pregnant belly to just below mid-calf. Our blue Gloriavale dresses hung all the way to our ankles, because showing any skin would be a stumbling block for our Christian brothers who must not be tempted by the sight of flesh.

The parents had three small boys and two girls, one a toddler and the other a teenager. The teenage girl was short and round with rich chocolate skin and black hair, unlike the rest of her family who had pale complexions. Her black eyes had lashes so long I thought they couldn't be real and she had an infectious giggle. I decided we would be friends.

The family spoke English but every now and then would break off to speak with each other in a low, guttural language that I couldn't understand. Grandad Hopeful announced that the family were the Hoovers and they were visiting to discover what it was like to live in intentional community.

He asked that the head of each family (the man) stand up and introduce himself to the newcomers.

After introductions, the meal ended and we got up to clear the dinner table. 'I'll help you,' I told the dark-skinned girl.

'Where do we take them?' Her accent was strange to my ears.

'To the kitchen. We stack them into the dish racks and the team on dishes will do the rest.' I gave her a big smile. 'I'm Lilia. What's your name?'

She giggled. 'Graciela. Nice to meet you.'

'Oh my goodness, how do I pronounce that?' Her name sounded so foreign. I was clueless.

She laughed. 'It's GRAY-SEE-EL-LA. It's Spanish. You can call me Grace.'

We laughed as I tried to say it.

The Hoover family moved into a spare room on our hostel floor where they could be close to Grandad Hopeful who would instruct them in living a practical Christian life.

My predication we'd be friends was right. Grace and I were a match made in heaven. I was two years younger and fascinated with her world. I begged her to tell me about life beyond the walls of Gloriavale and at night-time we snuck out of our rooms to meet in secret. Even her life history was different and interesting. She explained that her dark skin came from her Chilean heritage. Peter and Susan Hoover had adopted her at birth because her mother didn't want her. I felt sad. Why would anyone give their child away? In our community, children were prized as a blessing from the Lord. The leaders were right: the world outside Gloriavale was wicked.

The Hoovers had been living in Puerto Octay, a small town and commune nestled on the north shore of Llanquihue Lake in the Los Lagos Region of southern Chile.

I found it difficult to fathom what Chile was. The idea of any place other than Gloriavale seemed bizarre. Even when my father described foreign lands I found them hard to imagine.

Grace told me that in Puerto Octay, their house was on the edge of the Chilean–Argentinian border. So close, in fact, that they could peer out the window and see the fuzzy borderline in the distance.

The strange language they spoke was Hutterisch which had been brought to Puerto Octay by German settlers in 1852. It was a Carinthian German dialect originating from Austria and Grace told me it was spoken in all Hutterite colonies across North America.

It shocked me when Grace spoke highly of the Hutterite communities, because Gloriavale despised many of their teachings even though the dresses we wore had been modelled on theirs. Unless a church followed everything to the letter that Grandad Hopeful commanded then they were not a true church.

Peter Hoover had discovered Gloriavale on a business bulletin and was ecstatic. For months, he'd been soul-searching and researching what it meant to live a practical Christian life. Gloriavale's unusual lifestyle was exactly what he'd been looking for. He wrote a letter to Shepherd Fervent Stedfast and arranged a visit.

Grace's parents were also hoping the visit would cure Grace of her wicked ways. Already she'd run away from home once and a strict environment was exactly what she needed to curb her rebellion.

As the weeks flew by, the family began to adopt our customs as was expected of anyone who stayed longer than a week. They began wearing the compulsory blue uniforms, although Susan and Grace still wore their smaller headscarves instead of the large white headdresses we wore.

Hopeful knew that the Hoovers had been interested in joining the Hutterites so his response was to give long sermons at spiritual meetings and meal tables preaching against the evils of such communities. The sermons dragged on for hours. We were told the Hutterites were far too traditionalist and they didn't practise immersion baptism, the only baptism Hopeful believed to be biblical.

Peter and his heavily pregnant wife were put through many Leaders' Meetings as Gloriavale sought to reform their beliefs. Both Peter and Grace were pressured into accepting baptism by immersion. Gloriavale women would tell Grace, 'Immersion will help you fit in better.' Susan Hoover, though, didn't want to be immersed so she told the leaders it wasn't a good idea yet seeing she was in the last term of pregnancy.

Praise and Christiana, who were rostered on the same working team as Grace, told her the sprinkling she had received as a baby was not adequate for the kingdom of heaven. When Peter and Grace agreed to be immersed there was a big announcement made. Everyone clapped and cheered as we always did to celebrate a happy announcement. The sinners were coming to the cross.

But there were still problems with the family. Peter refused to stop reading his New International Bible—absolute heresy in Gloriavale's eyes. We were only permitted to read the King James version because, '. . . if any man shall take away from the words of the book of this prophecy, God shall take away his part out of the Book of Life*'. (Revelation 22:19.)

Grandad Hopeful thundered, 'People change the Word to suit themselves instead of changing themselves to suit the Word.'

Nobody wanted their name struck from the Book of Life, because that meant damnation to an eternity in hell. We would not be admitted to heaven unless God recorded our names in the Book of Life.

---

* The Book of Life is the book in which God records the names of the saints who receive admission to heaven.

Another problem for our leaders was that Peter was a passionate writer, and Gloriavale didn't warm to the idea of allowing free thought and self-expression into their church. It was dangerous ground because sheep could be easily led astray.

People were to submit their will to the church.

The Gloriavale leadership began to exercise authority over Peter, heavily scrutinising his work. When he spoke on the phone with people outside the community, Fervent would listen in on the conversations and reprimand him for speaking Hutterisch.

Shortly after their arrival, Susan home-birthed a beautiful little daughter, Maria. Then three months into their stay Grace brought me sad news. Her family was leaving. Peter had a dream he believed to be a warning from God to leave Gloriavale. In the dream, he was strolling through the Haupiri Valley gazing upon the hills when he suddenly became overwhelmed with a heavy sense of claustrophobia. Gloriavale's control had become too much.

Gloriavale didn't respond kindly to the news of the Hoovers' decision to leave. A Leaders' Meeting was immediately called to confront the couple. Susan emerged from that meeting in tears. The men had yelled curses and accusations of heresy at the couple. Only when Peter threatened to call the police did the leaders quickly change their tone. Grandad Hopeful said, 'No we can't have that happening. It will upset the young people.'

The community threw a massive farewell dinner to wish the family Godspeed instead.

I was greatly saddened to see Grace go. When people left Gloriavale we never saw them again—unless they confessed their sin, repented and obeyed the leaders, which wasn't very often. We said our goodbyes and the Hoovers were gone.

ELEVEN

A lake of brimstone

All men are born sinners, and unless they are saved
by God's grace they shall perish in hell.

—*WHAT WE BELIEVE*, P. 6

Dante's Peak isn't the movie I'd choose now to show to an
audience with many small children in it. But Gloriavale has never
shied away from scaring its youth, so for the Sixth Day movie this
night I wasn't the only ten-year-old to clutch her throat in terror
as we watched a small town fight for survival during a monster
volcanic eruption.

That night I couldn't sleep. The bedroom was pitch black and I
lay in my bunk wide awake with fear. I could just make out a tiny
dot on the bottom of my brother's bunk above me, so I focused
on it, trying to distract my brain. The terrible thoughts wouldn't

leave me alone. What if Mt Brian O'Lynn was a dormant volcano? We would all die! The biggest question was: Where would I go when I was dead? I couldn't go to heaven because I hadn't been baptised. Did that mean I'd go to hell?

Leaders had assured us that Jesus died on the cross to save us from hell, but we wouldn't be covered by the Blood of the Lamb if we weren't baptised. 'He that believeth and is baptised shall be saved; but he that believeth not shall be damned.' I'd heard that said so many times, always uttered with fervent conviction.

Dread clawed my chest. Hell was a terrible place. Leaders preached at meeting and meal times to make sure we knew what would happen if we didn't serve God. '. . . the fearful, and unbelieving, and the abominable, and murderers, and whoremongers, and sorcerers, and idolaters, and all liars, shall have their part in the lake which burneth with fire and brimstone: which is the second death', they promised us.

I didn't want to be cast into hell and tortured forever. In my mind's eye, I saw a huge, roiling lake of lava burning the flesh off my legs and fingers. I saw myself screaming in horrified agony as Satan and his demons, sneering with malice, thrust hooks into my body and lashed my chest with metal-barbed whips. I squeezed my eyes shut and pulled the covers over my head, trying to block out the images as tears pressed my eyelids.

Jesus couldn't save my unconverted soul. If the Lord returned I'd be left behind with the sinners. My parents would go to heaven and there would be no one to look after me. The thought made me sick with distress. 'Tomorrow I will ask to be baptised,' I resolved. The promise of eternal anguish was too much to bear. What other choice did I have?

The leaders approved my request for baptism. I felt limp with relief.

The following First Night my heart leaped when Communion was passed around the ring of brethren gathered for worship. I was thrilled to think that after my baptism I would be granted the right to partake in the unleavened bread and dark grape juice symbolising the death of Christ. Only those who had been baptised were permitted to take part in the rite. Soon, that would be me and I'd be able to go up to heaven with my parents when the day of judgement came.

Baptism in Gloriavale wasn't simply a matter of deciding you wanted to be baptised. You had to go through months of rigorous preparation before the leaders granted the immersion ceremony. They conducted weekly meetings after First Day lunchtimes to screen the baptism participants. The reason for this was because previously some of the young boys had been baptised but afterwards had fallen into sin. They rose up in disobedience against the leadership with some even leaving the church. The leaders decided the rebellious had been baptised too young and didn't fully understand what they were doing. Thus, baptism meetings were instigated to carefully instruct and question candidates. The leaders were determined there'd be no room for backsliding once we'd passed through the waters of baptism.

On the afternoon of my first instruction meeting, my family went home to rest and I pushed open the heavy door to the classroom where we'd been told to meet. Desks had been moved to the side and the chairs placed in a circle. I nervously clutched my Bible and found an empty seat.

The two instructors came in, Shepherds Fervent and Howard.

'There are two types of godly baptism,' Fervent informed us. 'First is baptism by water for remission of sins, and second is baptism by the Holy Spirit which is Christ's gift to his followers.'

He read to us the New Testament story of Christ's apostles who were filled with the Holy Spirit after Christ's death. The Spirit had manifested as flames hovering over each apostle's head. During this phenomenon the apostles claimed the Spirit had gifted them with the ability to speak in tongues, uttering the language of many nations without prior understanding of that language. In this manner they had been able to witness the Gospel of Christ throughout the land, spreading the good message to the Gentiles who did not speak the Hebrew language.

I was intrigued by this concept and it reminded me of the stories we'd been told about Grandad's plane crash where one of the missionaries had this gift. I hadn't seen anyone at Gloriavale with a tongue of flames on their head, but Grandad Hopeful had talked about the Holy Spirit many times. It seemed strange to me. How could someone speak a language they hadn't learned?

'What is "being filled with the Spirit"?' I asked Fervent.

He paused, looked thoughtful for a moment. 'When one serves God then God's Spirit comes to rest on them and takes over their body. He gives them spiritual gifts.' He opened his Bible to 1 Corinthians 12:10, and read aloud. 'This is an example of the gifts which are given; "to one the gifts of healing . . . to another the working of miracles; to another prophecy; to another discerning of spirits; to another divers kinds of tongues; to another the interpretation of tongues".'

I knew about healing as it was something that was strongly taught by the church. If there was sickness or disease, then the

Gloriavale leaders would anoint the ailing with oil and pray that they be healed.

'I don't get it,' I protested. 'I don't understand how this can be. What does it look like to be filled with the Spirit?' My audacity shocked me.

Fervent shocked me even more when he threw his hands towards the heavens and began to call out alien noises that made no sense and didn't sound like a language either. '*Hum ma re sha cu te ma she gaan.*'

I sat in stunned silence. What on earth was he doing? The babble kept going and all the time I was asking myself, 'Where's the tongue of fire?'

For a full half-minute, Fervent continued to speak in tongues, lifting his hands to the sky in rapture. Maybe he was praising the Lord? I was confused. This looked totally outlandish and I wasn't sure it was something I wanted to do. The babble ended and I looked down at my Bible.

Would my baptism give me a spiritual gift? If it did, I hoped it wouldn't be that one.

The months of instruction passed and the day of our baptisms arrived. It was March and the early autumn sun didn't come out at all that First Day. It stayed hidden behind grey West Coast clouds, with rain looking to be just around the corner.

After lunch I changed into my good clothes and Mum got a towel for me. I pulled a blue jacket over my dress, trying to get some warmth as we made our way down the hill to the Graveyard Pool in Jacks Creek.

The boys had used a digger to transform a section of the creek into a swimming hole. We called it the Graveyard Pool because it was about 20 metres from the community graveyard. As we passed the graveyard, my heart tugged at my chest. Grandma Gloria was buried there under a flat white headstone.

Even though I had never met my grandmother I felt I knew what she sounded like. How could that be when my mum had been pregnant with me when Gloria died? I wondered if she was watching over me from heaven.

Today, for the baptisms, the community members gathered along both banks of the creek, scrambling for a good view of the purification ritual. The baptismal party was called to step forward and I lined up with a few other boys and girls. One of the boys, Cory, was a new convert. He hadn't been born in Gloriavale, but joined a few months ago. Light rain began to fall and I looked down as the droplets stained my dress a darker blue.

Grandad Hopeful took his Bible in hand and stood before the brethren to preach. 'Peter of old said to the church, "Repent, and be baptised every one of you in the name of Jesus Christ for the remission of sins, and ye shall receive the gift of the Holy Ghost",' he said. 'Jesus, when he was baptised, came up out of the water, the heavens opened and the Spirit of God descended on him like a dove.' He pointed to us. 'These children have come today to be baptised of their own free will.'

I heard my name called and stepped towards the waterhole. Howard and Fervent had waded fully clothed into the depths and were beckoning me to join them. The water looked very deep. The boys must have recently excavated the creek bed. I slid my feet into the water, shuddering at the icy bite of the creek. *This looks too deep!* My frozen brain wouldn't let me go further.

'Take my hand, love,' a voice said.

I looked up. Howard was holding his hand out to me. I clutched it and held on for dear life. The water was freezing and I gasped with fright as it struck my chest. The long blue dress clung to my legs, hindering my steps. Fervent took my other arm so that I stood between the two Shepherds.

'Tell these people why you are getting baptised today,' Fervent said.

I was shaking, it was so cold, but this had to be done. My lips trembled as I spoke. 'I believe that Jesus is the Son of God. He died on the cross to take away my sins. I'm going to serve him and when I go under these waters I'm going to come up a new creature and all my sins will be washed away.'

'We baptise you in the name of the Father, the Son and the Holy Spirit,' the men cried out. Their strong hands gripped my shoulders and plunged me under the water.

For a moment, I was terrified. I couldn't breathe. I opened my eyes to see light stream through the surface of the water, and then a strange thought popped into my mind: Maybe God would open the heavens for me.

Hands pulled me up and I gulped fresh air as my head broke the surface of the water. It was done. I threw my hands to the sky imitating what Fervent had done at the baptism meeting but I spoke in English. 'Hallelujah! Praise God! Thank you, Jesus!' I screamed.

The whole church clapped, hooted and burst into a baptism song. 'Up from the grave he arose, with a mighty triumph o'er his foes.'

I waded to the bank and Mum wrapped a towel around my shoulders.

One by one the other participants were baptised. I clutched the towel to my neck, shivering as the cold wind stung my flesh. It didn't matter. 'At last I'm free,' I thought. 'My sins have all been cleansed so I'm going to go to heaven now.'

After the baptisms were complete Dove and I ran up the grass trail towards the hostel. 'How do you feel?' she asked.

'Oh! I feel just so free,' I exclaimed. 'I feel so clean. Now that I've gone under the water and come up again I can start fresh. All my sins are gone.'

'That's so awesome.' She threw her arm around my shoulders. 'I'm so happy for you. This is a massive step of faith.'

That night at First Night meeting when the Communion was passed around, Grandad Hopeful invited all the new baptisms to participate in the remembrance of Christ's death.

I was so proud as I broke off a tiny square of bread. The grape juice tasted sweet and delicious. I knew in my heart that I was now acceptable before God. Also, with my public demonstration of faith, the community now accepted me as a converted Christian and child of God. If I died I would go to heaven.

I was truly part of the fold.

TWELVE

The fate of a rebel

It was through pride that sin first came into existence, when Lucifer, now called Satan and the Devil, rose up in rebellion against God.

—*WHAT WE BELIEVE*, P. 98

I always tried to fit in, to do the right thing, but my older siblings were different. Their fearless spirit and endless curiosity landed them in trouble with Gloriavale's ministry countless times.

The leaders had very strict rules about the simplest of things and it seemed Sara and Sam were on a mission to break those rules. Somehow they managed to get their hands on contraband such as worldly music, headphones, pocket knives, chewing gum, sunglasses—anything small enough to stash in a metal case. They'd bury their booty deep in the garden or hide it in places no one would think to look.

Both of them loved me but they didn't appreciate my attempts to convince them to obey the rules and stop getting into trouble. They would laugh at my pleas, call me 'Bossy Boots' and do the rebellious thing anyway.

They thought they were untouchable and were a constant source of worry for my parents. If they were discovered in possession of illicit goods, or doing something that was forbidden by the leaders, the community would be called together for a revival.

I hated revivals. The meetings were a tirade of vehement lecturing to remind us of hell punishment for sinners. I'd try to hide in a back storeroom to avoid going to the meal table. Prayer would find me and I'd be sent to sit with my family, tail between my legs.

We were taught about the evils of the world and the wisdom of Gloriavale's decision to live in a secluded environment. Leaders warned us against people who had rebelled against the church and who might try to steal our souls from the Lord. Unbelievers and backslidden Christians were sheep in wolves' clothing.

We were forbidden to commune with people who'd left the church. We were not to live with them, eat with them or be in community with them.

'What concord hath Christ with Belial? What fellowship hath righteousness with unrighteousness?' Hopeful challenged us. 'Light hath no communion with darkness. Be ye not unequally yoked together with unbelievers.'

I was confused because I'd read the Bible myself. Didn't Christ himself eat with a whore? And when the church leaders of the time had berated him for it Jesus told them that because the woman had shown greater kindness to him than they had, she was worthy of respect. But I kept my opinions hidden. The leaders were sent from God so surely their counsel was to be trusted.

During a revival, the consequence for a rebellious child would be public shaming before the church. Children would be marched up to the stage where they were made to face the wall in shame for two to three hours. Their food portions would be confiscated and they would not be permitted to eat, as further punishment.

Parents who had rebellious children were denounced as not having fulfilled their godly parental duties. The Church held them accountable for the disobedience of their children. The scripture flung at them was, 'He that spareth his rod hateth his son'. The pressure on them to curb their rebellious children was immense.

The harsh punishment would be softened if a child showed repentance and their parent demonstrated proper discipline to curb their evil behaviour.

The parent would be praised for their good works and the child would be told they were forgiven for their sins.

If Mum discovered the leaders already knew about Sara or Sam's misdemeanours she walked them up on the stage herself. As a result, they'd sometimes be allowed to come down from the stage sooner and possibly be given some food. The mark of shame was lifted.

As Sara got older, the expectation that she would submit to the church grew stronger and more forceful. Some of her sins could be put down to childish mischief she would eventually outgrow, but as an adult she was expected to 'put away childish things'.

But she didn't want to and didn't see why she should. The

rules were so petty. So what if she wanted to wear sunglasses or roll her sleeves up over her arms? The disciplinaries came down on her for tucking the corners of her headscarf in and for wearing it too far towards the back of her head. They were always scolding her for wearing her belt too loose. She was nothing like the sweet submissive woman Gloriavale expected us to be. Every day, they imposed their rules more bullishly upon her life. When she turned fifteen, they declared her a rebel and set an older woman named Chastity to oversee her every move.

My poor sister. She began to be hauled through Leaders' Meetings, where she would be interrogated for hours, forced to admit her sins, made to publicly confess before the church and repent from following the Evil One. I was only eleven but I could see her free spirit suffocating under the enforcements. She got thinner and didn't smile as often.

If only she would listen to the church, then all this punishment could stop.

It was hard on my parents too. They were despised and looked down on for their parenting. I would often find my mother in tears over what her daughter had done.

Things limped along for a few months, with Sara becoming more and more withdrawn. One night a knock sounded on our bedroom door. Mum opened it to find Chastity there, looking for Sara yet again.

'She's in the shower,' Mum said.

'Let her know we're looking for her,' Chastity said. 'She's to attend a Leaders' Meeting.'

'Why?' Mum asked. Nobody had told her Sara had been called to yet another one.

'She's been asking Prudence what it's like to leave Gloriavale and live in the outside world,' Chastity growled.

Mum looked stunned. 'Um, OK, I'll go find her.'

As soon as Chastity took herself off, Mum headed to the Main Bathroom. She knocked on the door of the first cubicle where Sara had been showering. There was no answer.

'Sara,' she called out. 'Chastity is looking for you.'

Still no answer.

'Hello? Are you there!'

Nothing.

'Sara?' She turned the handle, the door swung open and she gasped in horror. The shower was empty but the walls were stained with streaks of blood. No! She threw back the curtains.

She raced to our cousins' rooms. 'Is Sara here? Have you seen her?'

'Wasn't she in the shower?' Lydia said.

'No and there's blood in there!' Mum was so scared.

Sam ambled over to her. 'Don't stress, Mum. She had a blood nose. But she headed off before I finished my shower.'

Sara emerged from nowhere and Mum ran to her. My sister's eyes were swollen and cheeks puffed. Mum wrapped her arms around her.

She put Sara to bed and, when they hugged goodnight, Sara clung to Mum longer than usual. The next morning when Mum woke me up there were tears in her eyes. 'Lil, Sara's left.'

She'd run away in the middle of the night, taking what belongings she could carry on her back. The note she left on my mother's bedside table was heartbreakingly simple. *I can't do this any more.*

I couldn't bear the news, but somehow I wasn't surprised. The leaders had been so hard on her. Poor Sara. She was only fifteen. How could she take care of herself?

My whole family was stunned and my mother's heart was broken. She was sick with worry. Where was her daughter? Was she safe? Who would care for her? She was so young.

The wound was still fresh when my mother heard Righteous Servant reprimanding a young person who was grieving the loss of a sibling who had also fled Gloriavale. In an act of defiance, Mum confronted him. 'Righteous, I heard you rebuking young people who weep for their lost ones. How can you justify that? Even I weep for my daughter.'

He puffed himself up and told her off. 'When someone turns their back on God, they are no longer your family. You can't cry, Miracle. You have to disown her. Your daughter is a sinner and should be dead to you.'

My mother didn't back down. 'How dare you criticise me? Your wife is allowed to cry when she buries her dead father in the ground and he's going to heaven, yet I'm not allowed to weep for the soul of my daughter, who is damned for eternity? I'll weep if I care to.'

From that moment on I had little love for Righteous even though I was fond of his wife, my cousin Forbearance. Men who were greedy for a position of authority in the church commonly used such displays of religious fervour to demonstrate their piety.

Sam didn't take Sara's disappearance well. Instead he became depressed. He cried a lot and when he wasn't crying he would sit in silence for hours and stare blankly. Mum attempted to console him, but he became more withdrawn and shut out everyone except for Bethany's brother Jared. They were fierce friends and did everything together.

I loved my rebellious sister and missed her a lot. Her top bunk was empty now. She wasn't there to climb into bed with and cuddle if I'd had a bad dream or was scared of the dark. It was difficult to come to terms with the fact that someone who'd been such a big part of my life was gone forever.

But it was a sin to love or think about those who had left the church. They'd turned their back on Christ and the one true church. So we must turn our backs on them.

I grew closer than ever to Mark and Lani's family, who still loved Sara even though she'd left. If there was one thing I learned, it was to savour the moments you had with the people you love because you never knew when they could be taken from you. Sara would always be in my heart. I prayed for her when no one was listening.

THIRTEEN

Blood on my hands

I confess that I have sinned against God, and against my fellow men.

—*WHAT WE BELIEVE*, 'THE COMMITMENT', P. 23

Cherish's mother, Prayer Darling, could flip in an instant from being a loving, sweet woman into a hard-faced tyrant.

I felt sorry for her because Grandad had her under his spell ever since her husband, Phil, left the church. Anything that Grandad said, she obeyed. When she did well in her position he praised her highly, but if she didn't submit to him he would shout at her in front of everyone.

Even though she could be nasty and callous, Prayer was also caring towards me during tough times such as when Sara left.

However, her position in charge of the kitchen gave her a

lot of power and she was intent on enforcing every strident rule. None of us were permitted to help ourselves to food from Prayer's domain. Food belonged to the community and we were only allowed our strictly rationed portion—too bad if you got hungry in between.

To curb the hunger, a few of us became adept at uplifting bread slices from the kitchen racks. You could see Prayer coming from a mile away with her buttocks swaying out either side of her apron. She watched that bread rack like a hawk and it wasn't long before she swooped down on a few young thieves. It was clear to a number of us that Prayer, ever the diligent slave, reported the sin of theft to Grandad Hopeful. The upshot of this was fierce—a revival campaign.

Campaigns were initiated by an appointed church leader and could last for weeks. The entire community would be forced to sit in long sessions where we rehearsed what to believe.

Some philosophies were drilled into us so often that obeying them was like muscle memory. The most important one was about submission to the church and repentance of sin.

A revival would end when Shepherds decided that the purging was complete. The Lord would send them a new message and the church would start a whole new campaign.

When Prayer snitched on the thieves, Grandad called the church together. Attendance was compulsory. 'Is anyone not present? Put your hand up if someone in your family is not here,' Grandad commanded.

A few hands went up among families whose men were out on the farm or working at something urgent for one of the businesses. Grandad sent somebody to fetch them. Nobody was allowed to be absent from a campaign.

When everyone was present Grandad took the microphone and began the drill. For hours he preached, drumming the same teaching, the same message into our minds over and over until the beliefs were hardwired into our brains.

It wasn't comfortable, either physically or emotionally, to undergo a campaign but even so, I was in awe of my grandfather's charismatic oratory. The man was a genius. He would back his teachings with countless scriptures quoted from memory and he never failed to provide solid references to his arguments.

No wonder he'd been one of the most accomplished evangelists of his time. His manner of speech was eloquent and everything that came out of his mouth made logical sense. When the leaders told us Hopeful was the Star of God it was easy to believe.

Grandad reminded us of the consequences of stealing. 'If your hand or foot causes you to sin then it's better for it to be cut off than have all your limbs and be cast into everlasting hell fire.'

I shivered as I imagined an axe slicing through my hand. Would I be willing to lose a hand so that I could go to heaven? It seemed quite extreme.

'If you can't curb the lust to steal then it's better to tear the eyeball out of your head than your whole body be thrown into hell,' Grandad thundered.

I shifted uncomfortably in the blue plastic seat and glanced at the clock. Meal table sessions could go for two to three hours. We were only forty-five minutes into this one.

'Would you be willing to cut off your hand or foot to save your soul?' Grandad said. He looked at me and I lowered my head. Victor and I had stolen rolled oats and fresh cream from the cooler. I was sure his words were aimed directly at me.

'Confess your faults one to another, and pray one for another, that ye may be healed.'

Confess, repent, be forgiven. The only path to salvation.

Condemnation swirled over my head like a dark, heavy force. I had to repent, to confess my theft or I'd go to hell.

My pride fought with me. Surely God would overlook the odd missing cupful of rolled oats? I had good, logical arguments to counter my grandfather's.

If Gloriavale gave us nice food more often then nobody would need to steal. Treats weren't that common on the farm. It was a decadence to have cream and sugar with our porridge once a week. It was a good day if we had eggs or pancakes for breakfast.

But there was no escape.

Grandad Hopeful's voice was stern. 'He that covereth his sins shall not prosper: but who so confesseth and forsaketh them shall have mercy.'

People were nodding in agreement. The sermon was striking home. Repent, repent, repent. I could almost hear a chant.

Brethren stood to their feet to confess. First one and then another. Soon over twenty were standing. Grandad handed the microphone to the first sinner who confessed taking bread and asked forgiveness.

My cousin Humble stood and his voice sounded over the speaker system. 'I'd like to say I'm sorry. I took some bread when I was hungry and it wasn't mine to take. Please forgive me.'

I wanted to ignore my conscience but the guilt was too much. Condemnation festered in my soul. If I didn't cleanse myself then I'd be damned to eternity with Satan.

Condemnation was cancerous and I'd seen it crush people's mental health and drain their happiness. I'd rather look like an idiot now than lose my salvation. So what if my selfish pride and ego got hurt. Better the short-term pain for the long-term gain.

Terror struck my heart as the sinners confessed. I hated public shame before the church. It was humiliating and terrifying but I knew that if I didn't apologise, the guilt of sin would stick in my mind.

I slowly got to my feet. In utter humiliation I kept my eyes glued to the ground. Grandad handed me a black microphone. It stank of bad breath and there was food stuck in the mesh. I held it as far from my face as I could and rushed the words out in a tumble.

'I took some rolled oats from the kitchen. I'm sorry and want to repent of my sins. I want the Lord's forgiveness and I'm going to stop living in sin. I claim the Blood of the Lamb to wash me white as snow.'

I couldn't sit down fast enough. Everyone watched as I almost fell on to the seat and nearly toppled over.

Way to go, Lil.

Even though I felt like an idiot, there was a feeling of lightness in my heart. At least now I didn't have to worry about going to hell or chopping off my hand.

FOURTEEN

The thief

Covetousness, the desire to gain or to keep this world's good, is idolatry, and is equal with murder, adultery and theft.

—WHAT WE BELIEVE, P. 42

'Lilia!' My cousin Cherish rushed in, dramatic as always. I looked up from Mum's sewing machine and laughed. Cherish Darling was now nine and just two years younger than me. We did everything together and were inseparable. Her love of turning simple situations into a massive cause for excitement made her orange freckles pop out and her auburn hair was always frizzy. Mum said she was just like her father Phil.

I heaved an exaggerated sigh. 'What is it now?'

'Guess what . . .'

'What? Tell me!'

'Mmm, I don't know if I should. Mum said not to tell anyone.' She looked thoughtful.

'Well, why did you mention it in the first place!' I exclaimed.

'Because I'm so excited.' She kept bouncing on her toes.

'Fine. I won't tell anyone else,' I assured her. 'Cross my heart and hope to die.'

She grabbed my shoulders. 'Grace Hoover is coming back! They've gone to pick her up from town already.'

I was stunned. Graciela, the Chilean girl with the longest lashes I'd ever seen. It had been almost a year since the Hoover family had left Gloriavale. Why was she returning?

I jumped up. 'When's she arriving?'

'They'll be here any moment now. She's going to live in the room with Prayer, Dawn and me.'

'We have to do something to welcome her!' My heart was doing a happy dance. Grace!

'What if we sing her a welcome song?' Cherish suggested.

Good idea.

We chose a hymn then rehearsed it, continually peeking through the high window in our family bedroom for a sign of her arrival. *There!* A van had pulled up and parked on the front lot. I grabbed Cherish's hand and ran, half dragging her to Prayer's family room. We perched ourselves nervously on the edge of Prayer's single bed and waited.

'I hope she likes the song,' I whispered.

The bedroom door swung open and we burst out singing. Grace stood in the doorway with a gigantic smile on her face. She held some bags and wore a short floral dress and dark purple hoodie.

The song was terrible. We were such idiots and she loved it. We all collapsed with giggles at the insane performance.

I threw my arms around her before Prayer shooed me out of the room. Grace seemed tired and there was a world of sorrow in her face. Something wasn't right. I took my leave and swore to find her later.

'What happened? Why did you come back?' It was dark and we'd found a quiet pocket where we wouldn't be overheard.

Tears glistened in her eyes. 'I was forced to come. We were living in Minnesota at a community called Elmendorf when a few rebels stole a car and crashed it. The next day a child came forward and accused me of stealing the vehicle and trying to kill her.'

I stared at her in disbelief. Was it true?

'It was a lie!' she burst out. 'I didn't know anything about it. They wanted a scapegoat to blame and an excuse to get rid of me.'

The agony of the deceit was plain on her face. 'No one knows about this. Not even Gloriavale. Hopeful thinks I'm here because I want to finish my schooling in New Zealand. The Elmendorf church leaders kicked me out and shoved me on a plane. I was boarding my flight in Sydney before they phoned and told Gloriavale I was on my way.'

I couldn't believe it. How could a church be so hateful? How could an institution that preached the love of Christ treat people with such malice?

My heart wept for my friend. Grace couldn't hurt a fly if she wanted to, let alone try to kill a little girl. This was a church deception, plain and simple, and Grace was also suffering from the rejection of her family who'd decided to side with Elmendorf.

I longed to hug her but Grandad Hopeful discouraged women from showing affection or emotion. Instead I listened quietly as she poured out her soul. 'Well I'm glad you're here now. I've been needing a partner in crime.' I squeezed her hand hard.

Having Grace back in my life was electrifying. She was an outsider and brought worldly habits and influences with her. I loved her strange accent and the way she spoke was so different to anything I'd ever heard. She called me 'Babe' and said things like 'Cool' or 'Shut up!' when she thought something was awesome. She wore hoodies over her uniform and pushed her scarf as far back on her head as possible to expose her hair. When Prayer reprimanded her for rolling her sleeves up over the elbow Grace simply waited till she left then rolled them up again.

On top of that, Grace had a stash of forbidden music tapes and endless stories about the outside world. My fascination with her life experience drew us into a deep and unbreakable friendship.

'Tell me a story,' I would plead, and so for hours late into the night, while the rest of Gloriavale slept, we would sit on the lounge couches whispering about her adventures. She described what it was like to collect maple syrup in winter when she lived in Canada and how the snow fell so thick it could reach her thighs. She told me how she would wear black leather jackets and trousers—clothing utterly forbidden in Gloriavale—and what it was like to kiss a boy.

Grace's worldly stories thrilled me and my imagination went on fantastical journeys about what was possible. I wondered what it would be like to live on the outside, meet a boy—not someone that Gloriavale had picked for me—and fall in love. What would it be like to drive a car or wear trousers or drink a beer?

Grace quickly became my most trusted confidante. In a world where saying the wrong thing to the wrong people could land you in all sorts of trouble, it was comforting to have someone I could trust with my most private thoughts.

I told her in strict confidence about the struggles our family had faced and the circumstances of Sara's leaving. I was furious when she informed me that certain church members were saying my Mum and Dad were not good parents because they were friends with their children. In the eyes of the church good parenting did not entail parents befriending their children. The role of a parent was to discipline and the role of a child was to obey.

~

After hearing the wonders of Grace's travels I was desperately hungry for knowledge of the world, even though the leaders always preached that the world was a place of sin and corruption.

'One day the Lord will return to destroy this earth with fire,' Fervent warned us over and over.

The only place I could go to satisfy my curiosity was to the strictly censored books Gloriavale allowed in their communal library. The shelves were high and there was no ladder. Too bad, the lack of one wasn't going to defeat me. I climbed by grasping a shelf above my head, setting my foot on any ledge I could find and hauling myself up until I reached the prize at the top—a set of encyclopaedias.

I wanted to know more about the places that Grace had spoken of and I was eager to know what life was like outside

Gloriavale. I read about wonders—the Eiffel Tower, the Golden Gate Bridge, New York. Grace got used to me asking, 'Have you seen this? What about this?'

During play breaks at school I would rush again to the library to pick up where I'd left off. I'd scamper up the tall shelves and hover precariously at the top, searching for hidden gems of knowledge. More than once I feared the shelves would fall and I'd be dashed to death. But the fear couldn't stop me. The search for understanding had bewitched me. In six months I'd read every single volume in the collection from A to Z, cover to cover.

When I found out that the Wisdom and Virtue girls possessed Jane Austen novels, I knew I must get my hands on one. Gloriavale leaders were more lenient with this type of content as they felt the women in such books used proper etiquette and wore modest dresses the way women should. I was ecstatic when one of the girls loaned me a copy of Jane Austen's *Pride & Prejudice* and I spent every spare minute I could hiding in the corner of my bunk bed with my nose buried in its worn, musty pages. If the hostel was relatively empty I would claim the kitchenette couch as a semi-private reading space. Only there, for just a moment, could I be transported to a different world, lost in the story of romance and drama.

∼

One day Grandad Hopeful announced that I and the other girls in my class would be taken to Greymouth, the closest substantial township, for dental checks. We were all hyped with excitement because this was a rare opportunity to get outside Gloriavale.

We changed into our good clothes for the special occasion and bundled ourselves into the van along with a few other town goers, chatting non-stop during the hour-long trip. The two older women appointed to watch over us for the duration of the expedition were tolerant of our excitement and didn't try to shush us.

I looked out of the van window, admiring the lush West Coast greenery and small, cosy townships. Little did I know what grave decisions awaited me.

Our dentist visits finished early and we looked at our carers for instructions.

'Granny is still doing the community shopping,' they said. 'We'll have to wait another hour or so.'

Time to look around! We left the dentist's office and spilled out on to the street, gasping in wonder at the captivating sights. Massive store windows lined the streets. They held enticing glimpses of colourful clothing, strange objects in gorgeous, glittering displays—things whose purpose we couldn't begin to guess. I pressed my face to the glass trying to see what was going on behind the windows. If only we could explore without governance.

Our watchers hustled us away from the stores and ushered us into a building. 'This way girls. We'll wait here until the van is ready to pick us up.'

I read the large serif letters marking the side of the building. 'Grey District Library'. My heart leaped. Books! This was better than the stores.

The library was quiet and the librarian peered over her glasses with a disapproving look.

I pushed ahead, barely able to contain my excitement. 'Don't get into trouble and don't leave the building,' our carers hissed. They sat in the corner with a couple of books and we girls were left to our own devices.

Oh, such wonders! The library shelves were lined with hundreds of books about topics I'd never heard of. Gloriavale's library was nothing like this. I wandered the aisles tracing the shelves with my eyes. My fingers tingled as I ran them across the spines. This journey could take me anywhere.

I shut my eyes and breathed deeply. When I opened them I saw a sign.

'Romance' it read. I stopped. What was in this aisle? My mind reeled. These books were forbidden. The pictures on the covers were more graphic than anything I'd ever seen. They showed scantily clad women clinging in ecstasy to handsome men and there was no lack of kissing or sexual innuendos. Picking out a single book, I ran my finger over the cover. The title was written in a thick, flowing Balmoral font and embossed with gold foil. I replaced the book with awe. If only I could stay here forever.

I plucked story after story from the shelf, poring over the covers and scanning the blurbs. I felt giddy with excitement. Then a new thought crossed my mind. Perhaps I could read a book. I hadn't thought of that. Surely it would be a sin . . .

But a cover on the lower shelf caught my eye. It pictured a dark-haired man who wore black leather boots and a loose white tunic. In his arms was a gorgeous woman. She was barefoot and wore a gown that was pushed off her shoulders to highlight her breasts. In the distance, a ship floated on the ocean. Something about the picture drew me in. This was the book I would read.

Hysterical giggles from behind the shelves made me jump. It

was Hosanna and Blessing whispering to each other and giggling. 'Oh my goodness! Look, there's a naked man in this book!'

I turned away, clutched my prize and headed for the corner of the library where a few beanbags lay scattered on the floor. I snuggled into one, opened the book and discovered a world of dreams.

'Darien,' I whispered, the main character's name. It felt sexy and spicy on my tongue; a worldly name that I would never be allowed to call anyone in Gloriavale. He was a sailor, in love with a woman of high breeding who he could not have. She loved him too, but felt torn between her family's expectations and her heart. Time slipped away as I devoured the pages.

'Lilia!' The call jolted me out of my reverie. Bethany was beckoning me. 'We have to go.'

I looked at the clock on the wall. What! In the blink of an eye, a whole hour and a half had passed. 'Hurry!' she called over her shoulder and headed towards the front.

No! We couldn't go now. I hadn't finished the story. I looked down at the book in panic. Would Darien and his love be together in the end? Would he perish in the trip from the castle to the city? My mind was frantic. This couldn't be happening. What should I do?

Take the book.

The thought was clear and simple. I was shocked. That would be stealing and I'd surely be sent to hell. I hesitated. If anyone discovered my sin I would be severely punished. Was I willing to suffer the shame in front of my friends and family?

Take the book now. Hide it and go. I couldn't resist. With horror I watched my hands slip the book inside my thick jacket. When

I walked towards the front of the library the librarian looked up from her computer. She had sharp owl eyes that scanned across me.

I forced a weak smile. *She can see what you're doing! You're going to get caught*, the voice in my head screamed. The stolen book burned a hole into my side. My heart pounded and my hands trembled.

When the automatic doors slid open I almost ran through and caught a breath of relief on the other side. The other girls were waiting in a group and I hurried to stand with them. I pretended to be cold and wrapped my arms around myself to keep the book secure.

'What took you so long?' Bethany asked.

'Nothing. I was just packing up,' I mumbled.

Our van rolled up to the front of the library and we clambered in for the ride back to Gloriavale. I felt awkward and stiff as I removed my jacket to better conceal the book.

My stern conscience reprimanded me. *God can see you even if no one else can.*

No, I desperately need this book, my freedom fighter argued. *I know what's best for me. Hush now.*

It was dinner time when we pulled into Gloriavale. The girls were groggy, most of them had fallen asleep on the trip home, but I was wide awake. I went directly to our room and hid my contraband deep in the back of my drawer.

No one will find it here, I thought.

My secret could never be discovered or all hell would break loose.

Later, when no one was looking, I removed it to read in secret. Every snippet of time I could grasp to immerse myself in the story was precious. At night, when my family was sleeping, I held the book up by the window to capture the moonlight so I could read.

The following Sixth Day afternoon I was rostered on cleaning duty. I worked hard, sweeping the big kitchen floors and polishing them to a sparkle. If I finished my tasks quickly our team leader might let us knock off work early.

After she granted permission to leave I crept into the family bedroom, where my mother and younger siblings were bedded for the afternoon, to remove the book from its hiding place. The hostel was quiet because mothers and children were resting in preparation for the Sixth Night cinema. It was the perfect time to read in secret.

Sunlight flooded through our hostel kitchenette so I snuggled on the couch tucked in the alcove and began to read. Oh the excitement! Sword fights, love letters, loss and longing. The book swept me off my feet. I was enthralled.

'Raaaaah!!!'

I yelped with fright and leaped off the couch, dropping the book in my haste.

Sam laughed at my ridiculousness. 'What are you doing?' he demanded.

'Nothing. Leave me alone.' I shoved him away and tried to sweep the book into the couch cushions.

'What's that?' He pounced on my book.

'Go away. I'm not doing anything,' I cried.

'Don't lie,' he scoffed. 'You're hiding something. What is it?' He came around the couch and I snatched the book trying to hide it in the folds of my skirt. He grabbed my wrist and I gasped as it tumbled out. Darien and his lover were exposed. 'Where did you get this? There are no books like this here. Tell me how you got it.'

'Just leave me alone,' I protested. 'It's my book and where I got it is none of your beeswax.'

'If you don't tell me right now I'll take it from you and tell everyone,' he threatened.

I gaped at him, horrified. Who was he to be telling me about good behaviour when he was continually being rebellious to the church? I weighed up the options. Maybe if I shared the truth he would keep his mouth shut. 'I got it from Greymouth Library.'

'What! You stole it. You're a thief!' His accusations stung and I tried to plead with him.

'Please, please don't tell. You can't tell anyone. I'll be in so much trouble,' I beseeched him.

'I'm telling Mum.' He spun on his heel and marched off.

I was fraught with dread and loathing. I hated him, but more than that, I feared the church. What would my punishment be?

'How could you do this, Lilia?' Mum asked in disbelief. 'You know the Bible says "Thou shalt not steal".'

'Please don't tell Dad,' I begged. The punishment would be so much worse. 'I just wanted to know what it was like to read something different. It was so important to me, but I know it was wrong. I'm sorry. I promise it will never happen again.'

Mum confiscated the book. 'Do not tell anyone about this.'

For weeks I awaited a terrible fate, but nothing happened.

If the leaders knew about my sin I'd definitely be dragged to a meeting for discipline. So why had no one come to take me away?

When no one came for me, I realised what my mother had done. It was against her faith to protect a thief and she would be accused of conspiracy. But regardless, she'd risked herself to protect me from the wrath of Gloriavale. I would be forever in her debt.

The strangest thing was that even in the midst of my fear I felt cheated of my right to finish the book.

FIFTEEN

Retribution

Those who sin before all should be rebuked before all, that the others may learn to fear.

—*WHAT WE BELIEVE*, P. 55

I graduated from the ukelele to the violin when I was ten years old. Gloriavale was filled with skilful musicians, and music approved by the leaders was an important part of our life.

I loved music with a passion and resisted the restrictions that were imposed on us. I didn't think music was something that should be controlled or caged. In my mind, the best type of melodies were the ones that set your soul free, and enjoyment of music was purely subjective. So, just because the leaders didn't like something, that didn't mean they should impose their preference on the rest of us.

My beliefs would land me in a lot of trouble as I got older.

Like every child of Gloriavale I was taught to read a musical score and play a variety of instruments. My teacher, Victory Overcomer, told me I had a natural gift for music and her encouragement was my fuel. I laboured tirelessly as she took us through gruelling violin lessons.

Music practice was held straight after breakfast every single day and one morning our class of wannabe violinists gathered in the Main Foyer for practice. Victory attached a large piece of paper to either side of the shoe lockers. On it, she'd drawn a neat line of notes along a stave; a full C major scale.

I had to make sure I didn't gape when Victory stood to attention before us. She was an accomplished artist, chef and musician and, unlike most women in Gloriavale, didn't have a husband. She hadn't been born in Gloriavale like me, but I wanted to be just like her. She reminded me of a military officer in the way she threw her shoulders straight back. Her chin was always lifted high and regal and she spoke with such elegance.

The corners of her white headscarf flared in perfect symmetry out either side of her head like the pectoral fins of a stingray and not a single grey hair was out of place.

With a flick of her baton, Victory jumpstarted the practice. Our class stumbled our way up and down the scales.

After music practice we found our classrooms and took our seats. Boys and girls sat in different rows. The teacher, Peter Righteous, headed the classroom.

'Take out your Bibles.'

Every day began with a Bible reading.

I lifted my desk lid and removed the thick King James Bible

that had been issued to me. It was an old book that had been re-bound in the community print shop. I stroked the dull-red cover and held the book to my nose. I loved the musty smell of the pages.

'We're reading from Hebrews 13:17.' Peter pointed to the boy closest to him. 'Nathan, read one verse and then you others continue around the room.'

Pages rustled for a brief moment before Nathan began in a clear voice. 'Obey them that have the rule over you, and submit yourselves . . . '

The boy beside Nathan picked up the next verse. After each of us had read aloud Peter finished the chapter. For the rest of class we were taught that to sacrifice one's self-will and serve the church was the only way to salvation. There was a godly order established in the church—the highest power was God and then Church leaders—husbands were to submit to the church and wives must submit to their husband. Children came last and were expected to obey their parents who served the Lord.

'The leaders watch for our souls. If you are obedient to the church you will live long on the earth and the Lord will bless you,' Peter told us.

He began to pray for our salvation and we clasped our hands and bowed our heads. He thanked God for the wonderful place the leaders had built for us and prayed that we would be saved from the lusts of the world.

We had two more classes after that and I was impatient for them to finish. Today was Friday, PE day, and I couldn't wait to be out on the field, kicking a soccer ball around.

Peter dismissed us and we tore down to the field, with Jubilant messing around as always and making us laugh at his jokes.

Gloriavale didn't allow competitive games because it was cause for people to be lifted up in pride. We had to play soccer without keeping score, which I thought was stupid because the whole point of sport was to win. The long dresses were so frustrating to run in but I tackled the football off Jubilant anyway. I didn't care if my dress flung up, there was no way I was going to let our team lose.

Our teacher for the session was Nathaniel Constant so I knew to be careful not to make him angry because his fuse was extremely short. Grace and I called him 'Nathaniel Constantly Annoying' behind his back. We kept our distance from his aggressive temper. It didn't deter Jubilant though. He kept on with the jokes, kicking the ball to the wrong player—anything for a laugh.

Nathaniel yelled at him, then he yelled again. Jubilant cooled it for about five minutes but it wasn't in his nature to behave even though Nathaniel's anger was building.

It only took one more smart remark before his temper erupted. 'Get out! Leave! Now! Get up to the main building. Go!'

Jubilant grumbled and left the field, but not without throwing a last snide comment. Nathaniel tore after him, caught up and kicked him, then bashed him across the head.

The game halted and the class watched, stunned into silence as Nathaniel kicked our classmate again and then again. He forced him to walk and kept smashing him across the head and kicking him for the entire thirty or so metres to the Main Building. Jubilant was sobbing and trying to protect himself as he stumbled up the road.

Even though the church taught that it was godly for disobedient children to be beaten, this was so wrong. I was only eleven years old but as I stood there, helpless and watching, my hands to my throat, I knew with every fibre of my being that this was wrong. It was the most shocking thing I'd ever witnessed.

I couldn't keep playing and neither could the other kids. We were numb from the shock of what had happened. All of us left the soccer field and returned to the classroom. I couldn't concentrate and after school I found Grace and fumed in disbelief about what had happened.

That evening I poured it all out to Mum. She was furious, both at what Nathaniel had done but also because she couldn't do anything about it. She was a woman and had little power to intervene in the men's realm. Both of us waited to see what punishment the men would give Nathaniel. Nothing happened and he continued teaching us. I was disgusted.

~

The incident fanned my loathing for Gloriavale's stance on child discipline into a raging furnace. The leaders called it godly, but I thought it was abuse. I couldn't see how beating a child because you felt angry and full of rage was a demonstration of God's love.

Some leaders not only encouraged violent beatings but scolded parents who were lenient. This was a church that preached non-violence and was anti-war, yet it saw fit to punish their young for minor errors. The leaders defended their philosophy based on the scripture 'spare the rod and spoil the child'. Some men took this literally, using weapons like polystyrene pipe to beat their sons. Certain other members rebelled against the impositions and refused to treat their children badly, and I witnessed loving relationships between many parents and their children.

A wife would, in strict confidence, show me her young children, who had horrific marks on their legs, bottoms and backs where her husband had beaten them. Rage boiled in my chest when I saw those poor children suffering. I vowed to unleash the fury of hell if any husband of mine ever laid a finger on a child of ours in malice.

I was not the only child of Gloriavale to witness violent episodes of 'discipline' inflicted on other youth. One quiet morning I was in the high school with my head down studying, as were my 30 other classmates. I was having trouble with a difficult maths problem and bit my lip in deep concentration.

Suddenly a loud noise jolted me out of focus. We looked up from our books, all of us startled. It was Shepherd Fervent bursting into the room.

Fervent was dragging his son Willing by the collar of his shirt and he yanked him to stand before the class. I cringed.

'Children look here!' Fervent commanded.

We didn't want to look. Willing's eyes were puffy and red. He'd been crying and he hung his head to the floor.

Fervent puffed out his chest and threw back his shoulders. His balding head caught the light from the window and he smoothed down the sides of his oily hair. 'The Bible says, "Children, obey your parents in the Lord",' he shouted. His other hand held a limp leather strap. 'Proverbs says, "Withhold not correction from the child: for if thou beatest him with the rod, he shall not die".'

I couldn't stop looking at the strap because it made me sick to the stomach. Fervent was going to make an example of Willing?

How could he do that to a boy of thirteen?

'What do you have to say, son?' Fervent poked his son.

Willing stared at the ground and mumbled an apology for being disobedient to his father. I felt a sliver of hope. Maybe the apology was enough to clear him?

Fervent spat a lecture of how godly parents beat their children to submission.

Then he turned to his son.

I screwed my eyes shut, thinking Fervent was going to strap Willing's hand, but my stomach dropped with horror at his next words.

'Pull down your pants. Bend over.'

In that moment I wanted nothing more than to kill Fervent. To my eyes he was scum of the earth. Willing looked shocked, but obeyed his father.

Fervent took a wide stance and drew the strap back over his head. Without warning the belt flashed down and bit into Willing's flesh. He moaned and whimpered with pain. Fervent didn't stop. With all his strength he whipped the poor boy again, and again, and again.

Bile rose in my throat and I turned away from the appalling scene. Fervent was a pig and no man of God. My knuckles turned white and I gripped the desk in fury. How dare that man—a leader—treat a child this way?

I shut my eyes to block out the horror and covered my ears. I couldn't watch even though I knew I risked punishment for showing disagreement. The whole time I prayed, 'Please God, let it stop. Please make it stop.'

When the beating ended I still couldn't look up. My heart knew it was disrespectful to gawk at Willing's exposed flesh. At the very least, I'd offer the boy some respect in his shame.

I stared at the pencil groove on the edge of my desk, and my eyes burned with unshed tears. Fervent left his humiliated son standing at the front of the room. The room was deathly silent. When the overseeing teacher gave him a curt nod, Willing stumbled to his desk and buried his sobs in his hands. The class ended and I stumbled to the lockers in a daze.

From that moment I had nothing but love and compassion for Willing. I was popular and loved at school because I was a gifted student of high-status birth so I did my best to include him in my social circles.

An exclusive group of us would meet in the evenings to play basketball or soccer. We were the misfits and the ones who thought outside the box. Willing hung out with us and I developed something of a crush on him which I dared not tell anyone for fear of punishment.

The rules, though, didn't change my feelings. What I believed was that all children deserved love.

~

That week didn't get any better. At dinner the next night, Grandad Hopeful made an announcement. 'We need the Lord's blessing and unless we sacrifice our carnal flesh and come to Him in prayer and fasting we will not prosper.'

My heart sank. I hated fast days. Why would anyone want to go hungry on purpose? Besides, it was hard to keep my mind on prayer when my gut ached with hunger. On top of that, I couldn't see how starving the body of important nutrients was healthy for growing children, men doing heavy manual labour or pregnant women. But Gloriavale often practised abstinence, with fasting a common practice. We were taught that food was a temporary need of the earth. When the Lord took us to heaven we'd receive earthly bodies that didn't need food.

'Man shall not live by bread alone, but by every word that proceedeth out of the mouth of God,' Grandad said.

I wondered why we were fasting this time because there was always an intention behind the practice. Grandad might tell us to pray and fast for everyone to be filled with the Holy Spirit, or it might be that we needed more money for the farm or one of the other businesses such as Air West Coast.

We practised different types of fasting. Sometimes it would be a short-term fast where the body was entirely starved of food for a day or two. Other times it might be a month-long ordeal where we only ate rice for each meal, perhaps with a bit of sauce if we were lucky. The women tried as hard as possible to make it tasty without overstepping Grandad's boundaries. He set the rules for the fast and we obeyed, whatever he decided we could or couldn't do.

～

To be fair, pregnant women could eat a little bit every now and then during a fast if their husbands allowed it. Mostly it was the husband's decision and if he was an extremely strict Christian then his wife wouldn't eat. Some couples even abstained from the sexual act during the time of fasting. They could decide between themselves if they believed an absolute fast of both food and sex was God's will.

Grandad also granted leniency to young children who would be given some bread, rice or beans.

This particular day, Grandad gave us instructions. 'We're going to fast and pray for money to support our charity in India. The money we normally spend on food for ourselves will be sent to build a school there.'

It seemed like a good cause. I'd much rather go without food to send money to starving children in India than try to get more money for a business. One of the traits that made Grandad such a powerful leader was that he understood how to be unselfish and give to those less fortunate. He was extremely practical when instructing us in Christian unselfishness.

He explained that for this fast there would be one month where we could eat only rice. We would be given three meals of rice a day, but each First Day of the week we wouldn't eat any food and we were to gather for two extra prayer meetings. At the prayer meetings we would kneel for hours in prayer to beseech the Lord's blessing. The fast would save a large portion of funds to send to India and the prayer would invoke the blessing of God.

Once Grandad had finished explaining all the reasons why fasting was such a good idea he then asked the church to demonstrate their agreement.

A loud 'AMEN!' blasted through the hall as we 500 showed our submission to Hopeful's decree. I hid a deep sigh and picked up the glass mug of fresh skimmed milk. *Drink up, you'll be going hungry soon*, I thought as I drained it.

Those fasting periods were ghastly. Tempers got short and sometimes us girls would catch snippets of conversations about how one of the pregnant women had fainted, or how a man who'd been working on the farm had collapsed with fatigue.

When four First Days had passed the fasting ended and I couldn't believe how excited I was to eat some plain vegetables. In my deprived state they tasted like the most delicious food on earth.

I complained to Mum about the practice but I knew she couldn't do anything about something that had been decided by the men. I felt rebellious. Grandad Hopeful said fasting was a good discipline for us, especially for us children.

SIXTEEN

The fruit of the womb

To destroy a child from within the womb is just as much murder as destroying a child that has been born.

—*WHAT WE BELIEVE*, P. 69

Babies were a big part of life in Gloriavale. Birth control and abortion were strictly forbidden and we were proud of how we didn't murder children in the womb like so many people in the world.

Grandad was very fond of bragging that we had the biggest families in New Zealand. He liked to show visitors a photo he'd taken of all the children who were number three or more in birth order, saying, 'None of these children would be here if their parents practised birth control and didn't have a faith in God.'

A favourite sermon of his was to preach about how lucky

we were to have been conceived by Christian parents. He'd say, 'Guess where the most dangerous place in the world is. It's not on the road in cars. It's not flying through the air in planes. It's in the womb of an ungodly woman.'

My grandmother bore sixteen children to Grandad Hopeful before her death and I grew up surrounded by cousins' babies. Grandad Hopeful would say, 'Children are an inheritance of the Lord. The fruit of the womb is His reward.'

Mum taught me to knit all sorts of babywear—cardigans, booties, hats—I always knitted a matching set for each of Patie's babies. Some of the women could knit a whole garment in just a few hours.

Childbirth was highly celebrated and parents were expected to prepare their children for the practicalities of having a large family. Boys and girls aged ten and older would often attend their mother's births to assist and learn about the procedure.

We birthed our children at home. There was no need to visit a medical institution for something that was a purely natural part of life. God had promised us that women who continued in holiness and faith would be saved in childbearing. But if there were problems with a birth then a birthing mother would be taken to Greymouth hospital.

The district midwife made regular visits to pregnant women and attended the births to ensure nothing went wrong.

The first baby I ever saw born was my Aunt Patie's second son when I was ten. When he came out he had the umbilical cord wrapped round his neck, he was blue and wasn't breathing. He was fine once the midwife got him breathing. Afterwards she asked me if I was OK, but to me this was normal because I'd never seen a baby born before, so I was blissfully unaware of how severe the situation was.

I was there to observe and help with my mother's next four births: Asher, Judah, Serena and Melodie. Because I was now the oldest girl I learned all the child-rearing skills too. I bathed my younger siblings, changed nappies, helped with potty training and when the babies cried in the night I would climb out of bed to attend to them to relieve my exhausted mother. I watched the women help each other breastfeed, if one mother had an abundance of milk she would suckle the child whose mother didn't have a good supply.

Women were allowed about two weeks off after giving birth but then they were straight back into the workforce. I always wondered how some of the ladies did it. They would birth during the night and the next morning be at the meal table to present the child to the community. The husband would make a big announcement: 'The Lord has blessed us with a new baby boy and his name is Courageous.' Everyone would clap and cheer.

When Patie had her fourth child, complications arose after she'd gone into labour. Her waters had broken, she was fully dilated but the baby wasn't coming. I was rubbing her back, giving her sips of juice and bathing her face with a cool cloth. The midwife decided she needed urgent medical help but we were so far away from any hospital with no time to wait for an ambulance. We would have to transport Patie ourselves.

The boys brought round one of the stripped-out vans, threw down a mattress, blankets and pillows and we helped Patie lie down. I sat by her head and held her hands as her body was being wracked by gigantic contractions. About twenty minutes into the journey we went over a sharp bump. Patie groaned and gasped out, 'Something's moved. I can feel the baby coming. Right now!'

I shouted, 'Stop the van!'

Patie was clenching my hand, almost breaking it. I ignored the pain of it and repeated over and over, 'It's OK. Just breathe through it. Go with the pain.'

She was bearing down. The back doors of the van flung open, I scrambled out, the midwife climbed in and a few minutes later my tiny, screaming cousin Submissive was born. The midwife handed her to me after her mother had a cuddle. I cradled her squawking body in my arms. 'Welcome, little girl. You're going to be so loved.'

SEVENTEEN

Cursed with rebellion

All the people must obey the leaders in the Church in all things and submit themselves willingly to them as unto the Lord.

—*WHAT WE BELIEVE*, P. 52

Grace had to travel to Australia to renew her student visa so Fervent gave her money for the trip, telling her to return any left over to the church. She arrived back a couple of weeks later but the leaders forgot to take the money off her and she, for sure, wasn't going to remind them. Money meant the ability to acquire wicked, worldly possessions like chewing gum and music.

Sam loved the music and would borrow her headphones to listen whenever he could. Pretty rich seeing he'd tattled on me for stealing the library book. One day he came home to discover that someone had invaded our family room and gone through his drawers. The intruder had slammed the drawer on the headphones, smashing them to fragments. Not only that, but they'd left a note: 'Stop borrowing headphones from Grace or you will go to hell.'

My brother was furious. How dare they invade his personal space! He was getting sick and tired of the church leaders' endless rules and tyranny. Their attempts to control him simply set off his rebellious spirit. He spent as much time as he could getting into trouble with our cousin Jared the son of Mum's favourite brother, Mark. It hurt Mum that Mark, the brother she was closest to, disapproved of the boys' close friendship. He felt Sam was a bad influence on Jared and was taking him away from Christ.

But the truth is that Mark was coming under pressure from men such as Righteous who constantly got in his ear warning him of dire consequences. 'Watch you don't let Jared spend time with Perry's boy or you'll lose your family to the world.'

Nothing would split the boys up, though, and for the next two years Sam and Jared were an inseparable duo of trouble.

I avoided trouble by trying my hardest to live by the church rules. I didn't want to cause my mother any more worry than Sam already did. But it didn't stop me getting around the rules wherever I could. It just meant that if I did something wicked I had to be stealthy and smart about it. My correspondence course, for example, allowed me to get a pass to stay up beyond curfew to finish my assignments, so Grace and I used it as an excuse to hang out.

I'd been working late one night in the communal lounge when my eyes grew heavy. Time for bed. I packed up my books and tiptoed into our family room. Everyone was sleeping. It was pitch black, but there was a small amount of light streaming in the top window on to our top bunks.

The ladder creaked as I climbed and I checked to see if the sound had disturbed Sam. His bed was neatly made and he wasn't there.

I gulped in a sharp breath. He should be lying there asleep.

I jumped to the floor and felt my way through the dark.

'Mum.' I shook her shoulder. 'Mum, wake up!'

She sat up. 'Oh, Lilia, what is it?'

'Sam's not in his bed. Shouldn't he be here by now?'

In an instant she was wide awake. She flicked the lamp on and light flooded the room. She climbed the first couple of rungs of the ladder to check for herself that his bed was empty. Then she was down again and grabbing her dressing gown to run out to the main lounge to search for him.

I hurried to the cot to make sure the baby was sleeping and that's when I saw the letter.

I love you, but I have to go. I'm sorry. Sam

Mum read the note, her face wracked with anguish. She stood in the kitchen sobbing while Mark's daughter Rachel tried to comfort her. I wanted to rush to her, take her in my arms and tell her I would never leave her.

My poor mother had now lost her two eldest children. 'How can I bear it?' she whispered. 'It's worse than if they had died.'

I didn't want to believe it. Was he really gone? I was helpless as I watched my beautiful, strong mother crushed with grief. 'He's too young,' she sobbed. 'Where is he? I don't even know if he is safe.'

In the dreadful days that followed Sam's disappearance Mum's anxiety, grief and shame weighed on me. Often I'd huddle on the couch in the kitchenette.

Tears trickled down my face. My throat was thick with misery. My nose began to run and I wiped it with my dress sleeve. How could Sam have done this? Did our family mean nothing to him? I wanted to be angry but my heart knew that he couldn't have stayed. He was miserable living in Gloriavale.

I didn't know how else to help so all I could do was pray for him. 'Dear God, keep Sam safe. Please bring him home. If you bring Sara home too I promise I'll never leave Gloriavale.'

Even as I repeated the words, my heart told me a different story. Who was I fooling? We would never see Sam or Sara again.

EIGHTEEN

Illicit music

To be a friend of the world is to be an enemy
of God.

—*WHAT WE BELIEVE*, P. 35

Since Dad was in charge of marketing the sphagnum moss
business, he had to do a lot of computer work. The leaders
allowed him to set up a computer in our family room and gave
him internet access.

The workload was too much. He was running a business,
censoring the movies, travelling and developing the websites.

The computer and its possibilities fascinated me and so I
asked if I could help. He gave me an initial introduction then
left me to it.

It was thrilling to have this window into the outside world, to other lives, cultures and countries. Not that I was pemitted to look at anything other than what I absolutely needed. Huh!

There wasn't anyone in the community with the skills to teach me, so with the help of Google, I taught myself website coding and design. It turned out to be such a good move on my part because I soon got asked to do more design work. *Thank you, God!* Before long I became so busy I could no longer work full time on the domestic teams. I was ecstatic because for a while now I had felt as though my talents were being wasted cleaning toilets. This was my chance to shine.

~

The deer business was expanding rapidly because wealthy hunters with deep pockets loved the big game we bred. Haupiri Valley was one of the most rugged yet beautiful places in the world to hunt and fish, they said.

My cousin Christopher who oversaw operation of the deer businesses was a thoughtful, intelligent man. He bit his fingernails when he was concentrating hard and was a complete workaholic.

Chris was very different to other men in Gloriavale. There was something about him that felt safe. It was easy to share openly with him as he knew how painful my siblings' departures had been, since he'd been very close with them before they left.

Our personalities complemented each other so we were a dream team and loved achieving deadlines together. It was unique for a girl to work with a guy and we created a close and loyal friendship during the long hours we worked together.

One day after I'd mocked up some brochures for Wilderness

Quest, I was walking to the print shop when Grace's American drawl sounded across the lawn. 'Yo, Lil! Wait up.'

She waved at me from the verandah of the First Hostel, jumped over the rail and slid down the one-storey pole where she landed at the bottom in a puddle of skirts, then leaped up to dance across the grass to join me.

I raised my eyebrows. '*Yo, wait up*? What's that supposed to mean?'

She grinned. 'It's slang for *wait for me*. Naughty, eh!'

I laughed, she was so rebellious. 'Yeah. We'll both go to hell so you'd better explain what slang is. I don't want to go to hell for something I don't understand.'

'It's kinda mixing words around so like instead of saying "Hi how are you?" you say, "Heya, what's cracking,"' she explained.

I liked it. It sounded strange but also very cool, especially as Gloriavale leaders didn't like us to talk like that. It was too wordly. I rolled some slang words over my tongue. It felt strange hearing them come out of my mouth.

Grace giggled at my awkwardness but then she pulled her mouth down. 'Prayer doesn't like us spending time together.'

I shrugged. 'Prayer doesn't like much that I do.'

'Apparently you think that you're special because you're Miracle's daughter.'

I'd heard this a million times already. 'People are jealous. It's got more to do with them than it does with me. They can think what they like. I am who I am.'

She touched my arm briefly. 'They don't like that I'm different either. Faithful Pilgrim's been taking me out of class and asking if I miss my family. He says I'm wrong to still love them. He keeps on about how following the Lord is more important than family and I should be willing to forsake them.'

I looked around to make sure the coast was clear before I whispered, 'I still miss Sara and Sam. I think I always will.'

Grace gave her eyes an angry swipe. 'The leaders don't want me talking to young people about Australia and Tasmania either. They say I'm trying to be different and worldly. They think I'm rebellious.'

I laughed. 'That's probably because you are.'

The joke put a smile back on her face. Her dark eyes glinted with fun. 'Guess what? I've been assigned a bodyguard. Praise Standfast is supposed to keep an eye on me and report when I'm misbehaving.'

'Bet she's got a full logbook,' I chuckled.

The laughter eased the seriousness of the situation. I had a big space in my heart for Grace. It made me angry to see her being treated so harshly. I made sure she knew I'd always support her no matter what. She was one of the very few people I could trust with my own rebellious thoughts and questions.

She was such a good friend. One day when I was complaining to her about being rostered on the hated cleaning duty she said, 'Tell you what, Lil—I'll come and wake you up. I've got a uni assignment due. I'll study while you work.'

I cheered up. It wouldn't be nearly so bad if I had her company.

∾

'Lil, wake up. It's time to get up.' Grace's voice whispered through the dark as she shook my shoulder. I rolled over, groggily rubbing my eyes. My Chilean friend was perched on a rung of my top bunk ladder. I could hear the deep breathing of my sleeping family.

'What's the time?' I groaned.

'Five-thirty. Cleaning roster. Remember? I'll wait outside for you.'

I sighed and pushed the covers back. I detested cleaning bathrooms. Scrubbing toilets wasn't at all the way I envisaged spending my life. I managed to avoid some of the domestic chores because of the computer design work, but that didn't start until 8.30 am so I was expected to bear a portion of the early-morning duties too. I dragged myself slowly out of bed. Chris and I had been staying up late at night to finish the deer catalogues for the livestock auction, which was fast approaching, and I was exhausted. I shushed my inner grumbling, though; it wasn't a Christian attitude. The community couldn't function unless everyone helped out, and the bathrooms needed to be sparkling clean before breakfast. If I didn't do it then one of my Christian sisters would have to, and that wasn't fair to them. Plus, if I was a willing servant to the church, then God would reward me in heaven.

I fumbled in the dark for a uniform, threw it on and went to find Grace who was sitting on the blue couch outside our room. She was wrapped in a worldly, purple jacket and had her Religious History books perched on her lap. Study was a requirement of the Student Visa she was on.

We climbed to the attic floor. No one was living on this level so the bathrooms weren't as filthy as others got. I silently thanked the team leader, my cousin Serena, for giving me the easiest assignment. Bless her soul.

I pulled out the buckets and mops while Grace set up a study space on one of the tables. 'Want to listen to this?'

I looked over. Her eyebrows were lifted mischievously and in her hand was a cassette tape labelled 'The Early Church'.

'Grace, it's too early. Let me wake up a bit before you hit me with Anabaptist baptism rituals or whatever.' I was ashamed of myself for being grumpy but I so wasn't in the mood for a lecture.

She laughed at me. 'You'll love it. I guarantee it.' She headed for the stairs, calling over her shoulder. 'Back in a mo. Don't go away!'

Very funny. As if I could. I pulled a pair of clumsy yellow rubber gloves on my hands and set to work on the first toilet. Disgusting as always. I reminded myself about the reward waiting for me in heaven.

Grace reappeared, clutching a stereo set in her arms.

I stared at it, then at her. 'How did you get that?' There was a stereo set on each hostel floor to be shared between the families for special occasions. On our floor it was kept in a locked cupboard, but no one had access to that cupboard except Hope Standtrue who made sure it was only used for legitimate purposes.

Grace held up a key. 'I went through Faithful Pilgrims's desk in the high school and found this tucked away in a drawer. It's a universal key.' She waved the tape at me. 'So, do you want to hear this?'

By this time I was fairly sure the tape was contraband so yes, I definitely wanted to hear it. 'Of course I do! But we'll have to be quiet or people will hear us.'

Grace rewound the tape, pressed 'play' and the old stereo coughed for a moment before music spilled out. I closed my eyes to let the experience soak in, rocking gently to the music.

I sighed. It was beautiful and I wished we could freely listen to music. Very rarely did we get to listen to music of this sort. Any music used in the church was under strict command of the church music keeper.

The leaders had shown us documentaries about the Illuminati and Satanism in the music industry as well as handing out comic books depicting satanic rituals to show us how evil the world was. This was the way Gloriavale exposed the evil method of backward masking in rock music to send subliminal messages to listeners, but this music that Grace was sharing couldn't be anything like that.

'Who's the artist?' I asked.

'Steven Curtis Chapman. Cool, isn't it?'

'I love it. Why can't we listen to music like this? There's nothing wrong with it.' It didn't make sense to ban something so beautiful.

Grace quoted a well-worn scripture in answer. 'Lilia Just, we must "come out from among the sinners and be separate".'

Neither of us could feel the truth of that but the odd thing was that we could feel truth and goodness in the music.

The songs softly continued as I went on washing down the bathrooms. I felt happier and more content than I had in a long time. Surely this couldn't be wrong.

I jumped as a door slammed. Footsteps rat-tatted angrily up the stairs. I looked at Grace in horror and she pounced for the tape recorder. It was too late. Prayer was in the room and she'd caught sight of it.

'What are you girls doing?' she demanded.

'I'm studying and Lil's cleaning,' Grace answered.

'You shouldn't even be here. Does Lilia need a babysitter?' She stabbed a finger at the tape recorder. 'Where did you get this?'

'Hope Standtrue gave it to me,' Grace lied. 'I have to listen to recordings for my Religious Studies.'

Prayer looked at me standing silently in my bright yellow cleaning gloves. It was a good story. I held my breath.

'You're listening to worldly music,' Prayer spat. 'Pack your things right now and get over to the kitchen.' She confiscated the evil tape.

Grace scowled, grabbed her books and stormed out of the room. I shot her a helpless gesture as they left. This was not going to end well. Why couldn't people just leave us alone?

I finished cleaning the bathrooms in a rush of fury and raced over to the dining room for breakfast.

Grace's place at the table was empty. Where was she?

After breakfast I searched for her in the hostel with no luck. It was getting late and Chris would already be expecting me for work. I should have asked Grace what her duty was today but there wasn't time now to keep searching for her. I snatched up my laptop and papers and sped on my way only to stop in my tracks as I passed the cheese room. The window was slightly open and Prayer's voice ripped out through the gap.

'That evil music of yours is going to send you to hell. The Devil is taking control of you and using you to lead others astray.'

I crept near the window where I could see but remain unseen. Prayer stood in the doorway, arms akimbo on her rotund hips. She trembled with fury. Grace cowered under the barrage she was yelling at her.

Poor Grace. Prayer often cursed her like this in front of the entire team of women. It didn't surprise me; I'd seen Grandad treat Prayer in exactly the same way. Could it be possible that she was projecting her own pain on to others?

I almost gave myself away when I heard her start on me. 'Lilia thinks that because she's Miracle's daughter she should have special treatment. *She* doesn't need your help. You should be helping one of the lesser girls.'

I started to tiptoe away but stopped when she again spoke my name.

'Lilia's independence will be her downfall. She's been falling asleep on the couches in the lounge room. The only girls who do that are the types that get into hanky panky with men.'

What! How dare she! I fell asleep so often because I was forced to wake up early to work when I was also staying up late to get the catalogues done. Maybe if the community didn't overwork us so much it wouldn't be an issue.

I ground my teeth in anger and wanted to burst in on the scene, but I knew that my interference could only result in Grace and me being taken before a Men's Meeting. Two men appeared around the building and looked in my direction. I ducked away to the back porch.

Gosh! Couldn't Prayer be a little understanding? I couldn't believe how she treated Grace. Surely she'd understand how humiliating and hurtful it was after receiving similar treatment herself from Grandad Hopeful.

Not long after, Prayer was again growling at Grace in the main kitchen. When Grace didn't subordinate herself adequately, Prayer raised her hand and slapped Grace hard across the face.

The blow left a red mark and she began to cry. I was filled with sorrow and felt helpless. I listened to Grace's burdens and did my best to console her woes, but what I found difficult to understand was how much my friend loved Prayer, regardless of the nasty treatment.

When I thought more deeply about it, I realised that beneath Prayer's hard exterior lived a kind but broken-hearted woman. I wondered if being forced to sacrifice her husband and children had made her sour and unforgiving. That night I prayed that Prayer's family would come back to Gloriavale so that she could be happy again.

A week later, Grace stole another stereo and began playing the same music. I was confused. 'Didn't Prayer confiscate that tape and deliver it to the church leaders?'

Grace winked. 'I made a ton of copies and hid them in the forest.'

She took my hand and led me deep into the bush, where she dug under a rock to reveal a hidden treasure of *Reader's Digests*, chewing gum, jewellery, money and cassette tapes.

I was both shocked and inspired by her audacity. 'Can you make me a music tape?'

Grace giggled and rubbed her hands together.

The next day, she slipped a tape into my hand. I hid it at the back of my bunk drawer.

～

Since Grace spoke fluent Spanish the leaders put her to work as a telemarketer for the sphagnum moss export business.

Her work day began at 2 am to fit in with USA time so she had plenty of treasured privacy alone in the main office. She grabbed the opportunity to add more forbidden music to her stash.

Google was blocked but she discovered if she went through Outlook Express there was a way to access the internet and download music without it being tracked. We snuck under the radar many times without being caught by Aaron Courage, the ICT manager who trolled Gloriavale's servers looking for evidence of banned activity.

Banned music wasn't the end of Grace's 'worldly rebellious behaviour' either. Occasionally she'd steal money from the cash box in Shepherd Fervent's desk to spend on trips into town. 'We work fourteen hour days for nothing,' she grumbled to me. 'I deserve to have $10 once or twice a year. It isn't hurting anyone.'

If Grace could do it then so could I, but I only managed to steal $10 once. With Sara absent I needed a strong female role model and took cues from Grace's behaviour. The year after Sam ran away I had the chance to go into Greymouth. This was too good an opportunity to miss. I went to Hope Love in the office and told her Mum wanted $10. She handed it over without questioning me. If Miracle wanted it, then that was fine.

I used it to buy Shania Twain's new album, *Up!* I knew who the singer was because Sara had shown me some of her music and I really liked it. Listening to her was a connection to my older sister and I wondered if she was listening to the same songs I was. I took the tapes home and Grace and I hid behind the bed in the guest room, sharing a set of headphones and listening to the sassy beat. We mouthed the words and sang about wearing men's clothes and short skirts, and used a hairbrush as a microphone. We knew we were sinners but loved it at the same time. I'd do a crazy dance and perform while Grace rolled on the floor in fits of laughter.

The risk of sin was intoxicating and we'd go to any length to experience some taste of the outside world.

The farm was so isolated that outside radio signals were extremely weak, but we managed to find a couple of stronger spots. The tape recorder was only supposed to be used if we were prepping a song for weddings or working on a Young People's tea performance. But we used it for much more. There was an antenna that you could put up and tune the stations to hear staticky radio. We had it up one day, concentrating on it so hard that when we heard someone coming to the door I half broke the antenna off trying to hide it.

The guilt was crushing. I thought I needed to apologise to the church because I'd been sinful by listening to worldly music and breaking property which didn't belong to me. But if I apologised for the broken stereo they'd know I'd been listening to wicked music. I kept quiet and suffered the guilt.

∼

Prayer continued to rip into Grace and it was always the same two complaints—I thought I was privileged because I was Miracle's daughter, and Grace was rebellious and worldly. We stayed silent under her tirades, our friendship becoming stronger as we did our best to cling to a sense of freedom while living as Christian women in Gloriavale.

NINETEEN

The purging

This whole world lieth in wickedness, and none of
the people of this world love or obey God, but they
follow instead their own lusts and fulfil the will of
the Devil.

—*WHAT WE BELIEVE*, P. 35

When a child turned twelve they were permitted to attend the
young people's social events on Seventh Day evening. Activities
on Young People's nights were varied. Often we'd form a working
bee to husk a couple tonnes of corn, preserve fruit for the off-
season or clear the farmland of rocks and ragwort for sowing.

The mixed-gender events were so much fun and a welcome
relief from domestic labour. It was the only time we young
women got to mingle, but under strict supervision, with the

young men. Aside from my job with Chris I spent most of my time with women.

Thank god for the chance to gawk at yummy church boys on the weekends because I still had a crush on Willing Stedfast, Fervent's boy who'd by now grown into a handsome young man. When I lay awake at night I dreamed that perhaps one day we could be married.

I still hadn't told anyone, not even Grace, about my fantasy. It was not our choice who we were to marry. God would decide for us and he would tell the leaders. It wasn't good to have a rebellious heart against arranged church marriage. Even looking at someone lustfully was sin of the heart.

Grace had kissed a boy outside Gloriavale and I was jealous that she had more life experience than me. Dating, touching and kissing were forbidden by the church. Gloriavale commanded we live in modest shamefacedness, putting aside wanton lust. Even engaged couples were not to touch until the wedding day.

On this particular night the youth leaders told us young people to gather for a time of worship and cleansing up near the stopbank. I hugged my Bible and slipped one of Sam's old V-neck sweaters over my dress for warmth. It reminded me of his crooked smile and wild eyes. Women weren't supposed to wear men's clothing, especially not those of an insurgent, but I didn't care about the rule in this case.

'Come on Vic, let's go.' I tugged at my younger brother's shirt.

I laughed as he peered in the mirror to check his hairdo for the hundredth time. We looked nothing alike even though we were full blood siblings. Vic had inherited Mum's blonde hair and pale skin. He stood tall for a fourteen-year-old and walked with a lanky swagger that was distinctive from a mile away.

Darkness fell as we trudged up to the back of the property. A blazing bonfire cast light and warmth around the circle of young people. Vic and I found a dead tree trunk to sit on. It was comforting to have my brother with me to represent our family. For years I'd attended the gatherings alone after my older siblings ran away.

From the corner of my eye I noticed my crush Willing where he sat with his family. 'Does he notice me?' I wondered.

The young people were watched over and led by Salem Temple, son of Shepherd Howard. He was a tall, red-faced man with a high forehead and reddish-brown hair. Salem was married to the daughter of Shepherd Fervent Stedfast.

He addressed the couple of hundred of us who had assembled.

'I challenge you,' Salem called over the roaring bonfire. 'Is your life in order? If the Lord returned to take his followers to heaven, would you go with him or would you be left behind?' He paused and rubbed his cracked lips together. The gap in his front teeth appeared larger in the light thrown by the flames.

'Are you submitted to the church? Have you gotten rid of your pride in the way that you dress and the way you comb your hair? Are you listening to worldly music?' He turned to my brother. 'Victor! Are you going to be with the Lord or does this world have a hold over you?'

Vic's face fixed in a sullen snarl as he ignored the intimidation.

My conscience began to scream at me. The forbidden Shania Twain tapes were hidden in the back of my drawer.

'You're living in sin. You will surely be damned to hell,' Salem bellowed.

'Amen, brother.' David Stedfast got up to speak. He was

another of Shepherd Fervent's sons and even in his early twenties was heavily balding. 'Our brother Salem is right,' he shouted. 'I challenge you young people tonight. Are you living for the carnal man? Are you following the lust of the flesh? Declare your faith. Those of you who possess worldly tapes, books, clothing or anything that is of this world, bring it here and burn it in this fire. Your sins will be washed away.'

A murmur swept through the crowd. Was this really happening? We all knew that some of us young people had worldly goods we were keeping hidden, but I could sense the zealous energy gathering force in the crowd.

I hated it. Salem's confrontation of Vic lit an angry fire in my heart. How dare he? Both Salem and David were arrogant and prideful in their own way. The display of religious fervour didn't fool me. Men who acted righteous were praised as being valiant servants of the church. They got privileges and freedoms granted to them as well as promotions to managerial positions in the workforce. My lips curled. I had no respect for people who bullied others for selfish gain.

The spiritual intervention kept on. 'Are you living for the Lord or are you living for the world?' cried Salem. 'Go now and bring anything that is keeping you from Christ. Burn it in this fire and cleanse yourself from sin.'

Young people began to leave the bonfire, run to their hostels and return with items of contraband. A flurry of books, tapes and clothes landed in the fire while Salem and David commended the sinners and began to pray for them. 'Amen, brother! Praise God.'

The bonfire raged high, fuelled by the sinful objects. The heat burned into my skin and I shuffled back away from the flames.

It upset me to watch Grace throw her favourite T-shirt with 'Australia' printed across the front into the flames. Dawn's new husband, Abraham, had made her fetch it. The hungry fire bit into the material, consuming it.

Although I despised the preachers, I couldn't stop thinking about the cassette tapes and CDs hidden deep in the back of my drawer. If anyone knew about these I would be shamed just as Vic had been.

I was so fearful that I would go to hell, but I couldn't bring myself to tell anyone I had them. My family was under so much public shame already with the rebellion of my older siblings. I was not about to add to that.

As the crowd began to dissipate I grabbed a handful of newspaper and raced over to our family room. Removing all the contraband I lay it out on my bed, hesitating. The music was something I really loved, but the promise of hell fire burned in my ears. My salvation was more important. I seized the cassettes, broke them in half and tore out the tapes and reels. The CDs I snapped in half. Shania Twain was destroyed. I gathered everything up and wrapped it tightly in the paper. As soon as the kitchen was quiet I would discard it in the wood fire. The sooner it was over, the better.

The next Young People's night, Shepherd Steady Standfast got up to speak. Isaac Love, who'd left Gloriavale, had come back home with some worldly possessions. On the night of the bonfire he had thrown everything into the flames but when no one was watching he took a pocket knife out from the embers. 'He just couldn't give up the world and its hold on him,' Steady told us.

Issac left Gloriavale for good shortly after.

TWENTY

A loving community

It is what must happen when brethren truly love
one another as Christ loved them.

—*WHAT WE BELIEVE*, P. 41.

Even though Gloriavale had strict rules and regulations, it was
also a place of fun and love. One night after serving, Bethany
and I loitered in the kitchen to avoid boring mealtime sermons.
Suddenly the kitchen light flicked off and footsteps sounded on
the vinyl. We ceased our chatter and pretended to be very busy
cleaning the dishes. Prayer's head poked through the door. 'Stop
that now and go sit at the table. There's an announcement.'

I looked at Bethany, who grinned and snatched my hand.
'Let's go!'

She dragged me through the dark kitchen, navigating benches

and equipment at top speed. I pulled my dirty apron off as we burst into the dining space. People turned to frown at the commotion. We dropped our eyes and hurried to sit with our families.

'What's happening?' I whispered to Victor as I wriggled into a seat beside him.

Mum put a finger to her lips. 'Hush!'

The air tingled with excitement.

A man's voice sounded through the loudspeaker system. 'A precious shipment was lost in transit over the Amazon jungle,' he began, then he paused to let the drama build. Everyone was looking at one another, eyes bright with expectation. The man's voice dropped to a thrilling whisper. 'For days, rescue parties have combed the forest, trying to retrieve the cargo and now, success! The treasure has been found and—'

'What's that? A delivery!' A man had jumped to his feet. He was pointing at the front door, and I spun round to look. Ten costumed men burst through the doors and streamed into the room. They began to dance, as The Marvelettes' 'Please, Mr Postman' boomed through the loudspeakers. The crowd went wild, screaming and hooting with delight, as the performers burst open their satchels to reveal envelopes, which they threw to lucky recipients.

I caught mine and cheered with happiness. The front of the yellow envelope read: *LILIA . . . Is this what you've been waiting for?* I looked at my cousins, who held envelopes too. 'I'm opening mine!' I burst out, then tore the seal off the back. The sides of the card flew open in my face and I screeched as a green octagon sprang out.

'Ooh! Ahh!' The dining room shook with joy as others opened their envelopes.

I giggled and snatched up the octagon. It was an invitation. Bold capital letters popped off the front.

FOOD . . . *Feed your fantasy with your favourite food!*

Fantabulous FUN for the fearless!

Finish with a forbidden FILM!

Bring your friends to the Foyer on the Fifteenth at 4.44 pm.

The Young People's Tea! It was finally here. We'd been waiting for this announcement for weeks. Vic and I jumped for joy and looked at Mum and Dad, who both had massive grins on their faces. I hugged them. 'Thanks, Mum! Thanks, Dad! I can't wait.'

⁓

For the next six weeks, Gloriavale buzzed with excitement. Special teas only occurred about once every two years. They were the biggest shows in Gloriavale and a highly anticipated part of our lifestyle. Grandad called the events 'a gift of love', and said it was a good time for us to work together as a team and demonstrate our creative talents. He was so right.

This event was called the Young People's Tea, and the Married People organised the entire shindig for us in secret, which only heightened the excitement. What we knew for sure was that it would be a night of feasting, fun and excitement. The Young People would reciprocate the special treat by planning a similar feast and show for the Married People at a later date. Planning, practice and design of these events could sometimes begin up to twelve months ahead. Each event was given a theme, such as

'Ice 'n' Ocean Cafe' or 'Cultures of the World', and the main dining hall would be transformed into another world, with backdrops and props painted by artists like Victory Overcomer or designed and handmade by the organisers.

During preparations for the feast, the main hall was off limits to Young People, and the windows were covered with black plastic. The Married People took care to ensure that nothing would reveal the wonderful mysteries that awaited us.

The weeks seemed to drag by, but at long last the big day arrived. We were allowed to knock off work early and gathered on the soccer field, wearing old clothes as we'd been instructed.

I sought out Grace. 'I bet we're going to get so muddy,' I said to her.

My prediction was right. The first part of the evening consisted of fun outdoor games and activities. We were divided into teams and played tug of war, mud-pit wrestling, obstacle-course races and much more. The men had built a hydroslide down the side of the river embankment, so Grace and I jumped on a slippery mat together and screamed with joy until we splashed into the pool at the bottom. The whole time, I wore the long blue dress. It got annoying, but I'd worn leggings underneath, so I knotted the side of it up a little.

After the games, I arrived home wet, soggy and elated to discover all the showers on our hostel floor were occupied by young people getting ready. I went to the large bathroom, where I could hear someone showering.

'Who's in here?' I called.

'It's Hope Love,' my cousin shouted over the noise of the shower.

'Hey, can I use the shower after you?'

'Bethany is already in line, but ask her if you can go next.'

I retreated to the lounge to put my name down with Bethany.

Since tonight was extra special, I took out my best camisole, half petticoat and panties. The cami was silk with lace inserts and too sexy for a single girl to own. I'd scored it from a secondhand store in Greymouth while there for an optometrist appointment, and I kept the naughty underwear a secret by handwashing it instead of running it through the communal laundry baskets. Wrapping the silks in a clean towel, I took a bar of soap and some shampoo from the back of my drawer. Gloriavale provided communal bathing necessities, but I refused to use a bar of soap that a hundred others had used before me. How disgusting! Fortunately, my cousin Sweetness had gifted me some sweet-smelling products she'd 'purchased' from Gloriavale's lock-up using the allowed budget system.

I showered in privacy, then slipped into the soft, clean undergarments. The bathroom mirror caught my reflection and I stopped to admire my curves. My body was developing and it felt powerful to see such revealing clothes draped over it. My fingers traced down the cami strap and over the lace cup. What would it be like to wear something like this for a man? Grandad had not yet chosen a husband for me, but I hoped it would be someone I liked.

Back in our room, I opened the closet and selected my newest blue dress. It wasn't faded like the others and the material was still crisp. The garment went over my head and I pushed my arms through the long sleeves, zipped the back, tied the belt then straightened the frills.

I brushed out my hair, which by now had grown to my waist, and donned the scarf, pushing it forward to create a hair poof at the front. I was careful not to overdo it; Grace always created such a big poof in her hair that she got reprimanded for the sin of vanity.

I threw on socks and my best white runners, then sprayed on a cloud of body spray. I couldn't wait to get married. Then I'd be permitted to use real perfume like Mum did.

On the way to the Main Building, I chatted with Grace. She smelled like a goddess, and I knew she'd been using real perfume that she'd brought from the world. I spotted my crush, Willing Stedfast, and was glad I looked my best.

It was time for the unveiling!

All the young people gathered in the foyer and a few organisers split the crowd into small groups. Vic and I were grouped with our Māori cousins, the Overcomers. I bounced on my toes as each group entered the Main Hall, trying to catch a glimpse of what was happening, but the door swallowed each group and tassels blocked my vision. Finally, our names were called. I took a breath and stepped through the black curtains.

Wow! My senses went into overdrive. Darkness, coolness, shadows, animal sounds—it was like stepping into another world. I shivered. My eyes took a moment to adjust. We were standing in a cave. Green lights threw beams across the tunnel walls, and the sound of jungle creatures filled the air. It was magical. Two people could fit in the tunnel side by side, so Obedience and I stepped forward into the shadows. *Whoosh!* Mist shot out from a ledge.

I seized her arm and jumped up and down. 'This is amazing!' I whispered.

She squealed. 'Look at that!'

A snake was coiled on a branch and as we crept past it raised its green eyes to hiss at us.

'Thank God it's not real!' I exclaimed.

The end of the tunnel opened into the Main Hall area. A large sign overhead read:

WELCOME TO THE RAINFOREST EXPRESS!

Backdrops of jungle scenery covered the walls, while ponds of flowing water littered with lily pads, flamingos and parrots filled out the scene. An Amazon warrior with a painted face crept through the grass, eyeing visitors with wonder.

'Who is it? Who is it?' We all tried to guess, prodding at the actor to try to snap him out of character.

'It's John Ready!' exclaimed one of the boys.

My cousins and I giggled and wandered past a stand where refreshments were being offered to all the new arrivals. Juice in hand, we continued to explore the jungle wonderland, inspecting the incredible workmanship and mechanics that had gone into engineering such a scene. After twenty minutes, an usher escorted us to an area where long polished tables had been set in tiered rows for the dining and concert experience. Once we'd taken our seats, the orchestra opened the performance with a brilliant ensemble. We were on our way!

Grandad appeared to make his traditional speech, then said a prayer of blessing over the night. Servers delivered us an entree of shrimp vol-au-vents with beurre blanc, followed by the main course. I was ravenous and the menu looked extra delicious. *Discover the mysteries and delights of a rainforest cuisine as you bite into the unknown* . . . it read. There was a choice of succulent pork with apricot glaze, or roasted chicken stuffed with exotic nuts, or steak cuts with creamy mushroom sauce. The Gloriavale butchers had obviously been hard at work preparing the best home kill for this celebration. I ordered the pork and it was divine.

While we ate, act after act flew across the stage. Amazonian dancing, duelling banjos, a steam-engine captain singing of his adventures, then Zion Pilgrim and my uncle Mark performed a beautiful rendition of the famous 'Classical Gas' guitar piece. Even the younger children were involved in the acts, dressed up in the cleverest animal costumes. The sound and lighting was on point and we all screamed when, during one act, the tiered flooring beneath us simulated a light earthquake and mist burst from overhead sprayers. The experience was all-encompassing.

At intermission, Mum came out of the kitchen in her hat and apron. It was so nice to finally see her—the House Mother. She'd been rehearsing each part of this event for weeks: rosters, budgets, food stocks, menu design and much more. She was a fussy organiser as well as an accounting whizz and her leadership was pivotal for Special Teas.

'Are you having a good time?' She smiled.

'Mum, this is amazing. The food is delicious and the set-up is incredible. How did they make the birds fly? We got the biggest fright when the ground shook. We thought it was a real earthquake. Luke and James are hilarious.'

Her face lit up. 'I'm so glad. We've worked so hard to make this night as special as possible for you.'

At the end of the night, the Married People gathered on stage.

Grandad stood before us and spread his hands. 'This night has been put on by the Married People to show their love to you. Don't take it lightly. Each of you young people is alive because your parents chose to come out from the world and refused to practise birth control.' He paced the stage. 'Children are an heritage of the Lord. The world disobeys God. They live in sin and kill their children in the womb. Here, in this valley, is God's true church. Here, you are safe from the world and its evil temptations.'

I nodded at his words.

After he'd finished his sermon, Grandad shot his hands into the air. 'Praise God!'

There was a deafening pop and confetti blasted out of the stage. The married people jumped into the crowd, laden with gifts, and we all clapped and whistled. Mum had her apron off now—her House Mother duties were over and it was time to be a parent. She and Dad presented gifts to Vic and me. Everyone was ripping open presents and there were lots of hugs, tears, 'oohs' and 'ahhs'. I discovered a new pillowcase, underwear, soap and body spray in my gift, as well as a laminated book that held stories and photos from my childhood.

I noticed there was no mention or photos of my two eldest siblings. I looked sadly at Mum. The pain was even more intense for her and Dad, who wished their eldest could be with us tonight. I threw my arms round Mum. 'I love you so much. I'll never leave you.'

My aunt was there and she hugged me too. 'I love you, Lil. I'm so sorry that Sara and Sam aren't here, but you have to be even stronger now. Your parents need you. Don't break their hearts.'

Choked up, I nodded, trying to hold back the tears.

There was a thick envelope in the bottom of the gift box and

I slit it open. It was full of letters from those Married People who had cared to put their thoughts into words. I began to read the first letter.

My dearest daughter Lilia,

I know that I probably don't tell you enough, but I do really, really love you. I am proud that you always want to do what is right. Most of all, I cherish your faithfulness to God. That means more to me than anything. It pleases me to see that you have hate for the world and it's wonderful to have the confidence that you will never be entrapped by its snares. Thanks for helping me with the kids and the washing. Thanks for being concerned about Victor and encouraging him and his walk with God. Thanks for being my friend and listening when I need someone to talk to. I hope that tonight you will feel my love three times over and fill the gap in my heart from the two missing seats.

Love forever, Mum xxxx

Dear lovely Lilia,

It was so much fun doing this tonight for you young ones. I hope you never take for granted that you have one of the best mothers in the world. She worked so endlessly because of her love. Thank you for loving God and giving yourself to others. Always remember, when you are feeling low, look around: there is always someone worse off than yourself. Have a lovely night and remember we love you!

Love, Prayer Darling xxxxxxxx

Dear Lilia,

I think very highly of you and admire the strength that I see in you. It's been really hard for your mum with her two eldest leaving, but I know she has a strength in you and she can always depend on you to do what's right and stick to the path that has been set before you . . .

Love, Peace Stedfast

Lil,

You have a leading spirit and many girls will follow you. Always remember to keep yourself in humility and a sweet tongue. Don't let others' wrong bring out the worst in you. Keep the love of Christ always before you. God will give you strength for each new trial if you trust him. Remember, ahead of every closed door is another door opened . . . I love you with all my heart.

With love, your friend Serena Christian

Dear Lil,

Thanks a lot for your kind and friendly ways. I have been really surprised with your progress in every way. It's lovely to see you grow into such a sweet girl and so capable. Thanks for being a good friend to Mary. It's really important to parents to know their children are in company you approve of. I'm always blessed with the challenges Mary faces in having you for a friend, because it encourages her to develop simply to keep up. Enjoy your night, sweetie. We've enjoyed doing it for you. Remember, the most important thing we aim for in this life is to live a life completely acceptable to God. As we do this, we cannot help but radiate that love and care to others.

Love, Virtue Pilgrim

There were many more letters, and almost every one of them gave mention to my mother's ceaseless hard work and contribution to the church, as well as of the heartache my parents bore over the loss of their children. I closed the envelope and hugged it to my chest. I'd never forget this night.

After dishes, we watched a movie that we'd never seen before. New movies were a treat, because we'd seen everything in the video room so many times already. As usual, Dad had edited out any scenes or words that, in the eyes of the church, could be a bad influence on us.

It was midnight by the time I stumbled to our hostel room bearing armfuls of leftover goodies. The fridge was bursting at the seams and I stuffed as much as possible on to the shelf that we shared with Aunt Patie's family, then stowed the rest on my top bunk.

I felt full and satiated as I flopped into bed. The sweet snoring of my younger siblings drifted up from their bunks and lamplight peeked through Mum's curtain. I closed my eyes.

'Dear Lord God, thank you for sending your Son to die on the cross. Thank you for an awesome night, and for the Married People, who love us so much. I pray that you will forgive me for all my sins and that you will bring my brother and sister home. Amen.'

TWENTY-ONE

A witness for Christ

Such a person is to be delivered unto Satan for the destruction of the flesh.

—*WHAT WE BELIEVE*, P. 55

My life was a constant struggle between following the religious teachings of the church and doing what my heart told me was right. It was easy to follow my heart where Grace was concerned. Having a partner in crime who despised petty religious teachings was liberating. Where I was concerned about little sins Grace thought nothing of breaking the rules. We could talk to each other about anything. Even so, Gloriavale's hold on my mind was strong and I still struggled to reconcile my love for my brother and sister with the nasty picture the leaders painted about them.

For weeks Hopeful had been preaching at the meals and

meetings about spreading the gospel to unbelievers. It seemed his sermons were aimed directly at my family. 'Forsake those who forsake you. Preach the gospel to the wicked and the damned. It is your Christian duty to witness to the lost. He that believeth and is baptised shall be saved; but he that believeth not shall be damned.'

His words dug into my mind. Sara and Sam had left the one true church and they were doomed. I became convinced that their fate was damnation to a lake of fire where they'd suffer eternally for their sin. I had to save them! No matter how strenuously I tried to ignore or banish Grandad Hopeful's words they would not cease. They were there, sewn into my mind and jabbing at my conscience. His message was unequivocal: it was my Christian duty to pull my siblings back from the path to hell fire and damnation.

How to do it though when I hadn't seen Sara for five years and Sam for three?

In the end I decided to speak to them. It would have to be by phone. I was sure my parents had been in touch with them a couple of times, because legally they had to exercise parental duties as both my siblings had been underage when they ran from Gloriavale. Mum would surely have a contact number.

It felt like a big step and I dithered about asking Mum to ring but another mealtime sermon from Grandad Hopeful where he thundered out how it was our duty to redeem the lost by preaching the gospel persuaded me.

I decided to start with Sara because I knew Sam would follow where she led and they'd both return to us.

I asked Mum to make the phone call for me. She dialled the

secret code for an outside line from the landline in our room. I was nervous and anxious but this was the right thing to do. I had to warn her, I had to tell her she was going to hell if she didn't come back.

Mum talked to her for a while but I was too wound up to hear what she said. Then it was my turn.

I took the phone. 'Hello?'

'Hey, Lil.' I was taken by surprise. This wasn't the voice I remembered. This was an adult's voice, a much more confident one than Sara's had been. She seemed far away, like a complete stranger. I wondered what she looked like. She would be, what, twenty now?

I heard Grandad's voice like he was in the room. 'Your sister is an evil sinner bound for hell. Tell her the gospel. You have to save her.'

Before I could stop, I blurted out, 'I just need you to know that you're going to hell.' The moment I said it regret washed over me.

There was a thick silence on the end of the phone. I looked at Mum and her expression was painful. My stomach sank and the phone in my hand felt like a hot iron. I thrust it back to Mum. What had I done?

I rushed out of the room with tears burning my eyes. My breath was short and ragged. Sara! Oh no, no, no. I needed space to think. I ran to the old blue couch in the kitchenette where Sam had discovered me reading the stolen book.

I hated myself. *What have you done? What have you done?* The agony pounded through my mind, setting a seesaw argument to rage in my head.

'You were being righteous,' insisted a voice of command. It

ABOVE: Lilia (yellow dress, third from left) and her high-school classmates in costume for a concert event. The females are allowed to remove head coverings for theatrical purposes, but must always wear modest clothing.

BELOW: Lilia (back row, second from left) with some of the girls on her rostered working team, including Integrity Hopeful (far left) and Lilia's cousins Serena Christian (centre, blue sweater), Bethany Christian (second from right) and Promise Overcomer (far right).

ABOVE: Lilia's baptism by Shepherd Fervent Stedfast (right) and Shepherd Howard Temple (left).

BELOW: Lilia pictured with her grandfather Hopeful Christian (aka Neville Cooper), making her Commitment.

RIGHT: Lilia at her 'first' birthday, proudly showing off her new shoes.

BELOW: Lilia learning to wakeboard at Lake Brunner.

ABOVE: Lilia's parents, Perry and Miracle Tarawa, at home in Christchurch in 2016. (Photograph: *Woman's Day*.)

ABOVE RIGHT: Lilia Te Aroha Maia Tarawa in 2017.

RIGHT: Lilia's grandmother Nga Honore Roimata Tarawa at a wedding in 2017.

sounded indignant and self-righteous. 'You were a witness to your sister. If you hadn't spoken, she'd go to hell and it would be your fault.'

'But she's your sister,' the voice of my intuition sobbed. 'Aren't we supposed to be loving towards each other? Perhaps you could have asked her how she was? Maybe shown her some love.'

Five years I hadn't seen Sara. Five years . . . and to damn her was all I could muster.

'This is love!' the first voice snarled. 'It's your responsibility to share the gospel message with the lost. If you refuse to confess Christ before man he will deny you before God in heaven.'

The gentle voice disagreed. 'Lil, you shouldn't treat people like that. This is your blood family. Rather than spitting hell fire and brimstone we should connect as understanding humans.' This gentle voice was strong, but was it right?

Apparently not. 'That's weakness!' the first voice sneered, 'The church would be proud of you for doing this, Lilia. You've done your duty to Christ.'

The words of Matthew 10:37–38 that Grandad Hopeful hammered into us at meetings and mealtimes rang in my ears. 'He that loveth father or mother more than me is not worthy of me: and he that loveth son or daughter more than me is not worthy of me. And he that taketh not his cross, and followeth after me, is not worthy of me.'

Was I worthy?

But the gentle voice refused to be cowed. 'Love one another,' it urged.

I pressed my hands over my ears. 'Stop, stop, stop, please stop!'

I curled up, resting my chin against my knees, and stared out at the endless fields of Gloriavale's farmland. These were the same paddocks where I'd herded cows, gone eeling and enjoyed bareback riding with Sara and Sam. All I wanted was for them to come home.

TWENTY-TWO

Bearing one's burdens

Those who will not work hard at what they are
capable of doing should not be given anything to
eat. No lazy people will be accepted in the Church.

—*WHAT WE BELIEVE, P. 71*

Dad was in the States on a business trip again. I hoped the leaders
would ease my mother's life as a sole parent by lightening her
burden as House Mother, but there was no way Mum was going
to ask for help and risk being called 'soft' or 'lazy'. Such weakness
would have gone against Grandad's rule that women were there
to serve the men.

Dad asked Uncle Mark to watch over and care for Victor
while he was gone because he knew Mark would treat Vic with
love. However, Mark was so busy running the men's domain that

instead he appointed his second-in-command, Righteous, to take up the task.

Righteous, ever the vigilant master, watched Vic's every move to make sure he was behaving—best be certain he didn't follow the wickedness of his siblings or influence others into sinfulness.

The scrutiny was suffocating. He expected to know what Vic was doing every second of the day, but the more he tried to get Vic in order, the more my brother acted out. It was a repeat of how the church had treated Sara. I was angry with the leaders for sending our father away. Shouldn't Dad be here taking care of his family so he could guide Vic? Where was he to protect us in all of this?

I could see Mum needed support, a lot of it. Because I was the eldest of the seven I sought to relieve her burden as much as I was able. It wasn't easy and we were both worried about Vic's continual bucking of the rules.

Grace, as always, was my go-to person when I needed to vent my frustration about him. 'I wish he'd just behave. Doesn't he understand how his rebellion is hurting our family? He needs to knuckle down and get his act together.'

❧

The trip Dad was on was one of the long ones. The leaders knew that it wasn't a great idea to split a husband and wife apart for so long, so their next move was to send my mother with her tiny baby, Melodie, to visit him. The absolute care of our entire family, including my rebellious brother, fell on my shoulders.

I was only fifteen. How on earth was I to care for five children the way they needed? Vic minded himself and didn't listen to much I said anyway, but the well-being of Gloriana, Asher, Judah and Serena was my responsibility. For the first time I was living the role of a mother. I'd wake up early to finish chores then return to rouse and dress the children. After they'd been fed I'd kiss them goodbye and send them to school and kindergarten. At the end of the day I collected them, fed them dinner, bathed them and put them to sleep.

I loved and protected those children like a tigress. When they misbehaved I did my best to train and discipline them nicely. It was also my responsibility to maintain Bible study in the home and pray with them.

Righteous kept after Vic, increasing my stress and worry to the max.

Vic wasn't fitting into the church's cookie-cutter box though. True to form, he actively rebelled against the church. His sins stacked up to those of his older siblings' but the church wasn't going to tolerate another rebellion. The whip cracked down hard.

Dawn's husband came into our family home to direct Bible readings. His weak chin quivered as he sat in Dad's seat and read certain scriptures from the Bible that highlighted our supposed sins.

When he ordered us to pray Gloriana began, 'I pray that you will protect Sara and Sam and bring them back to us—'

Dawn's husband burst in on her prayer. 'Stop! You can't pray for your sister and brother any more. They've made their decision to go to hell.'

The children were tense and I fumed under my breath. How dare he invade our home! Our family room was the only private space we had, but now even that had been stripped from us. Vic hated it even more and made nasty remarks under his breath. 'You're not our father.' I tried to hush him. His attitude reminded me so much of Sara and Sam. I couldn't bear the thought that he might run away like they had done.

I confided in Grace. 'It'll get to the point where the leaders won't accept it any more.' I was so worried and scared for him. 'This situation is going to blow up and it won't end well. What if he's banished or taken away from us?'

One morning somebody knocked on the door of our family room. It was early to be visiting. I opened the door and wasn't surprised to see Righteous standing there. Couldn't he just leave us alone? I was weary of the intrusions.

'Is Victor here?' He tried to look over my shoulder into the room.

He had no right to be barging into our private space, especially given his cold arrogance towards my mother when Sara left. Indignation rose in my chest. This was our family's territory and the man was not welcome. 'I don't know where he is. He's probably at work already.'

Judging by the look on his face, Righteous clearly didn't believe me. 'I can't find him. If you see him, tell him I'm looking for him.'

'Maybe he's in the hostel kitchen,' I suggested, sending Righteous on a wild goose chase. I knew full well Vic was listening to music with Jared.

I slammed the door and sat on the computer seat. There was so much work to complete before Chris arrived to review it. But I couldn't concentrate because anger seethed in my blood.

I desperately longed for my parents' return. I was weary of the mental bashings, weary of the religious chains and the personal invasions.

My head dropped into my hands as tears blurred my vision, but this was not the time for weakness. I took a ragged breath. 'Pull it together, Lil. The children need you.'

Mum and Dad returned home and I hugged them with relief. Finally, I'd been granted a break from the storm. The men eased off their intrusions in the presence of my father's authority. But the holiday was short-lived. Church duty called and we waved goodbye as Dad headed off again. 'Stay safe and come home to us,' I whispered.

Vic turned fifteen and for a few weeks the leaders sent him to be with Dad in America. It gave Mum and me a break but the moment Vic returned he was up to the same trouble again.

We did our best to keep his sins from being discovered by the leaders but he liked to flaunt his rebellion. After all, what was a good rebellion worth if no one knew about it? I was fearful for what he would do next. Sara and Sam had both been fifteen when they ran away. Surely Vic wouldn't do that to us. It was unthinkable.

Things didn't improve and often I had the rebellious thought that Grandad Hopeful and the men were inventing rules they knew Vic would break.

The day of the Hair Oil Rule was typical of what they were doing. At dinner time Grandad Hopeful's voice resounded over the speakers, ranting on and on. I sighed and reached for another glass of milk.

High on the wall of the main dining hall, the long hand of the clock hit the twelve again. It had been an hour since he'd begun preaching. I watched the second hand tick. Was time getting slower? I hated sitting through these sessions and had tried to stay away from this but, once again, Prayer discovered Grace and me hiding in the cheese room and roundly ordered us to get to our seats.

Grandad Hopeful's sermon this time was about men's hairstyles. For goodness sake! Was God really going to send a boy to hell if he combed his hair the wrong way?

'We've created an excellent formula for hair oil so there is no reason any of you boys should be walking around with scruffy hair.' Hopeful pulled out his comb and ordered his young son Faithful to stand up. He stood behind Faithful and grabbed his hair, pulling it up to show the community how long it was. 'This is how long each of you are to have your hair cut. None of you young men are to cut your own hair. If you need a haircut then Willing Disciple or Enoch Upright will do it for you.'

I winked at Grace and she ducked her head to hide her giggles. We had another name for Enoch. Enoch Up-tight.

I glanced at Vic. His face was fixed in a scowl. He, Jared and Gideon had been under the pump recently for their worldly hairstyles. Vic hated the homemade hair oil they were forced to use and honestly I didn't blame him. It was slimy and oily, plus it smelled revolting. The insubordinate boys had used sewing scissors to cut their hair very short. Vic would spray his hair with water to spike it up at the front, an act absolutely prohibited by church orders.

Hopeful rolled on with the instructions. 'This is how I want to see you young men comb your hair.' He parted Faithful's hair on one side then combed it over, slick and flat. I stifled a snigger. It looked so ugly and there was zero possibility Vic would ever do his hair like that.

It was just one more worry to pile on Mum's head.

~

Only a day or two after the hairstyle sermon Vic swaggered towards me with a cool, smug look on his face. I rolled my eyes. The boy was incorrigible. His hair was flicked high at the front and his blue pants rode low on his hips.

'You're going to get in trouble for wearing your pants like that,' I warned him.

He shrugged. 'Don't care. They can't tell me what to do.'

'Son! What's this?' Hopeful's loud voice echoed through the empty dining hall. I was dismayed. This was exactly what I'd been afraid would happen. Why couldn't Vic understand it was better to comply?

Grandad Hopeful stomped up to us and grabbed my brother's shoulder. 'Look at you. You look like a scruff. Pull those pants up.'

Vic gave his trousers a weak hoist.

It wasn't nearly enough for Grandad Hopeful. 'If you boys aren't going to start behaving then you'll have all your privileges taken from you.' He grabbed the top of Vic's trousers and yanked them up to the waist.

A dark look flashed in Vic's green eyes. A wave of energy burst out of him, hateful and angry and he yanked away from Hopeful's talons.

My heart pounded. *Keep your mouth shut!* I silently shouted at him. If he dared defy Hopeful the retribution would be severe.

Hopeful towered over him, spitting in fury as he roared at my brother. 'You've had one too many chances. If you're not going to do what you're told then we'll find a way to get the Devil out of you.'

I shivered. What was the punishment going to be?

It was so excessive and so typical and so demeaning. He marched Vic and Gideon to the sewing room where he ordered them to surrender their shirts and trousers. He then measured where the trousers were to sit on each boy and commanded the women to sew the trousers on to the shirt so the boys couldn't adjust where the pants sat on their hips. The trouser and shirt became a one-piece coverall which looked very uncomfortable.

The rebels were forced to wear the one-piece in front of the community. It was a symbol of shame and a warning to any who might defy Hopeful's authority.

It didn't stop with the set of clothes the boys had been wearing that day. Each item of Vic's clothing had to be sewn together. He took one look at the garments when they were delivered back, headed straight for Mum's sewing kit, grabbed the stitch ripper and cut all the stitching off. It was a blatant act of rebellion.

Mum was horrified. 'Victor, how could you! You're going to get us in so much trouble. Don't you know they'll take you to a Men's Meeting for this?'

'Let them,' Vic spat. 'They can't control me. Who do they think they are? I hate this place.'

Mum shook her head helplessly. She was still under extraordinary stress from the demands of her role as House Mother as well as caring for her seven children without a husband there to help. Vic's disobedience increased her worry tenfold.

Even though I hated that Vic was causing her so much stress, I felt for him. He didn't want much—just a small sense of freedom from the strict regime. Being told what to do didn't sit well with his DNA, and as luck would have it, he'd been born into a church that expected utter obedience.

He'd more or less followed orders his entire life but now he was fifteen and the petty rules grated on him. They were so ridiculous. What was wrong with wearing sunglasses? Why couldn't he listen to worldly music on the radio? And if our grandfather had had any sense or maybe a smidgen of compassion, he'd have worked out that the fashion for low-riding pants would pass if he left Vic alone and didn't make it an issue. And as for the hair-styling rules—idiotic. Grandad Hopeful's dominance was excessive, to say the least.

I knew what it felt like to be bawled out for infringing one of the leaders' petty rules. Victory Overcomer got on my case for tying my cardigan around my waist rather than carrying it.

'You're just trying to draw attention so the men notice your hips. The Bible says not to be a stumbling block for your brothers in Christ,' she scolded.

I stared at her in disbelief, but obeyed her because I liked her. It was the most outrageous thing I'd ever heard. Although, thinking about it, it was similar to the way Prayer would walk around the kitchen while we girls worked, checking our uniforms. Not only were we expected to wear the blue garb, we were also under strict regulations about how the outfits were to be worn. If any of us tied our belts loosely, which I often did, Prayer would undo it then tie it back in place on the waist where Grandad Hopeful had dictated it should sit. The act felt like such an invasion of privacy, but I bit my tongue and as soon as she turned away I'd angrily loosen my belt.

TWENTY-THREE

The Commitment

He must declare that he will submit to, be guided
by and obey the leaders of the Church.

—*WHAT WE BELIEVE*, P. 22

The full sound of the grand piano poured through the dining
hall. I shut down the vacuum cleaner in a hurry. It was Grandad
Hopeful playing and I dared not disturb him.

I loved this side of my grandfather, it was the creative, soulful
aspect of him that felt oh, so human. I sat down and closed my
eyes to let the notes of the hymns flood into me.

It was easy to see why God had chosen Grandad to lead his
church. There was no one as multi-talented and charismatic as
he was. I remembered the stories of how police and evil men had
come to persecute him when I was young. They'd locked him in

a prison cell. Fervent had warned us that persecution could again be waged against our church. Would we be willing to lay down our lives to protect Hopeful?

As the music sang to me, I vowed to willingly follow Grandad Hopeful to the ends of the earth. It would be an honour to become a martyr for Christ. After all, this earthly life was fleeting compared to the promise of an eternal life in heaven with God.

But right now I had duties that wouldn't wait for Grandad to finish playing. I crept away, my thoughts turning yet again to my wayward brother. If only he could sit still and listen to the music, it couldn't help but calm his soul.

It was becoming clearer, though, that my poor brother's soul was anything but calm.

❦

With Vic acting so defiantly I desperately wanted to give my mother peace that I would never leave her or break her heart. Dad returned from the latest business trip but the shame of my older siblings' defection and Vic's disobedience hung over our family like a dark, indelible stain.

Something extraordinary needed to happen to restore the honour of our family. But what could do that?

The question troubled my mind, weighing heavy on my shoulders in a dull, unceasing ache. There must be a way to right the wrong and reinstate the honour of the Just family, but how?

The answer dawned on me. Of course! I must make the public Commitment at once to protect my parents from scrutiny and clear our family name. If I declared my obedience, the blemish on our family name would be removed.

It was early October 2006 and my sixteenth birthday was rapidly approaching. Already, I could feel the pressure mounting to take my Christian vows before the church because both Sara and Sam had left the church when they were fifteen. Both of them had run before they had to take the vow.

I was well aware of the whispers spreading through the church. 'Miracle and Perry's next-in-line is coming of age. What's she going to do? Will she follow in the footsteps of her siblings?'

I would silence those whispers by making my Commitment, the rite of passage whereby a child moves into adulthood.

Once we were baptised we were allowed to take Communion, but Gloriavale children were expected to make their Commitment at age sixteen because that was the time ordained by the church for a child to 'come of age'. Coming of age meant displaying the mental, physical and spiritual qualities expected of an adult ready for marriage. By sixteen an individual's walk with Christ was expected to be firm-rooted.

To 'come of age' also meant taking a fair responsibility in the workforce. For men this meant participation as a labourer or manager in the commercial or industrial workings of Gloriavale. For women, it meant willing involvement in the domestic duties of the community and preparation for inevitable marriage and childbirth. Nothing would actually change for me because I was already fully in the workforce but I knew that unless I made the Commitment vow I would not be permitted to marry, and I wanted to marry Willing.

My mind was clear. I would do this for my mother. In the

evening I sat with her in her office as she worked on the rosters. 'Mum, I think I'm ready to make my Commitment.'

She stopped working and swung around to look at me. 'OK, Lil, why don't we talk about it at the next family night? You can ask Dad. Then you'll have to get Grandad's permission as well.'

'Yeah, that sounds good.' Some of the weight I'd felt in my shoulders fell away.

A week later I went to Grandad's family room and knocked on the door. It swung open and I peered inside. The beds were all neatly made and the room was empty. Where was he? I crossed the walkway bridge and there he was, striding to the kitchen, marching along like a war general.

'Hey, Grandad!' He stopped and turned to me. 'Um, I'd like to make my Commitment,' I blurted out.

'Well, love, why do you want to do that?' He gave a hitch to his cardigan, placed his arm around my shoulders and we walked together. He'd become nicer to me because his young wife spoke highly of me.

I gabbled words I'd heard other members recite. 'I believe Gloriavale is the one true Church of God and I want to commit my life to serve the Brethren here.'

'Have you talked to your parents about it?' he asked.

I assured him that I had.

'Right. Now, our way of life is different to the world. It's about giving up your selfish wants and needs to serve your brothers and sisters in Christ.'

I nodded. Yes, I knew that. I just needed him to grant me passage. I should have known it wasn't simply a matter of him saying *Yes, Lil. Go ahead.*

He began speaking in his preaching voice. 'Some people have decided they don't want to be here and that's their choice. They will face God on judgement day and give account of their sins. All of us will stand before God and give account for our life on earth. If you want to make your Commitment then it's important you understand the full consequences. There'll be a Leaders' Meeting for us to make sure you do.'

I didn't like the prospect of going to the Leaders' Meeting. I'd heard stories from Grace and others about how terrible they were. But this situation was different, because I wanted to become a full member of Gloriavale, so surely the leaders would be pleased.

First Day lunchtime arrived and I sat nervously at my family's allotted place looking across the six long dining tables. Butterflies were spinning in my stomach and I felt self-conscious, yet excited. Today was a big day. After lunch I'd be called for questioning by the Servants and Shepherds.

Grandad ended the meal by announcing that the Servants and Shepherds were to convene in the Staff Room. Residents knew to keep away from the meeting room to avoid disturbing them.

Grandad spoke the closing prayer of thanks, and all 500 residents hummed into motion, clearing dishes to the kitchen for the team on wash duty. Afterwards, most people broke out to their respective homes for an afternoon of rest before the First Day Meeting at 6 pm.

Dad, who was by this time back from his travel, told me to wait in our family room for him to come and fetch me when the leaders were ready for me.

I waited on the middle bunk bed, my Bible in my hands. I

couldn't read it. My focus was off and I couldn't concentrate on anything. Out in the communal lounge I found Grace reading on one of the couches. 'I'm so nervous. My hands keep shaking,' I told her.

'It'll be OK. Don't worry,' she reassured me.

'Can you wait here for me until it's done?' I begged her.

She promised just as Dad came hurrying through the front door. 'Lilia, it's time to go.'

I jumped up to run after him. I turned to make sure Grace was still there on the couch. 'Don't leave. Don't go away.'

The commune was deathly quiet as we walked across the lot and passed the main office. Dad opened the Staff Room door for me and I stepped through. Fifteen men turned towards me. I jumped as the door closed behind us with a heavy thud.

The circle of Servants and Shepherds sat on blue chairs, silent and waiting. There were two empty chairs and I dropped my gaze to the terracotta-coloured carpet tiles and followed Dad to sit down.

The room was eerily quiet except for the pinging sound of heat running through the pipes of the big steam heater on the wall. The atmosphere felt tight and claustrophobic. *Someone, please talk.*

Grandad broke the silence. 'Lilia, you've said you want to make your Commitment. That's why we're here today. Now tell the Men what's been on your heart.'

I felt strange, really detached, but the words were imprinted on my brain so it was easy to recite them. 'I believe that this is the one true Church of God. I want to do the Lord's will and serve him for the rest of my life. I want to forsake the world and have my name written in the Book of Life.' I paused and looked up. A couple of the men were nodding. Most held Bibles.

'Amen, sister,' Howard said in his Southern drawl. 'Sister, we need to make sure you understand the full consequences of the Commitment. We're going to ask you some questions. Think carefully on your answers.'

I took a deep breath, and the inquisition began.

Fervent got things going. 'Once you make this commitment before God and the church, God binds it in heaven as a spiritual vow. This means that if you are to ever break your vow on earth you do so to the peril of your soul.' He lifted his Bible to the heavens and shook it. 'God has prepared a special place for those who deny him; a lake of hell fire and brimstone for sinners who do not repent. Do you understand the consequence of breaking your Commitment?'

'Yes.' The concept wasn't new. I'd heard the foundational teachings of the church at every spiritual gathering and meal-table sermons for the last fifteen and a bit years.

Time ticked on as I answered their questions. Did I accept the role of a woman in the church to be meek and quiet? Did I promise not to teach men, or speak or preach in the meetings, but to go quietly about my duties and submit myself to the leaders?

I remembered Prayer accusing me of unsubmissive independence and wondered what she'd think of the lie, but I nodded. Of course I'd submit . . .

Was I willing to put aside the lust of the flesh, the lust of the eyes and the pride of life? Did I promise to put aside my own selfish desires in order to serve my brethren? Would I willingly renounce all my earthly possessions to the church?

Yes, I agreed to be unselfish.

My heart was beating abnormally fast and I felt hot and flushed. My knuckles turned white as I gripped the edge of my seat. 'Relax,' I told myself, releasing my fingers and inhaling a breath of air. 'You're not the first young person to do this. All your friends and family have made their Commitment with no drama.'

The questioning continued.

Was I willing to forsake all that I had to follow Christ?

Was I willing to forsake my family members who had fallen into Satan's snares? I stopped for a moment. That meant forsaking my siblings and never even thinking of them ever again.

Hopeful saw my hesitation and launched into a scripture. 'If any man come to me, and hate not his father, and mother, and wife, and children, and brethren, and sisters, yea, and his own life also, he cannot be my disciple.'

What difference would it make? I didn't have a relationship with Sara or Sam now. We didn't mention their names and even the photos which held the memories of our youth were stored away. *You can't love someone you don't know*, I thought. *There's nothing left to lose and everything to gain.* I looked at the men. 'Yes, I am willing to forsake all my family that forsake the church.'

The inquisition seemed to be over and I could sense Dad relaxing beside me.

They hadn't finished and instead, slammed me with one last question. 'Lilia, the *Sunday* TV programme is going to make a documentary about our way of life. The Commitment is a big step in showing the world what the Church is about. Are you willing to go on TV, make your Commitment and declare your faith to the world?'

National television? The world? My heart stopped for a moment. Sara and Sam would see this. I couldn't speak.

One of the men quoted Mathew 5:14: 'Ye are the light of the world. A city that is set on a hill cannot be hid . . . Let your light so shine before men.'

I found my voice. 'I am willing. If it's the Lord's will.'

Eight weeks passed. One week before my scheduled Commitment date a van arrived on the Gloriavale property. Two men and a woman all wearing strange clothes emerged from the vehicle, carrying cameras and equipment. The *Sunday* crew had arrived. Hopeful made an announcement at the breakfast table, telling us the TV crew were here to report on our way of life. Everyone was to be on their best behaviour.

After breakfast, I was washing the gluten bowls from bread-making when the TV woman came to the nearby water cooler and collected a drink. She paused and looked at me.

'Hello' she said, in an interested, engaging voice that made me feel warm.

I smiled at her. 'Hi.'

'I'm Janet,' she said. 'What's your name?'

I cocked my head to look at her properly. Her eyes were bright and questioning and she seemed interested in me. The leaders must have asked her to wear something respectable because she was wearing a simple top and scarf with a beige skirt that fell to the floor.

'I'm Lilia,' I replied. 'I'm Miracle's daughter. Hopeful Christian is my grandfather.' I figured they would have been introduced to my mother by now seeing she was the one woman of note in Gloriavale.

'And what are you working on here?' she asked.

The leaders mustn't have been able to impose all of our beliefs on to her because her scarf was round her neck and not covering her head. She had pale skin and dark red hair that fell to her shoulders in a thick, soft waterfall. She fascinated me. We didn't often get to interact with people from the outside world—only at the biennial concerts we performed for outsiders who were interested in our way of life. We hoped they would see how enlightened our lifestyle was and choose to join us. I couldn't remember another time when we'd been encouraged to talk to outsiders, unless the purpose was to witness the gospel.

'I'm cleaning these gluten bowls from the batch of bread I made for the community this morning.' I noticed that Janet's lips were darker than natural and her skin seemed too flawless to be natural. Could she be wearing make-up? The leaders preached that only women such as Jezebel, who was a wicked queen in the Bible, would paint their skin, but Janet seemed to glow in my eyes.

'Wonderful.' She smiled at me. 'How often do you do this?'

'About once a month,' I said. 'It depends how the roster is set up. If I'm on making bread then I'll get up at three am to start so the dough is risen by the time the girls on kneading arrive in the kitchen at five-thirty.'

We chatted for a few more moments before she had to leave and I was left staring at a sink full of suds with an idle brush in my hand. Would these people be a threat to our life?

The leaders chose me, Mary and Sarah to be interviewed by Janet for the programme. First, though, we had to go to a meeting where the leaders talked with us about what we would say and how we were to behave. Much of it we already knew, because we'd rehearsed the teachings our whole lives.

Interview time. I changed into my best clothes (that is, the newest of my five identical dresses), took my Bible and met the girls outside the First Hostel.

The weather was overcast but warm as we walked together with Shepherd Fervent Stedfast down to the gardens where Janet, a cameraman and a man called Chris Cooke were setting up to film.

We three girls perched uneasily on a picnic bench while Chris Cooke explained how the interview would run.

Janet added her encouragement. 'Just be as honest as possible.'

We smiled dutifully; we already knew what we would say.

The interview didn't last long. Janet appeared shocked when we told her we believed we were ready to be married and have children at fifteen. She didn't seem to understand it was really all a woman in Gloriavale could want. I wanted to help her understand. What else was there that we could even possibly do?

She asked if we had any desire to pursue a career. Mary, Sarah and I stared at her blankly. 'That's not our place. A woman's place is in the home. Why would we want to do the men's work?'

That seemed to shock her too. Next she asked what we thought of outside women.

Mary Pilgrim piped up. 'I think outside women look hard and

ugly. They dress like men and walk around with unhappy faces. I wouldn't want to be one of them.'

I recalled a sermon from the meal table where Grandad had told us the same thing. A thought flashed through my mind. I'd been browsing catalogues from The Warehouse in Mum's office and I really thought some of the clothes and make-up were nice. Immediately my heart flushed with guilt for my rebellion.

The interview finished and I returned to my hostel to prepare for tonight when I would go before the church to make my Commitment.

That First Day afternoon I was allowed the use of the spare Guest Room on the First Hostel floor because I needed a place of silence to prepare my vows. During the past week I had read *What We Believe* from start to finish, familiarising myself with every belief of the Gloriavale church. Some of the beliefs I didn't understand because they were quite complex, but the Commitment included a clause to declare I had read it so it had to be done.

I cringed at the section on birth control which told the story about Onan. In the Old Testament, Onan was supposed to procreate with his dead brother's wife to ensure offspring to carry on the family name but he didn't want to fulfil his duties so when he went to the bed of his brother's wife he would spill his seed so as to not get her pregnant. God had slain Onan for his sin and *What We Believe* clearly stated the same punishment for those who practised birth control.

Over the past weeks I'd spent every spare minute choosing which Bible verses to reference in my Commitment. It was really important to me that I get the script right.

My notebook was a mess of crossed-out words, so I hurried

across to Mum's office to use her computer. I typed out the Commitment script in a Word doc and printed off a neat copy.

I needed Grace. I found her and asked her to come and help me. I paced back and forth, reciting the words over and over. Grace sat in the corner giggling at my nervousness.

'Stop laughing at me!' I snapped. 'I just need you to listen to me. The whole Church is going to be there and TV is filming. This has to be perfect!'

'OK, OK. Calm down,' she said. 'I'm here aren't I?'

I sat on the end of the bed and buried my face in my hands. 'It's just so much pressure. I'm stressed out and my skin has broken out in pimples. I'll look so ugly. What if I mess it all up?'

'It's going to be fine.' Grace smiled at me and I knew she'd help me. 'Look here.' She opened her bag and pulled out a small bottle. 'It's make-up,' she whispered.

I jumped up with fright. Here I was taking the strictest of church vows and she was thinking to smear forbidden paint on my face! She giggled and concealed the bottle.

'Don't worry, we'll only use it if you're so ugly no one can look at you.' I slapped her arm and more giggles spilled out of her. My distress was a little bit funny, I guess.

I ran through the whole script twice more but when I went to do it again she shooed me off to have my shower. 'Time's a-marching. I'll be here when you get out. Off you trot.'

I went through to the Guest Room ensuite, grateful for its privacy and cleanliness. There was a big mirror in the bathroom. I stopped and looked at myself. *It's OK. You can do this, Lilia.* I took a deep breath and relaxed my shoulders. 'You're going to be perfect.'

I picked up my ironed scarf, twisting the crisp corners before securing it to my head. That way the corners wouldn't flare all the way out. I didn't want to look like a dork, but sometimes girls got in trouble for tucking in the corners of their scarves so I had to be careful not to overdo it.

Grace watched me write key notes from my script on the palm of my hand. I felt supported and almost calm to have her there.

It was time to go. I folded the script so that it nestled in my Bible.

Grace wished me luck. She had to sit with Prayer.

Mum and the kids were heading to the Main Building for the First Night meeting. I caught them up and picked up the baby. It felt safe to cuddle her and stopped me feeling so self-conscious.

The TV crew and their equipment were set up in the meeting hall when we arrived. After about ten minutes all of Gloriavale had arrived and the meeting began with a song.

My foot tapped anxiously as I waited. Grandad stepped into the middle of the ring and began to preach, 'Brethren, we are gathered here today . . . ' His voice faded. I don't know what he said or how much time passed before I felt someone slip a cool microphone into my hands.

My palms were damp and I wiped them against my dress.

'Our sister, Lilia.'

I looked up. Grandad Hopeful was asking me to join him in the middle. I stood, clutching my Bible and walked across the room towards him. One foot in front of the other. It seemed like a mile before I reached his side. I turned to face the crowd. The long black lens of the camera intruded into my vision and I blinked rapidly.

My grandfather began the ceremony. 'Lilia, are you making this commitment from your own heart?'

I clutched the microphone. It was on. The green light was glowing. I had to say something. 'Yes.'

'And is anyone trying to make you make this commitment?'

'No.'

My heart was thumping so hard I thought I might collapse.

He kept on asking the ritual questions. 'Do you really want to make it?'

'Yes.'

The questions seemed to go on forever even while somehow the clock raced towards the moment when I'd have to recite my vows.

At last I heard him saying, 'And now you can make your own commitment from your own heart, Lilia.'

I began reciting the words I'd practised with Grace. 'I love the Lord and I'm grateful to him for sending his Son Jesus to die for me to take away my sins. The least I can do is to give my entire life in faith and obedience to him. I've been baptised and committed myself to being a Christian . . .' My vision faded and my mind went blank. What was next? I checked my palm to read the prompt. No! The writing was a blurry mess, the words destroyed when I'd wiped my sweaty hand against my dress.

I looked up, the camera was waiting. Five hundred pairs of eyes and the eyes of an entire nation were looking at me. *Breeaaaathe. You know this off by heart. Speak now.*

The words came back. 'I realise there is a place that God has given to women in this life and I will always keep that place by submitting myself to the men and being a keeper at home and having a meek and quiet spirit. I will always dress modestly and walk in purity without fornication or adultery. I will never accept divorce or the remarriage of any people who are divorced. I will never accept birth control or abortion. I know that Christ must be the most important thing in my life. And I will love and obey him before anyone, before my family, before myself, and I will forsake anyone who tries to turn me from Christ and his church.' I recited the speech carefully, trying to utter the words with conviction but not show too much emotion because Grandad didn't like that.

I did as was asked of me, renouncing my earthly possessions and dedicating all the works of my hands to the church. It should have felt amazing but I was dismayed by the energy in my body. It felt torn. On one side I was gaining a loving church community but at the same time I was losing my independence and renouncing my loved ones. Was I losing a precious part of myself?

Hopeful asked me to read some parts of the Commitment and I did so. I promised I would never take legal action against Gloriavale. I made a promise that stripped me of earthly relatives who did not choose Christ and I felt sadness wash through my body. I knew I was renouncing Sara and Sam. After this they would truly be dead to me. I comforted myself by remembering that I would always have everyone in this church as my family— Cousin Serena, Bethany, Chris and Grace. It was more important to have a community who loved God than to accept blood family who were sinners.

The final promise was the most important. I promised never to leave Gloriavale as long as I lived. Then it was done. My life was pledged to Gloriavale. It was no longer my own.

TWENTY-FOUR

Uncertainty

He should be assured and convinced also that
Christ holds the leader of this Church directly in
His hand, and that he can therefore entrust his
whole life and faith to the decisions and leadership
of this leader, knowing that he is thereby placing
his life in the hands of God.

—*WHAT WE BELIEVE*, P. 22

Soon after I'd made my Commitment Vic couldn't stand the
tyranny any longer and ran from the church, just like his older
brother and sister had done. When we woke up in the morning
his top bunk was empty.

I couldn't believe it. I just couldn't believe it. Although I'd
seen it coming, the reality punched me in the face, hard. At

breakfast that morning it was as though, once again, the eyes of the entire commune looked disapprovingly at us. It took a couple of weeks for me to reorient and I attended to my chores in a daze while the other women shot looks at me. Cousin Serena rubbed my back and hugged me. 'Sorry honey, I'm here if you need me,' she told me.

I was devastated, yet at the same time strangely relieved. Both Vic and I were suffocating under the church pressure. Even in the midst of tragedy I knew he would be happier than if he had stayed.

My heart went out to my mother who would surely be heart-broken but Mum didn't seem to grieve as deeply for Vic as she had for Sara and Sam. Instead she and Dad began to whisper long conversations into the night. I could hear them murmuring on the other side of the thick curtain but couldn't quite make out what they were saying.

I got the feeling something was afoot, but I couldn't quite put my finger on it. The first real sense I had that things were changing was when Dad asked me if I'd like to come to Greymouth with him. 'I'm going to fix some plumbing at the Chinese restaurant in town and also there's someone you should meet.'

I was intrigued, and of course jumped at the opportunity to score a day off work and go into town.

The Chinese family were fun to spend time with and I laughed as they taught me how to eat food with chopsticks. They had an old box TV bolted high on the wall of their restaurant so, while Dad worked, I spent a good hour watching a cartoon called *Pokémon*. Human trainers would catch and teach fantastical creatures to battle each other. The show was like nothing I'd ever seen before. When Dad came to fetch me I didn't want to leave.

After lunch we drove to a motel where Dad introduced me to an elderly woman. 'Lilia, this is my mother, and your grandmother, Honore Tarawa.'

Uh, what?! I stared in disbelief at this woman. My father's mother had left Gloriavale before I could remember and we rarely spoke of her. I didn't even think she was a real person sometimes.

But Honore, with her golden, glowing skin and thick, almost-white hair cut to her shoulders, was more than real. Her eyes crinkled in the corners when she laughed and she fussed over small details.

'Let's make tea,' she suggested. Dad smiled and left us to catch up while he fixed the plumbing.

I'd never made tea in my life. Gloriavale had strict religious boundaries about consuming any foods containing stimulants. Tea contained caffeine and was prohibited.

Honore shuffled to the kitchen and stood on tiptoe to reach the pantry. She took a tiny perforated bag filled with dry herbs and poured boiling water over it. A rich, dark aroma filled the motel room.

'There's milk in the fridge,' she told me. 'Pour a dash into the mug. About two tablespoons is good.'

I was shocked. If that wasn't the strangest thing I'd ever heard! Why would someone put milk with herbs?

Being around Grandmother Honore was invigorating and we spent the whole afternoon together while Dad did the plumbing work.

Honore told me we were the descendants of Māori royalty.

I noticed that when she spoke, it was to share some meaningful wisdom and her eyes danced. When Dad came to fetch me for the drive back to Gloriavale, I was sad to go.

Honore didn't say anything about Vic to me but it turned out he'd been staying with her in Wellington. I'd been to Wellington once on a school trip to the Museum of New Zealand, Te Papa Tongarewa.

Our class had flown up under the supervision of Shepherd Steady Standfast on Air West Coast. Strangely I had discovered a book called *Devious Ways* in the seat pocket of the airplane. It was a gift from God. I consumed the entire volume during the return flight from Westport to Wellington. It contained some kissing between people who weren't married and other scenes that I knew the church forbade.

The day after I met my grandmother, Dad spoke to us during family Bible study night in our room. 'We believe that all our children are a gift from God.' He emphasised *all* our children. 'We feel that if God blessed us with children then it is our godly duty to care for and raise those children.'

I was confused. Where was this going?

'Mum and I have been praying about Vic. We aren't willing to let another child of ours go to the world,' Dad said. 'We've gone to Shepherd Howard to receive a blessing from the church.'

I was still perplexed.

He took Mum's hand and together they faced us. 'We've been given the blessing to live outside the community in a house at Moana. Vic will be with us and we will be together as a family. This way we can care for him and all of you kids at the same time.'

A stunned silence. I was shocked. He had to be kidding. Nobody left Gloriavale with the leaders' blessing. We'd be shunned. Anyway, I didn't want to live so far away from Grace and my cousins.

Dad went on explaining how it would all work when we moved. 'There are moss swamps out towards Moana that need harvesting. Vic and I will do that work for the church.'

My mind was spinning. We'd live in a house? What kind of house? What would it look like? We had lived in hostels in Gloriavale for as long as I could remember. The only houses I was familiar with were the two homesteads we used for holidays. The concept of living anywhere other than Gloriavale was bizarre. What about school and work? I shook my head trying to clear the bewilderment.

Dad was still talking but I couldn't make sense of his words through the stupor in my brain. *House. Moana. Vic. Focus, Lilia, FOCUS.*

'We will live at Moana in the evenings and Mum will bring you children back each day in time for school and work.'

Oh, so we wouldn't actually be leaving the church for good then? We'd have one foot in Moana and the other in Gloriavale. Made more sense.

I realised that my head was nodding and caught myself. I wasn't sure about this in the least. Perhaps my parents were just considering Moana as a possible option, but without the probability of it really becoming an actuality. 'I'm sure this will all blow over,' I told myself. 'Life will continue as normal.'

I ran to Grace the moment I could. 'Mum and Dad talked to Shepherd Howard. He's given permission for our family to go live at Moana part-time.' I still couldn't believe it. 'I bet if Grandad Hopeful wasn't in India he'd put a stop to such rebellious nonsense.'

Grace was just as dumbfounded as I was. 'How on earth did your parents manage to get that past the leaders?'

I shrugged. 'They're powerful members of the church. Their word has a lot of influence. They probably told the leaders that the influence of our family will persuade Vic to return to the church.'

Grace raised her eyebrows. 'Yeah? Not a likely happening.'

I put my hands to my head as if to force the Moana idea into my brain. 'I can't believe it. Nothing like this has ever happened in the history of Gloriavale. We'll be the first family ever to live outside without leaving the church.' I was nervous and unsure about the arrangement.

Grace's face lit up in a grin. 'How cool! Living at Moana is gonna be so much fun.'

I gave her a weak grin. 'Yeah and I don't have to put up with you following me around 24/7.'

She burst into uncontrollable giggles.

Her open-hearted acceptance of the coming change calmed some of the anxiety simmering in my belly but not entirely. 'We're moving next week,' I cried. 'What on earth should I take?'

Before we left for Moana, Grandad Hopeful sent a message from India to announce another fast day and to remind us he'd be returning in time to lead it. For the first time in my life I welcomed it. Surely this time of praying for the Holy Ghost to fill me with his spirit would calm my mind and take away my worrying.

True to his word, Grandad Hopeful was back in time to lead our final First Day living at Gloriavale. The community gathered as usual in the main meeting hall to pray. We fell to our knees beseeching God to send his Holy Ghost to fill us with gifts of tongues, prophecy and healing.

This was what I needed. I prayed to God to send me healing so that the questions whirling in me would no longer torment me.

Grandad Hopeful walked through the group of believers, laying his hands on each person to pray fervently for the Holy Spirit to rest on each individual. My heart beat fast while I waited for my turn to come. *Finally!* I clasped my hands together, squeezing my eyes tightly shut to concentrate. My grandfather's hands quivered powerfully as they rested on the top of my head. 'Dear God, fill this young Sister with your Holy Ghost. Bring your fire to rest on her heart.'

I held my breath and waited. Any moment now something extraordinary was going to happen. The moment stretched out. Nothing. Grandad Hopeful finished his prayer and moved to the next person. I was devastated.

What was wrong with me? Maybe I wasn't spiritual enough for the Holy Ghost to come into my life.

The experience left me with a hollow longing.

The next week our family packed a few boxes of possessions, piled into a van and we were off to Moana. The township lay a half-hour drive from Gloriavale and was situated on the northern shore of Lake Brunner. Beech trees lined the edges of the lake and coloured the water black. The township itself was tiny with a population of no more than a few hundred.

We arrived at a small tan-coloured house. The younger

children, who were itching to explore, jumped out and roared up the steps as soon as the van ground to a halt.

I got out to help unload as Vic emerged from the house. I had never been so happy to see his cool swag. 'Good to see you, brother,' I said, even though the outfit he wore was bizarre. He had on loose jeans and a white T-shirt with bold black graphics printed across the chest. One of his earlobes was pierced through with a clear, sparkling diamond stud.

His get-up looked peculiar to me after the blue uniforms of Gloriavale, but I thought he looked more comfortable than he had in a long time. A pair of white headphones hung unashamedly around his neck and I could hear thudding music coming from them. I laughed. What if Gloriavale could see him now!

I carried boxes up the steps into the tiny house. I'd best get used to this strange life. Who knew how long we would be staying?

Mum showed me the room that I would share with Gloriana. It was insane to think that I only had to share with one person. All the kids scrambled to claim their beds. Our new life had begun.

The next morning Mum and us kids travelled back to spend the day at Gloriavale for preschool, school and work. Dad stayed at Moana to help Vic in the moss swamps.

News of our family's situation sped around the church. Many people didn't approve or agree with it. It was not surprising that Prayer was one of them.

Each night, either Mum or I would need to prepare our family's dinner on the wood stove in the main kitchen separate from everyone else's dinner. I was doing it on the first day of our new life and, of course, Prayer came marching up. 'What are you doing?'

I looked up from where I was stirring beef stew. 'Um, sorting our family's dinner for Moana.'

'Oh.' Her right eyebrow twitched.

I prayed she wouldn't ask to taste it because if she did I'd be in trouble. I'd helped myself to some extra nice ingredients like soy sauce to make it more delicious than the often bland and tasteless communal stews.

After a moment she nodded and walked away. Phew. Lucky escape.

Because the leaders had given us their blessing most residents kept their opinions to themselves in public, but our trusted friends and cousins repeated some of the judgements being expressed behind closed doors.

'The Word tells us to forsake family members who leave the church.'

'Miracle and Perry are living in rebellion to God's will.'

All this was in my mind as I watched to make sure Prayer wasn't going to come back.

'Hey, honey, are you OK?' My cousin Serena stood by the bench tying her apron on. She peered into the pot. 'Looks yum. If you need anything at all let me know.'

I was so grateful for her kindness that I almost cried. She was a team leader so had the keys and permission to access ingredients in the lock-up. After all the judgemental, disapproving looks, her concern for me was balm to my soul.

My cousin Chris was awesome as well. He nibbled at a rough fingernail. 'If you need to talk to me about anything, anything at all, I promise I will never break your trust.'

The first afternoon of our new life drew to a close. It was time to return to Moana. I gave the heavy door of the preschool a good shove to pop it open. It was 3 pm and the little kids were still asleep on thin foam mattresses lined across the floor.

I tiptoed to Joy Temple and whispered, 'Mum wants me to pick up the girls. We've got to drive back to Moana now.'

It wasn't normal to be picking the children up this early but then nothing about this new life was normal.

I sidled down the row to where four-year-old Serena was sleeping and shook her shoulder gently. 'Wake up, darling. We have to go in the van now.'

She stretched and rubbed a wee fist into each eye. Both she and Melodie were dark haired with rich tan skin like me. I helped her up and dressed her in the clothes and shoes folded at the end of the mattress. Her dress was a miniature version of the navy blue frock we all wore. 'Look, we're matching.' I smiled at her.

We found two-year-old Melodie then the three of us headed out to the back porch behind the kitchen where Mum was loading the van up with goods needed at the Moana house. Cousin Serena carried the stew out and hugged me goodbye. 'See you later, honey. Miss you already.'

To us children the commute to Moana seemed like a long drive. We weren't used to travelling in motor vehicles and the kids suffered from travel sickness. Judah began to annoy the little girls who screamed in frustration.

'You kids better start behaving,' Mum growled from the driver's seat. Everyone was out of routine and on edge in the unfamiliar situation.

I sighed and looked out the window at the trees and mountains speeding by. That night I helped the kids into bed and then looked around me. What should I do now? Dad was working at his computer and Mum was cleaning the kitchen. Usually I'd skip a few metres to my cousins' room and hang with them for the evening but now they were miles away. The tiny house walls closed in on me and I went to sit on the porch step to gaze at the stars.

I wondered what Grace was doing. Hopefully Prayer wasn't telling her off again. I could almost see her waiting till Prayer left then giggling to herself as she rubbed make-up on her face. Cousin Serena was probably still cleaning the kitchen because she always worked too hard. I wrapped my arms around myself and tried to hum. Usually it made me feel better but this time my throat didn't want to work. I bit my bottom lip and covered my face. I missed my friends terribly. Perhaps the people who'd been gossiping about my parents were right. Perhaps Mum and Dad were in rebellion.

The entire living situation scrambled my brain. My parents had brought us to Moana to be together as a family but at the same time had taken us away from our cousins and friends. The rules we'd followed our whole lives were slipping away. We were living with Vic who was a sinner and we no longer stayed in the church hostels. I was scared of what might happen next and terrified of this spooky town.

The weekend came around and I asked Dad if I could stay back at Gloriavale in our old room. After all, it would save him from making a special trip from Moana to Gloriavale to pick me up after the Young People's night. He patted my head. 'Sure thing, Lil.'

Night was falling and the young men raised up gigantic

spotlights to light the soccer field. I laughed with glee as I tackled the ball from Willing and he was a total good sport about it. The soccer field was huge and when no one was watching I grabbed Grace's hand and dragged her to the adjacent field. We hid in the long grass and whispered.

'Tell me what Moana is like,' she begged.

I laughed. Usually I was the one who pestered her for stories.

'I miss you guys heaps, but the lake view is so gorgeous. In the mornings it reflects the mountains like a mirror. Has Prayer been scolding you?'

'Dawn's husband is a bastard,' she cursed. 'He's been going through my drawers looking for music tapes to burn.'

My hands flew to my mouth and I looked around to make sure we hadn't been discovered. 'Don't swear! You'll go to hell!'

She giggled. 'Bastard, bastard, bastard.'

I covered my ears. 'Stop it. Cursing is forbidden.'

She pulled my hands off my ears and continued the chant.

I couldn't believe how outrageous the girl was sometimes.

'Be quiet! Do you want to get your mouth washed out with soap?'

That made her splutter with laughter even harder. 'Well, you'll have to get your ears washed out for listening to me.' The comment was so stupid I couldn't contain myself and we tumbled into the grass howling with laughter.

After soccer ended we showered at the hostel and walked together to the meeting hall. Grace had to sit by Dawn's husband and scowled at the prospect. I found Cousin Serena and sat beside her. Salem preached to us a sermon that struck guilt into my heart. 'Are you willing to forsake your family for Christ and the church? If you're not willing to give up your life for Christ, to forsake all you have for the Cross, you are not worthy to be Christ's disciple.

'Having your earthly family together does not mean you will receive a mansion in heaven. You will not be rewarded for loving your family more than God.'

I looked at Grace who rolled her eyes then blew me a kiss. We both knew the preaching was aimed at my family and while her support was encouraging, I was still the sole representative of the Just family's young people. Vic's absence had never cut me so hard before.

Salem quoted a favourite scripture from Matthew 10: 'I am come to set a man at variance against his father, and the daughter against her mother. A man's foes shall be they of his own household.'

He hammered the message home. 'Those who have forsaken this Church have forsaken Christ and are not your family. Christ commands, "He that loveth father or mother more than me is not worthy of me; and he that loveth son or daughter more than me is not worthy of me."'

My religious conditioning got the better of me and the words of the sermon hung in my mind. Oh my goodness, he was right. This whole situation of living at Moana was a beautiful lie to cover the rebellion of my parents. If I didn't renounce my family I'd lose the one treasure I most valued—my salvation and God's promise of eternity in heaven. I would be stricken from the Book of Life.

My thoughts were frantic. *Maybe there are some sinners who will get left behind with me.*

My cousin Sweetness was very naughty and disobedient to her parents plus she'd been stealing lollies from the locked cupboards in Mum's office. 'I bet she'll stay here with me!' I thought. 'The two of us could eat all the lollies together.'

Grace would definitely be left behind with me. The thought cheered me, but only a very little.

~

Grandad had told me if I left the church I'd be sent to hell because I knew better. 'You were taught the truth right from when you were young. Don't be like Sara and your brothers. Watch that you don't fall into the snares of the Devil.'

For days, the words of Salem's sermon tunnelled into my brain until I couldn't take it any longer. I became convinced of the sinfulness of my parents' decision to support my brother and live outside Gloriavale. I didn't look forward to telling Mum what I was thinking but I had to confide in her.

The next day I talked to her as soon as I could before I lost my courage. I looked her straight in the eye and said, 'If you leave Gloriavale, I'm not coming with you. I believe Gloriavale is the one true Church of God and I'll be sent to hell if I leave.'

Mum said, 'What makes you think we'll be leaving? We're not leaving.'

I wasn't convinced. She looked very unsure. Having to choose between my family and my faith broke my heart. It was a no-win situation, I was going to lose something precious no matter what choice I made.

I tried to comfort myself by thinking about the advantages of living in the community. I had everything I needed at Gloriavale—no financial worries, a luxurious job as a graphic designer that often took me out of having to cook and clean. I couldn't fathom a life without Grace and the cousins and friends I'd grown up with.

There wasn't really a choice. I'd have to forsake my family for the sake of my immortal soul.

TWENTY-FIVE

A vessel for God's work

A little leaven of sin leavens the whole lump.

—*WHAT WE BELIEVE*, P. 55

Grandad Hopeful went again to oversee the church founding in India but I was fairly sure he was keeping a close watch over his flock back in Gloriavale. I was sure of it when the Shepherds announced there'd be a meeting. 'All those who have made their Commitment to the church are to attend. It's a special meeting to address matters that have arisen in the schooling department,' Shepherd Howard announced.

I almost snorted. It for sure wouldn't be to tell off teachers who used harsh physical punishment on their students.

At the appointed time everyone filed obediently into the upper meeting hall of the main building. White plastic chairs had been arranged in a series of inward facing rings. I grabbed a seat next to Grace and we chatted in low voices while we waited for the rest of the church to arrive.

Howard waited till everyone was present before he raised himself up to speak. His snow-white hair was combed back exposing a high forehead with two obvious balding grooves in his hairline. He didn't have Grandad's charismatic presence. He was sometimes nice, but I hated it when he slipped his arm around me in the kitchen.

The topic of the meeting astounded me. It was about being Māori and identifying yourself as Māori. Grace clamped her hand hard on my wrist, warning me to keep my mouth shut.

Howard stood there with the microphone in his hand and lectured us. 'It has come to our attention that there are some among you who've been saying that you enjoy being of Māori descent.' He paused to sweep his eyes across those of us belonging to one of the three families of Māori descent. One was our family. The second was the family of Dad's sister Serene and then Clem and Sharon Ready's tribe.

His accusing voice went on, 'You've been telling your children they are half Māori.'

I sunk a bit lower in my seat and looked over to where my Aunt Serene sat. Had she known they'd called this meeting to specifically address us?

Howard's cheeks drooped from his cheekbones and his face was hard. 'This type of attitude will only create division in the church. It breeds contempt among brethren. Once we commit to the church we leave our previous identities. That's why we have new names. The Bible says "there is neither Jew nor Greek, there is neither slave nor free man, there is neither male nor female; for you are all one in Christ Jesus".' He was quoting from Galatians. 'We are all equal.'

Really? Women were definitely not equal to men in the church and it seemed interestingly convenient to share the scripture in this context then ignore it in another. When he said that, Grace nudged me and I pretended to vomit. She stifled a laugh.

Howard was on a roll—jaw clenched, voice strident. 'Once we commit to the church our lives are no longer our own. They belong to the church. When I took my vows to the church I shed my American heritage. Now I am a servant of God. I'm an empty vessel for God's work.' He paused again, possibly under the mistaken impression that it gave emphasis to his words. In reality it was annoying. Grandad Hopeful was an articulate and engaging speaker even when you absolutely disagreed with what he was saying. Howard was a poor second.

'Already the government wants us to include more Māori teachings in our curriculum. These people out in the world won't leave us in peace. They think the Māori people are special but we are all God's people. No man is above another.'

What a hypocrite. From my own observation and experience I knew only too well that Māori were treated differently from other residents. We were often targeted for tiny things, hauled up for 'sins and errors' that others always got away with. The racial playing field inside Gloriavale wasn't an even one.

Without warning Howard turned to me and pointed a furious finger at me. 'Lilia! What do you identify as?'

Hundreds of eyes swivelled to look at me.

I was stupefied. Deathly silence hung over the entire room.

I sat frozen and watched the moment stretch out.

Speak! my brain screamed, but I couldn't even move my lips. Somehow my shoulders lifted and dropped into a barely perceptible shrug. Still I said nothing. The silence was becoming exceedingly awkward.

Howard realised I wasn't playing along and turned the attention away from me. 'We are all God's creatures,' he reiterated.

Anger, defiance, embarrassment and contempt stung me. Late that night, after the meeting ended, I sat with Grace in the sanctuary of the tatty blue kitchenette couch.

'I can't believe Howard did that.' Disgust burned in my throat.

'I can,' she said. 'The leaders honestly do things like this all the time, Lil. It's just that you're so used to it you didn't notice before.'

'It's evil. What makes them think they can treat people this way?' Of all the people in Gloriavale, Grace was the only one to whom I'd dared express such blasphemy.

'Well, Howard was raised in the deep south of the USA. It's slave territory over there. Even to this day racist attitudes are prevalent. People are still looked down on if they have dark skin,' she told me. 'It wouldn't surprise me if your skin colour has something to do with it.'

'The entire thing makes no sense,' I argued. 'It's like he's trying to change facts of life that can't be shifted. My skin colour IS different. I AM a female. Saying, "You are no longer a female" or "You are no longer Māori" doesn't change the facts. I am who God created me to be.'

Grace nodded. How could she stay so calm?

I was too furious to keep quiet but at least I had the sense to lower my voice. 'They want to make me a blank slate so they can inject whatever beliefs they want into me. We have to be vessels for the church; serve the church, work for the church, be whatever the church wants us to be. It's why Sara and my brothers ran away and it doesn't sit right with me any more.' I couldn't believe the words coming out of my mouth. Such a way of thinking was pure heresy. If anyone heard me I'd be dragged before the Shepherds and Servants to repent. Perhaps living at Moana was having more influence on me than I'd realised.

After the freedoms of Moana this current campaign felt like the leaders were trying to steal my independence away. I no longer wanted to be a mere vessel with no identity. I no longer wanted to obey the leaders' whims.

It was an uncomfortable feeling. How could I think this way and still belong to the church? If I left, I'd lose my cousins and I couldn't bear the thought of never seeing them again. Losing them seemed as bad as the prospect of the hell that waited for those who no longer believed. My mind tormented me. Were the whisperers in Gloriavale right when they said my parents were in rebellion? Were they right to say we shouldn't have been allowed to live outside the community?

From their point of view, Gloriavale was right to object to us being at Moana. It was separate from Gloriavale but the main sticking point was the many worldly influences that could lead us astray. They must have been right, because the sinful rebellion of the world had started to take over my mind just as they said it would.

The leaders ordered us to move to Glenhopeful House just across the river from Gloriavale. We'd be closer to Gloriavale where it would be easier to keep control over us.

TWENTY-SIX

A new world

Whatever particular standards of separation are taken by the Church, they must be consistently followed by every member of the Church.

—*WHAT WE BELIEVE*, P. 36

Life at Glenhopeful House was much better than Moana for me. The daily commutes were a tenth as long and I could catch a ride with the farmers who frequently crossed the river if I wanted to see Grace or my cousins.

For the first time ever I was given a bedroom all to myself. I shut the door and leaped on the bed in joy. Finally, an ounce of peace. The silence was soothing and I loved the privacy. I danced around in my underwear singing Shania Twain songs.

The atmosphere Mum and Dad created at Glenhopeful had

none of the tension that pervaded the church across the river. Over there, I'd become accustomed to having someone looking over my shoulder at every move so when Dad gave me free internet access and a computer in my bedroom I was ecstatic. Freedom!

Mum didn't have time to cook porridge in the morning so she took cornflakes and Coco Pops from the church store to help feed us quickly. We pounced like wolves on the yummy treats and yelped with laughter. The cereal was so delicious after being served porridge every day of our lives. I was also grateful not to have to sit through the harsh meal-table lectures. In fact, I felt I could almost get used to living like this.

One evening I logged into my newly discovered website to kill some time while Mum prepared dinner. YouTube videos about every different topic under the sun had, for the last few months, been my connection to the outside world. I had begun to learn new things—everything from how to play the guitar, researching new music to following celebrities. I was a sponge for knowledge.

One video had me riveted. I saw a young woman with long, voluminous blonde hair. She was wearing a short dress with thigh high boots and singing a sassy song about an arrogant ex-boyfriend.

I was bedazzled. 'She's amazing,' I thought dreamily. I hadn't listened to much worldly pop music except for Shania Twain and this girl had the smoothest singing voice I'd ever heard. For the next hour I searched YouTube for everything I could find on Taylor Swift, listening to songs, interviews and TV shows over and over again.

Life at Glenhopeful suited me but I knew that Mum and Dad

were struggling with Vic. Being stuck on an isolated, rural farm with limited freedom bored him out of his mind. To create some excitement he snuck over to Gloriavale, stole a car and went hooning around the farm with Jared.

Once again, I found myself wishing he'd just behave. If he didn't buckle under he would ruin the paradise we'd been able to create here. Couldn't he just be happy? Life had opened up so many possibilities for us already and just when I thought it couldn't get any more interesting, Mum dropped a bombshell that was a mix of good and bad news.

'Your grandmother Honore is coming back to live with us.'

I was stunned. What did this mean? Would I have to share my lovely private room with a woman I'd only met once before?

Mum went on, 'She's coming back to help your father and me care for Victor. We're moving back to Moana.'

My heart sank. Moana! Not again. This was awful news. I was upset and that night I didn't go back to Glenhopeful with my parents. Grace slept over with me in our empty hostel bedroom to keep me company and talk things through.

Her helping me 'talk things through' was more like a wicked plot to rebel. 'It won't be so bad, Lil. Think of all the fun you can have. You can even fetch chewing gum from the store for me. Ah, yes!'

'I'm not buying you chewing gum. It's a one-way ticket to hell,' I told her.

'It's a good idea. You buy it. I'll chew it and we can go to hell together forever. No church will ever come between us.' She clapped her hands in glee.

I burst out laughing at her lawlessness. We talked into the night and Prayer knocked on the door ordering us to quieten down.

I whispered in the dark. 'Sometimes I don't wear headscarves during the day when I'm at Glenhopeful. Do you think that's wrong?'

'Oh, it very much is,' she assured me. 'Babe, you're taken with the Devil. Let me cast the demon out of you.' I swiped her hand away and hooted with laughter.

Prayer bashed on the door again and warned us to zip it.

'Quit joking and get to sleep before Prayer makes you sleep in her room,' I told her. We girls fell asleep beside each other and I slept soundly knowing Grace was there. God, I loved her to bits.

Grace's jokes cheered me up and the next day I returned to Glenhopeful with my family. For Mum's sake I decided to stop being so cranky and put on a happy face. Anyhow, didn't the Bible say 'Obey your parents in the Lord'? It was my duty to be an obedient child and a simple geographical move wasn't the end of the world, was it?

But what seemed like a small move suddenly became a maelstrom when Mum sat me down to talk to me. 'Lil, we've been talking with Sara and Sam. We're hoping they'll come back to the church but they're not ready to do that yet. They are going to meet us at Moana and they'll live near us. We can be a proper family again.'

I sat back in disbelief. The move back to Moana made more sense when Mum went on to explain how my older siblings desperately wanted to be part of our family again but refused to live at Glenhopeful. Of course Sara and Sam would hate living at Glenhopeful. It was so close to Gloriavale that they would be back under the church's thumb yet again.

My brain was still in a whirl. How could they be part of our family if they refused to go near Gloriavale?

There was more astounding news. Sam had a child, a little boy.

I stared at my mother. 'You mean he's married? Is his wife Christian?'

She looked sad. 'They're living together but they're not married. We hope living with us will help them decide to sanctify their union.'

The three of my siblings were all going to work in the moss swamps with Dad, even Sara—how typical of her to be doing men's work. They would be paid wages, because Gloriavale needed the extra labour. I was so jealous. I didn't get paid for the long hours I worked. 'Will they live with us?' The idea seemed outrageous. I hadn't seen them for years. I didn't know who they were now. Sam was living in sin. Even his child had been conceived in sin.

'Yes. Sara and Vic will live at our house, but Sam will rent a house with his own family,' Mum told me.

'How do you feel about it?' she asked.

How did I feel about it? I was struggling to respond. How on earth could I support my parents in this while still remaining true to the church?

'Did you get permission from the leaders?' If they had, then maybe it'd be all right.

Mum nodded. 'They hope your sister and brothers will return to the church. It's time for us to all be together as a family and we believe God wants us to be proper parents to all our children.'

I knew she wanted my support. My shoulders and chest ached from the magnitude of what was happening and there was a dull thudding pain in the back of my head.

Even though I understood logistically how the house at Glenhopeful wouldn't be able to accommodate my grandmother, Sara, Vic, and Sam's family, it still wrecked me inside to be so far away from my church circle.

I quashed my anxiety. I loved my mother with all my heart. She was my best friend as well as my confidante and we had been through so much already. I admired her immensely. She was beautiful—high cheekbones, sculptured features and porcelain skin—enough to make any man weak at the knees. But more than that, she had a heart of gold and gave so much to serve the church. My support was the least I could give.

'Sure thing. When are we moving?'

～

It turned out to be almost immediately. We packed our bags and piled in the van. Time for the next adventure. I felt nervous during the drive back to Moana because Mum had told me that Sam was already there. Four years has passed since I had seen my brother. Who had he become in the time we'd been apart? I guessed he was a grown man now. It seemed unreal that someone who'd once been such an important part of my life was a complete stranger. My brain kept worrying. What would he look like? What would he sound like?

When we drove into the township it felt comforting to be back in this slice of heaven. The lake rolled against a backdrop of Southern Alps that thrust towards heaven and I smiled when I saw that our new house had a lakefront view. It was much larger than the bach we'd had for our first stay at Moana. Awesome.

The new house was painted white and had plenty of light from huge windows that overlooked the lake. Once again, the view took my breath away.

Melodie screamed for me to unstrap her car seat and I patted her fat cheeks as I released her. The kids ran off to explore the house while I glanced around nervously. Where was Sam?

A gentle voice asked, 'Hey, Lil. How are you?'

I spun around to gawk at the man who stood in front of me. This couldn't be him. This man had a big chest and muscles, not at all like the boy I remembered. But he lifted the shades from his eyes and I saw that it really was him.

It was Sam, and I didn't know whether to laugh or cry. How did you greet people outside Gloriavale? Should I hug him? Shake his hand?

He opened his arms and I went in for a bear hug. When he kissed my cheek I almost broke down.

I just couldn't believe it. I couldn't stop thinking that this moment was all a dream. Nothing in the universe had prepared me to be reunited with him.

'I'd better forgive you for telling Mum how I stole the library book, then,' I joked.

He gave a loud guffaw and we walked to the house together. He was dressed in a black singlet that exposed his arms and I noticed a picture drawn on his arm.

'What's that?'

He lifted his arm to show me a name tattooed into his skin. I teared up when I read it. It said: 'MIRACLE'.

'I missed you guys like crazy, especially Mum. Life has been hard for Sara and me without you. We had to fight to keep our sanity and we had no idea how to survive in the outside world. I needed to have something to remind me of home.'

My heart broke. Sam and I were only walking to the house but this journey was far more than that and it had only just begun. I shook my head in wonder and thanked God for the return of my lost brother.

Sara's return was no less moving. She was so tall and she'd cut her hair short like a boy's and she was wearing jeans and had her nose pierced. I couldn't help gaping—it was so sinful for a woman to do all that. Her crooked smile hadn't changed a bit, but she was so grown up. She hugged me tight. It wasn't just a memory any longer; she was real. She was still my big sister who loved me. Oh, I couldn't believe how good it was for us to be all together again.

I rejoiced to have them with us but I still felt torn. I missed Grace and I missed my cousins, especially Bethany and Serena. I wanted both my families but I could see that was never going to happen. Sara and the boys would never return to the church and our parents must know that in their hearts.

TWENTY-SEVEN

Strange things

I will have no friendship with the people of this
world, nor find pleasure in their company or way
of life.

—*WHAT WE BELIEVE*, 'THE COMMITMENT', P. 24

I'd grown up around many older women in Gloriavale who
were kind, caring and loving like my grandmother, but she was
different—somehow brighter and more vivid. Maybe it came
from her being free to love us unconditionally, but whatever it
was, she brought life and fire into the household and each of us
children fell in love with her instantly.

She was so encouraging to my parents. She knew the conflict
in their hearts about what they were doing in supporting three
wayward children when the church believed they should have

been shunning them. 'It's good you're living here with Sara, Sam and Vic,' she told them. 'God gave you each child to care for. They are your responsibility.'

Grandmother Honore's return made my father so happy. She'd been gone for many years and he loved her dearly. He did his utmost to help her feel welcome and comfortable in our home.

~

We'd not been living at Moana for long when five strangers came to visit.

'This is your cousin Frank, his wife Ginnie and their children,' Dad told me.

Ginnie had jet-black hair cut short to her shoulders. She wore tight pants and a low-cut top that showed her cleavage. Frank and Ginnie's three children, Erica, Liam and Bella, smiled at us. Erica and Liam were only a couple of years older than me and Bella was just a year younger.

Our relatives began to visit regularly and my parents warned us to keep their visits a secret from Gloriavale. One day Frank and Liam drove up to the house towing a boat and two high-powered jet skis behind their trucks. Sara and my brothers were ecstatic. After the monotonous work in the moss swamps they were more than ready for some epic fun.

Our cousins were avid wakeboarders and during the summer months they'd bound out of bed to meet Sara and the boys at the lake. Early mornings were the best for watersports because the undisturbed lake surface was an excellent canvas for tricks and stunts of all sorts.

The group always looked so cool in their sunglasses, shorts and T-shirts or singlets. Envy blazed in me as I watched them jump into the utes, tooting and waving as they sped off to the lake.

I pulled Gloriavale's uniform over my head. It wasn't fair. Why did I have to go back to the commune when the three of them were having fun here?

It was hard to concentrate on work. Chris tapped my shoulder. 'Are you sure you're OK, Lil?'

'I'm fine,' I lied.

'Remember, if you need someone to talk to, I will listen. I'll never criticise or betray your trust.'

I choked up. I loved Chris dearly, but there was no way I'd be able to tell him the truth. We shared a great deal in confidence with each other but this secret was too painful to tell.

My Moana cousin Frank was Chris's brother who had left the church many years ago.

How could I tell Chris that his brother and his brother's family were my constant companions at Moana? How would he feel if he knew the truth? Would he be angry that I had betrayed him?

The moment our family arrived back at Moana I tore the headscarf off and changed my clothes. Shedding the long blue dress, I swapped it for a long skirt and T-shirt Ginnie had given me. I stared long and hard at my reflection in the mirror. Who was this girl? I looked like a Gloriavale outsider. Was I betraying Chris and Serena and all the people of Gloriavale? I didn't belong here, but I also didn't belong in the commune.

I picked up the house phone and dialled the number to the community. 'Can I talk to Grace?' After a few minutes Grace's voice sounded through the line. I began to cry.

'What's the matter, babe?' she asked.

'I can't do this any more,' I sobbed. 'I'm losing myself out here and I have no idea who I am any more.' The words kept tumbling out. 'Do I obey my parents or the church leaders? I'm living two lives and at some stage the lies are gonna stab me in the back. I can't keep living this way.'

Grace poured words of gentle encouragement into the phone. 'You are the strongest person I know, Lil. God has a plan for you and he's not about to let you down. Trust him.'

I felt stuck between a rock and a hard place. If I went back to the way things had been, I'd never see my outside brothers or cousins again. But if I left Gloriavale I would be branded a sinner and stripped of everything I held dear. I didn't know what to trust in any more.

~

One afternoon Bella popped over to our house to play with Melodie and Serena. Her clothes stopped me in my tracks. She wore very short white shorts, making her sculpted legs look smooth and tanned in the sunlight, a ruffled top that floated in the breeze, and sandals with too many straps to count. Her hair was so much shorter than mine and fell like satin around her ears.

Was she wearing make-up? Yes, I decided, she must be. Her cheek bones glowed a soft pink and the rich brown shadows emphasising her dark eyes had to have come out of a jar.

She looked absolutely stunning and nothing like the hard-faced, ugly women Gloriavale told us lived in the world.

She tickled Melodie to make her giggle, while little Serena

clung to our cousin's back, begging for attention.

'Hi, Lil!' Bella greeted me. Her lips glistened around her bright white smile.

I loved this girl and the way she and her family had been nothing but kind to us. When she cuddled the little children or played with them, all I saw was open-hearted love.

Even after all the nasty things Glorivale had told me about worldly outsiders, I reasoned there could be nothing wrong with this heart-warming scene of Bella and my sisters playing. As far as I could tell Gloriavale had got it wrong.

Bella stood up. 'Want to come wakeboarding?'

I was stunned and excited. 'I'd love to!'

'Cool. Dad and Liam are towing the boat down. Grab a towel and let's go.'

I threw on a jacket to keep out the cool breeze and ran down to the jetty where the boys were launching the boat. They grinned at us, possibly because I couldn't get the beaming smile off my face. We jumped into the boat, donned life jackets and sped off into open water.

The rush was exhilarating and that stupid grin stayed on my face. This was the most fun I'd ever had!

The boat was fast and the speakers boomed with music. I asked what kind of music it was and Bella told me it was hip hop. The rhythm was addictive and I swayed in time to it as Liam slipped into the rubber boots of his wakeboard.

The boat powered him out of the water and I was stunned by his fluid movements across the lake surface. I bet it didn't look this cool when Jesus walked on water. Liam charged into the wake and spun off the top flying high in a double flip. I clapped my hands and shrieked with joy thinking my heart might burst from excitement. How awesome!

'Want to learn to wakeboard, Lil?' Frank asked from the captain's seat.

Did I? Absolutely.

'Good girl. Get changed into this.' He handed me a wetsuit.

I left my skirt on and slid the thick neoprene on to my feet. 'Oh my goodness.' I tugged my skirt down. My legs looked nothing like Bella's smooth, shaved skin. Women in Gloriavale were not permitted to shave any part of their body so my shins were covered with a dusting of short brown hair. We'd been taught that a woman's natural God-given beauty was not to be altered.

I felt exposed and conspicuous as I pulled the wetsuit up over my hips, keeping my legs covered and stripping off items of clothing as I went. The neoprene hugged every inch of my figure, pulling tight around my backside and breasts.

'You look awesome,' Bella said as she zipped it up for me.

I might as well have been naked. It didn't feel right to wear such a revealing outfit but it wasn't going to stop me.

I'd waterskied at Gloriavale—wearing my long blue dress and headscarf—but Frank's boat was much more powerful and faster than anything I'd ever experienced. He and my cousin Liam taught me how to set myself up for success. They were loving and caring, and I couldn't believe that these were the same people Gloriavale had told us were wicked and evil.

The boat pulled, the rope tightened and I got jerked up out of the water. I turned the board to the side, the way the boys had instructed.

Yes! I was up! Wheee! I was shooting across the water, slicing through the crisp air. The wetsuit now made me feel powerful and strong. For the first time in my life I had a womanly shape I was allowed to show. It felt almost as good as the wake-boarding itself.

When we arrived back from the lake I whispered to Mum, 'I want to shave my legs. I feel ugly and unkempt when we go out with Frank and Ginnie's family.'

Shaving my legs would be a naughty act, but Grace did it and so did my cousin Prudence who had run away from Gloriavale for a couple of months so I wouldn't be the first one to rebel. I was a bit surprised that Mum agreed to it and when we next drove to Greymouth I chose a pink flowery razor and some foaming shave cream.

She also took me to the secondhand shop to buy some worldly clothes because I only had the one outfit Ginnie had given me and I didn't like wearing my Gloriavale uniform at Moana. People stared at me and I hated being so conspicuous.

The shop was a wonderland. Mum left me there, exploring unsupervised for a blissful hour while she went off to do the food shopping. I didn't want to miss looking at a single piece of clothing. There were so many options and for a girl who'd never worn anything other than the Gloriavale uniform all her life, this was an intoxicating opportunity of a lifetime. But I had no idea what to wear . . . What was normal for a worldly person?

Short skirts, dresses, blouses, T-shirts, pants . . . Pants! Maybe I should get a pair of pants. No, I shoved the idea aside quickly. Dad would never let me do that because it was a rule that women were not to wear men's clothing. Perhaps though it would be OK to just look at them, so I headed for the rack and found a pair of loose black pants. They looked cool and I was sure Sara had a pair just like them. If I copied what she wore I couldn't go wrong.

I'd collected a bunch of items when Mum rushed through the store door. She handed me some cash then turned to leave. 'The kids are waiting in the car. Hurry.'

I looked at the basket of items and then the pants. Should I do it? Almost without thinking, I shoved the pants into the bottom of the basket and paid for the goods. The woman serving me looked at the pants and then at my blue Gloriavale dress and raised her eyebrows. I blushed a deep red, grabbed the items and made my retreat.

At home I hid the pants in a drawer and instead pulled out a short skirt and singlet to try. I felt so immodest and naked when I put the outfit on for the first time but I was determined to fit in so I kept them on. My legs! The short skirt showed my hairy shins. This would never do.

Locking the bathroom door, I lathered up the cream, and slowly dragged the blade up my leg as close to the skin as I could. My heart was beating fast and I was jittery. Once this was done I couldn't go back and if anyone in Gloriavale found out I'd get in such trouble, but I was determined to fit in with my cousins.

Done. I washed the last bit of foam from my legs and sat back to inspect my work. Holy smokes. My calves rubbed together and I gasped. The skin felt like satin. It was the most incredible feeling. I loved how my legs looked. They were nice and slim and tanned, just like Bella's. I vowed to never let them get hairy ever again.

I felt more confident in the short skirt now. I could do this, although when I went back to Gloriavale, I had to be really careful not to let any of my girlfriends see my legs when we were swimming in our long blue dresses and headscarves, or just sitting out in the sun.

I lifted my dress to show Grace and she pulled her skirts up for us to compare legs. 'Mine are nicer,' I teased.

Shaving my legs was such a big change. There was no going back from such a visible misdemeanour. It was easy to get rid of little infringements like chewing gum or music tapes but shaved legs would stay shaved until the hair grew back, which I was determined it wouldn't be allowed to do.

The tidbits of outside life that I was experiencing were exciting but they were confusing and emotionally draining as well. I loved spending time with my Moana cousins and we were growing closer each day—they were so full of life, so happy and loving. But the guilt that I was betraying my church and my Gloriavale cousins was always there, nagging away at me.

There were good times with my family at Moana as well but they only added to my confusion because people at Gloriavale were expecting me to disown my family. Dawn's husband found me and warned, 'If you do not give up your worldly family then God will forsake you.'

One warm, golden night Vic came to find me. 'Want to go down to the beach?'

He was in a singlet and shorts. I couldn't help thinking how cool and relaxed he looked wearing worldly clothes. So different to the scowling, angry boy who'd been forced to use slimy hair oil and pull his pants up to his waist.

I changed out of my Gloriavale uniform and we set off.

It was relaxing to chatter with Vic as we walked through

the township, along the coastal bush track and across the swing bridge to the lakeside. He pulled out his iPod and turned on music with a cool, slick beat. We kicked off our shoes—such a treat to walk barefoot on the sand.

'What's this song?' I asked.

'Justin Timberlake. "My Love".'

I knew the name. Sara and Sam had shown me a few of Justin Timberlake's music videos and I'd relished the freedom and creativity of his performances.

We sat in silence on the sand for a while watching the waves lap at the beach. I let the lyrics wash over me. I wondered what it meant but the song was about falling in love. It seemed like the singer was talking about a whole other reality, something I'd never known but very much wanted to experience.

'What's going to happen, Vic? The leaders are putting pressure on us to go back to Gloriavale and we can't live like this forever.' My voice was thick with emotion.

'Dunno. But as long as we're all together, that's what matters,' he said.

I stared out across the lake. There was a war raging in my mind, but the presence of my rebel brother eased and comforted me. Suddenly I realised how much I loved him, and my heart swelled with emotion. How on earth could I ever cut him off the way Gloriavale were commanding me to?

The thought was so painful it pierced my gut. For a long time we both sat in silence, neither of us possessing the words to express what we were feeling. I was so connected and yet so lost. My mind flew out across the lake and looked back to take in the scene. There sat a Gloriavale girl on a summer beach with her rebel brother, wearing worldly clothes and listening to forbidden music.

By Gloriavale's standards everything was wrong with that picture, but in my heart I knew that what I saw couldn't possibly be wrong. The love in my heart dissolved the voices of guilt and as they began to disappear so did Gloriavale's expectation that I choose to hate my family. I could almost believe that the uncertain future seemed promising. The gentle opening of my heart ushered in new possibilities and my mind filled with truth and wonder.

TWENTY-EIGHT

Revelations

The true love of God is not primarily an experience or feeling.

—*WHAT WE BELIEVE*, P. 93

My brothers and Sara called our grandmother Taua.

'It's a term of respect for our Māori elders,' Vic explained.

I couldn't possibly call her 'Taua', not after the way Howard had shouted at me in the meeting about being Māori. He'd stripped me of that identity and for most of my life I'd been called by my Gloriavale surname of Just. We hadn't been allowed to use the name Tarawa. At first, when I heard my cousins use the term 'Taua' I thought it was wrong, but it also made me realise I missed being a Tarawa. A rebellious thought sneaked in; perhaps our Māori heritage was something to be proud of after all.

One day I decided to try using the Māori name my cousins used for our grandmother. My back had been very sore and I needed prayer. Usually the elders of the church would pray for the sick, anointing them with oil to heal them. It wasn't something women were allowed to do, but Taua had told us that we could ask her for prayer.

'Taua, can you pray for my back pain?' I asked. The Māori word felt strange in my mouth.

I sat on the bed and she took some baby oil from her closet.

When I closed my eyes she laid her hands on my head. It was just as Grandad Hopeful had done when he prayed for the Holy Ghost to fill me, but the energy in this room felt very different. It was clearer, warmer and more inviting.

When Taua began to pray for me I was riveted. No one in the world had ever prayed for me like this. Instead of quoting stiff scriptures and begging desperately for forgiveness, my Taua began to open up a whole other realm.

Her gentle voice was infused with confidence and power. 'Lilia, God loves you. He wants you to come to him. He desires healing in your body. He wants a personal relationship with you.'

A personal relationship? What was that? Taua seemed to have some unusual ideas.

The hollowness in my soul began filling with something far more expansive and nourishing. What was this feeling? As Taua's affirmations flooded into my soul I wanted to cry, but caught myself. *Don't cry. Your grandfather would tell you off for that kind of weakness.*

I managed to hold the tears back, but the way Taua prayed for me, the words she used to tell me God loved me, were just so foreign compared to everything Gloriavale pumped into us day after day. I struggled to reconcile two such different approaches to prayer and God. Everything about the way she spoke was unlike anything I'd ever heard or experienced in Gloriavale. There was no promise of hell fire for sinners and no harsh emphasis on punishment.

Over the next months I couldn't stop thinking about how incredible I'd felt when Taua prayed for me. What was it that she had and Grandad didn't? I had no idea, but I knew that whatever Taua had was what I wanted.

I often had to stay back at Gloriavale without my family when I was on an early or late roster. My life there was busy. I'd either be helping make the daily batch of bread, operating the laundromat, cleaning bathrooms or working in the office doing the graphic design work.

The quietness of our empty room in the hostel was, in a time of real uncertainty, comforting and gave me the chance to clear my head. The leaders encouraged us to be studious and earnest in Bible study, so at night I would pore over scripture. The stories from the Old Testament were exciting and the philosophies of the New Testament fascinated me.

My Bible lay open on the bed as I studied, carefully writing out notes from the Book of John. 'He that loveth not knoweth not God; for God is love.' The pencil froze . . . *for God is love.* That was it. *Love.* Love was the boundless energy that for months I couldn't find words to describe and love was what Taua had shown me that Grandad wasn't able to. Oh. My. God.

Understanding crashed over me. For all the years of my life I'd obeyed my grandfather to the letter. I'd starved my body of food, attended every meeting, undergone prayer, been baptised, made my Commitment, publicly repented of sin and yet none of that had really changed me.

What Gloriavale had been teaching me about God wasn't love; it was *obedience*. Obedience to their man-made laws and traditions, obedience to the whims and wishes of the leaders and obedience to a book of rules called *What We Believe*.

The Bible dropped from my hand and as if by magic fell open to Colossians: *Beware lest any man spoil you through philosophy and vain deceit, following the tradition of men according to the rudiments of the world, and not in accordance with Christ.*

I couldn't believe it. Gloriavale had been deceiving me. the rules of the church were of human thinking and I'd subjected myself to them for years because I thought that it was God's will. I shook my head in disbelief at the web of lies.

Tears welled in my eyes and this time I let them fall. Taua, my Māori grandmother, had finally shown me the truth. This was the answer to the question I'd been asking all along: *What was right?*

Opening my palms to the heavens I closed my eyes and whispered, 'Jesus, fill me with your Spirit.'

A new energy coursed through my body. A new seed flourished in my mind. A person didn't need to have the same beliefs as Gloriavale to be acceptable to God. My Taua didn't and I sensed the love of God that flowed out of her.

The conflict of having to choose between my family and God began to dissolve. Somehow there was a reality where I could keep both my faith and my family.

TWENTY-NINE

Unholy communion

If any person is put out of the Church, be he or she even a member of my own family, I will keep no company with that person nor eat with him.

—*WHAT WE BELIEVE*, 'THE COMMITMENT', P. 25

One night at Moana Dad switched on a television show, an American thriller series called *24*. I'd never watched a television show. It was addictive. Dad didn't censor or edit it the way he'd had to do in Gloriavale and so the characters used foul language and often there were kissing scenes. The stories made a lot more sense now.

This wasn't the type of show Gloriavale would have let us watch, not in a million years. Yet I liked it that the women wore men's trousers, painted their faces with make-up and worked in men's jobs. I loved having the freedom to observe how other people lived, without needing to worry about being discovered by the church.

But women in trousers? Was it really OK? The guilt of the trousers that were hidden at the bottom of my drawer troubled me. I broached the subject with Dad. 'What do you think about women wearing pants? Ginnie does but she says she's still a Christian. But how can she be?'

With Dad travelling so often he'd been spared much of Gloriavale's preaching that women shouldn't wear anything pertaining to a man but he knew the rule and the scripture well.

Dad thought for a moment. 'Well Lil, it does forbid women to wear men's clothing in the Old Testament, yet it also says not to mix wool and cotton, but Gloriavale do that quite happily. Also in the Old Testament the Lord allows his servants to go to war and kill people, so does that mean we should adopt that belief as well?'

It was such a relief to be having this conversation with my father. 'Dad, it seems highly convenient to pick and choose certain scriptures and ignore others. Is it right? Should the leaders be doing that?'

'It's important for us to remember that the leaders are only men and make mistakes,' Dad said.

I couldn't believe those words were coming out of his mouth. After being told for years that the leaders were messengers of God and their word was law, this was blasphemy.

And there was more. 'When Jesus came to earth he created the New Testament and did away with the Old. Gloriavale are living in the past. The Bible is a book of stories, many of them metaphors. Certain leaders like Fervent have interpreted those metaphors literally and that's why we have so many unnecessary rules. When you think about it, Jesus in his day wore clothing that would, in this day and age, be considered women's clothing.'

I'd thought about this often, wondering if it was right and trying to convince myself that it wasn't. 'Yeah, imagine if Jesus came and visited Gloriavale today. They'd probably kick him out because he was dressed like a woman.'

The conversation reassured me. Dad was a lot more clued-up to the ways of the world whereas in Gloriavale we knew nothing other than that women wearing men's clothing was an abomination to the Lord. He must have gotten used to the sight of women in trousers because he was on the outside so often.

There was a scripture in 1 Corinthians 11:5 about our hair that got hammered into us regularly. 'But every woman that prayeth or prophesieth with [her] head uncovered dishonoureth her head: for that is even all one as if she were shaven.'

Since I'd confessed to Grace that I often went bare-headed at Moana she and I had talked openly about this topic.

I repeated what Dad told me. 'Gloriavale have taken these scriptures and interpreted them so literally. But isn't a woman's long hair a covering in itself? If you look at the Bible stories in the context of the Old and New Testament then their dress rules are different.'

I got no argument from her.

The scripture about our hair was repeated so often we knew it by heart. I'd thought then that Gloriavale were taking the scriptures too far and choosing their own interpretation.

I concluded that what they'd chosen wasn't what the Bible actually meant.

However, their teaching was strongly ingrained in me thanks to endless mealtimes hearing Grandad Hopeful thunder about hard-faced, painted women on the outside, how we'd go to hell if we showed our flesh, how God wanted us to keep our hair long and modestly covered and more.

When I lay awake at night I'd ask myself—what do I believe? The voices in my head fought each other relentlessly.

Grace was a gem. We worked tirelessly through each different belief, deconstructing them for ourselves. Both of us struggled to accept everything the church leaders taught but we also had strong religious commitments that bound us to Gloriavale.

I especially was so up and down about what I believed because I could see more benefit in staying in the church than in leaving. How could I let go of Grace, Bethany, Serena and Chris? The prospect of severing myself from their love was agonising. If I left they'd be forced to speak hatefully about me.

I was also frightened of the outside world. Moana was a small escape. But to completely leave and never return? I didn't want to think about it.

The weekly Young People's meetings proved even more daunting. The loneliness of attending while Vic was absent isolated me and even though I sat with my cousins I could feel my heart being wrenched away.

I would enter a meeting intent on supporting my parents and I'd leave that same meeting with the belief that my parents were sinners. I tried to answer the questions Salem threw at me: Are you on the path to heaven or hell? Are you a child of God or Satan?

For me, the hardest of all the questions was: Are you putting the church before family the way God wants you to? I clenched my teeth and refused to look up.

After the meetings I always stayed back in my family's empty quarters to rest and recover. Grace had moved in to the room next door and during the night we whispered to each other through the partition wall. When I was there I felt I had to try to separate myself from the life my family was living at Moana because there were aspects that I couldn't reconcile with my religious beliefs.

My double life continued to throw up confusion and doubt for me. At the next Young People's night, the leaders suggested that we demonstrate our obedience to our parents by washing their feet. This was a common custom. In the days of the Old Testament people travelled by foot and it became a sign of respect towards honoured guests for the host to wash their feet.

At the last supper, Jesus had taken a bowl of water and washed his disciples' feet to show he didn't set himself above them. Jesus also saved a woman who'd been living in fornication from death by stoning. As a sign of her gratitude she took the most fragrant oil she possessed, washed his feet and dried them with her hair before anointing them with the oil and kissing them.

Gloriavale said that when we washed each other's feet we showed that we were the servant of our brothers and sisters in Christ. They called it a ministration of love. It also signified the washing away of sins—rebellion, envy, pride. I often felt confused as to whether certain thoughts or deeds were sins or not. Gloriavale's deception was so cunning they'd tricked me into believing the worst about myself. It was better to fall down in repentance than risk eternal damnation.

Foot-washing was also used as an act of repentance where one brother in Christ had committed a grievance against another. The brother or sister who had committed the sin would wash the feet of those they'd sinned against. Certain people who were often hauled before the leaders for their rebellion would do it to show their repentance.

When Salem announced that we were to wash the feet of our parents I almost laughed out loud. He had preached that I should forsake my family and now he preached that I should obey them. I wasn't confused at all . . .

That First Night Meeting, along with the other young people, I took a bowl, removed my parents' shoes then washed and dried their feet to show that I was an obedient child.

The church taught that if my parents were in rebellion then I must obey the leaders before my parents. This didn't feel right. My parents had never done anything to harm me. I'd only received love from them my entire life. I struggled between my intuition and my religious teaching over the next couple of weeks.

About this time, Sam's girlfriend, Sacha, and their small son, Jamal, moved to Moana to live just up the road from where we were staying. Sacha was so worldly, so cool! She was tall, with tanned skin and shiny black hair that fell down her back but was cut short to her shoulders in some places.

When she saw me studying it, she said, 'It's called layering.' Her pretty eyes sparkled with mischief. 'We should do it to your hair.'

I was shocked. Women in the church were forbidden to cut

their hair. Gloriavale had taught us that a woman's hair was the glory of her husband and a covering to show submission to men. Many women in Gloriavale had hair down to their calves.

I wasn't at all sure about this girl. She'd borne a child out of wedlock. She wore black pants that hugged her legs and backside. I thought the pants were revealing and immodest.

But my little nephew, Jamal, was so cute and he was just learning to walk. I watched him toddle across the lounge drooling happily.

I really wanted to love my brother, his son and partner, but all the while Gloriavale's teachings held me back. I could hear Grandad Hopeful's voice in my head preaching that if Jamal were to die then he would go to hell because his parents were living in sinful fornication. I worried for the salvation of my brother's family.

If I thought for a moment that I'd find relief from the uncertainty that plagued me, I was wrong. More events began to throw me out of my comfort zone.

A few weeks later I had another shocking realisation. Sam brought Sacha and his baby into our house to have dinner with us. I was surprised to hear a knock at the door.

My brother hugged me and Sacha's eyes sparkled. Sara and Vic bowled in the door roaring with hunger after their day harvesting the moss swamps and we all sat down to eat.

Gloriavale's rules forbade us to commune with sinners. The breaking of bread together was an act of holiness and those who had forsaken Christ were not welcome. But at Moana we all ate as a family, us in our blue uniforms and my rebel siblings plus Sam's family in their worldly clothes.

I was conflicted. The excommunication of sinners had been the strictest of rules since before I could remember, yet here we were blowing that rule to smithereens.

Unholy communion was forbidden according to the Commitment vow my parents and I had taken. We were breaking a rule of that Commitment and if we were breaking one rule then could we break all of them?

The more we ate meals with our worldly family, the more accustomed to it I became. After a while it wasn't strange at all. In fact, I began to look forward to spending the time laughing and chatting with Sacha. She was kind and funny and would place sunglasses on my face begging me to pose for her camera.

The joy of family time nourished my soul and I confided in Mum while we washed the dishes, 'This feels good, we feel like a family again.' She felt the same way and told me that the wounds of separation were being stitched together for all of us.

Taua's love surrounded us even more powerfully during this time and I started questioning more than ever the things I'd been taught at Gloriavale. I was beginning to realise that life could be quite different to what Gloriavale taught and that it was often better than what Gloriavale taught. Another knot fell undone.

I didn't know what the future held, but I knew no matter what happened it would work out for the best.

THIRTY

More broken rules

People must face the consequences of their
own sinful actions, and of their having lived in
an evil world.

—*WHAT WE BELIEVE*, P. 91

After we'd been at Moana for almost six months I went into
Greymouth with Mum to go to The Warehouse. I wandered
around, still unused to all the worldliness of outside, but then I
stumbled on the CD section.

Oh my gosh, what vain delights! I saw a cover showing a
bronze-skinned woman wearing gorgeous jewels. Her hair was
blown out and it was wavy and golden. There was a name—
Beyoncé—written across the front. I thought the way to say it
was with two syllables: *Be-yonce*. Something about her drew me

in, and the first thing I did when I got home was look her up on YouTube. Her music captured my inner goddess. She was nothing like the Gloriavale women. Beyoncé had an alter ego called Sasha Fierce who protected and guided her onstage. This intrigued me because the only voices guiding us were those of the church leaders. I was entranced. Would it ever be possible to go and see her perform? No. Of course not. I'd go to hell for sure.

But the music was magical. How could it be wrong? Perhaps it was because it tempted us to fall into sin and error.

Mum let me loose in the secondhand shop again and when I went to the counter I spotted a range of chewing gum. *Oh my God. Yum.* I badly wanted some and plucked some grape Hubba Bubba from the box. The moment I took it in my hand I regretted it and the guilt of Gloriavale came crashing down on me. I could have sworn every single person in the shop was judging me: 'Look at this girl in her Gloriavale garb buying forbidden chewing gum. What a sinner.' After I'd paid for the gum I ran out of there as fast as I could.

Dad started giving us pocket money and the local garage had a shop, which to us kids was a goldmine. Grace's constant begging for me to sneak her in some chewing gum eventually got the better of me and I smuggled a few packets into the commune.

'I feel guilty, though,' I confessed as I offloaded the contraband to my friend.

'Ah, forget it.' She shrugged. 'They can't control us. You're on the dark side now, Lil.'

I loved her headstrong defiance but I still felt bad. Surely God was watching and would punish me for my disobedience.

～

Living at Moana allowed me to push boundaries and I was desperate for new experiences so I shoved my guilt aside. I wanted my hair to look like Sara and Sacha's. I wanted Beyoncé hair.

I tried to make my hair free and beautiful too by twisting it in a bun, letting it dry and then letting the curls come out. It didn't work very well, my hair was too long, too thick and too heavy.

But then my cousin Mike came to visit us from Australia. He'd left just before Sara. She and Sam went to stay with him for a while after they ran away. He'd always been so kind to me and I loved him dearly. He came back to visit my siblings and spend time with our family for the first time in many years. It was so good to see him again.

We had a lot of catching up to do. Wow! He worked in a hair salon. I had thought that men didn't do that. But he was awesome and so manly.

'Hey, Lil, how about we trim your hair a bit. Don't worry. I'll make sure it's not too much. Nobody in Gloriavale will notice but I'll give you some layers. It'll be like Sacha's hair only I won't cut it short like hers.' He held up his scissors and snipped them in the air a few times.

I was freaking out. This felt just like being a kid again when Sara and Sam were always pressuring me to do naughty things but at the same time it was fun and exciting. I would never ever let either of them take to my hair but I knew I could trust Mike. 'OK.' My voice squeaked and he laughed.

I squeezed my eyes shut. I couldn't watch.

'There you go. You can look now.' He was laughing at me.

I opened my eyes. Oh my goodness! It didn't look very different but it felt so much lighter. I loved how I could run my fingers through it much more easily. It still hung down to my waist but somehow it just felt less of a burden and it would be easier to shampoo and keep it looking good.

Sacha hugged me and told me how great my hair looked. Two rules broken in one hit. She was like Sara and my brothers and took every chance to nudge me towards worldliness.

One night at dinner, Mum said, 'Lil, I tried to find you this afternoon. Where were you? I don't like not knowing if you're safe.'

Sacha actually bounced in her chair. 'You need a phone, Lil. I'll give you my old one.' Before any of us could say a word she was up and running off to get it. 'This'll be OK, this'll be such a great idea.' She was always suggesting naughty things for me, fluttering her eyelashes and grinning her naughty smile. She knew what a huge step it was for me.

I was rapt. Now I had this glorious, pink metallic object which I could use to send a message to Mum and Dad. 'This is so great! We could do this in Gloriavale.' Why didn't the leaders let us have phones? They were so practical.

Sam laughed at me. 'No good taking it to Gloriavale, Lil. The reception's useless out there.'

And he would know. Of course.

But I did take it. I smuggled it in, whipping it out of my pocket to show Grace when I was sure we wouldn't be seen.

I'd lie awake at night playing the games on my phone. I loved it. No way was I going to let anyone take it off me.

So sinful. So much fun.

~

There was sin all around us at Moana. I was fascinated by the bridal magazines somebody'd left in the house. Those weddings were a revelation. The women wore white. The dresses hugged their bodies. Lace, chiffon, sparkles, jewellery. All those naughty, wicked things. Oh my goodness. If only I could wear a dress like that one day.

We watched a movie where a bride's father walked her down the aisle. I thought I'd love to see my dad in a suit giving me away to a man of my own choosing. It was mind-blowing and empowering—the idea that I could choose my own husband. It felt so good.

Then I'd go back to Gloriavale to work and I'd grab any spare moments to talk with my cousins, especially Serena and Bethany. It was tough. I couldn't tell them the worldly things I was doing or the revelations I'd experienced about the truth of Gloriavale's teaching. It was heart-rending and made me feel lonely. I no longer felt one with them, especially with Serena who I'd always been so close to.

She told me she was getting married and asked that I keep it in confidence because it hadn't yet been announced to the church. Her marriage was due to happen very soon. She was excited about it and shared the love letters her husband-to-be sent her from India. He'd lived in Gloriavale for some months so she'd got to know him and they liked each other. She was happy and couldn't wait to become his wife. I was so happy for her.

THIRTY-ONE

Marriage decisions

When we assert our will against what our
brothers or sisters would ask of us, we assert it
against Christ.

—WHAT WE BELIEVE, P. 54

Afternoon sun flooded the space outside Mum's community office
with light. I basked in the warmth as I checked the pinboard
announcements. As usual, it was full of rosters, scriptures and
any newspaper articles the leaders wanted us to read. I was most
interested in the photos from Tamil Nadu, India. The leaders had
just announced that my age group of girls would be sent there
to visit. They'd snapped my passport photo, which I thought
looked ugly because we had to keep our headscarves on. Fervent
had given us documents to sign so the New Zealand government

would allow us to keep the headwear. But I was excited at the prospect of travelling to somewhere so different. Before Vic left home he and Dad had gone there to build the school and help found the church.

It was almost two years since Gloriavale had begun founding the community in the southern Indian state of Tamil Nadu. The leaders had been bringing Indian families to Gloriavale for a few months at a time to learn Christian living. They'd then be sent back to build a similar church there. Not only did it give Gloriavale a charitable project to work on but, as a bonus, it brought marriageable young men into the fold for single girls who needed husbands.

This was a blessing because there were more girls than boys of marriageable age living in Gloriavale, thus many of the girls had to marry men much younger than they were. The shortfall was a result of Gloriavale's strict stance to only permit their young people to marry those who had made a lifetime pledge to Gloriavale and signed the Commitment. My brothers weren't the only young men to run away rather than commit their lives to the church.

The Indian mission was also the answer to Gloriavale's refusal to allow inter-church marriages. The leaders believed that marriage to an outsider risked disrupting our way of life by bringing in conflicting religious beliefs, as had happened in Gloriavale's early years. Thus, marriages were now kept in-house.

The Indian mission seemed to have plenty of eager young men who dreamed of marrying Western girls. My cousin Serena's fiancé, Faithful, was a kind and funny Tamil Nadu man who she actually liked so I was happy for her. Their wedding would be the first of many.

All the people in the photos seemed cheerful and happy, judging by their wide, bright smiles.

I was so absorbed that I jumped when I heard Grace rushing towards me, 'Lil, help me. Please help me!'

I swung round. Her face was twisted in panic.

'What is it?' I ran to her. 'What's happened?'

She was gasping for breath as if she'd been running for hours. 'I don't know what to do. I mean . . . I can't . . . I just . . . I don't know what to do.'

Oh God, she was a mess. I made my voice calm, copying the way she'd helped me through panicky situations time and again. 'OK, calm down. Breathe. You're practically hyperventilating. What's going on?'

'Howard's been at me again about getting married. He says I need to make a decision about it . . .'

Oh no, this was worse than bad. We'd need privacy for this conversation and there were people in the kitchen. 'Come in here.' I towed her to the door of the First Storeroom a couple of metres away.

There wasn't anywhere to sit among the bags of flour and preserved fruit, but we wouldn't be disturbed. I snibbed the lock to make sure. 'Now, tell me everything. What did Howard say?'

The dim lights cast a shadow across Grace's dark skin. Tears began welling. 'They've chosen a husband for me. Howard says I have to marry him.' She slumped over, her hands covering her face.

'Who?'

'Christian from Tamil Nadu.' That was a shock. He was nothing like Serena's fiancé. Grace and he both knew they would be a terrible mismatch that could only end in heartache for both of them.

'I can't marry him, Lil.' She shook her head. 'I can't do it. The thought of it makes me sick.' She was crying hard by now.

'Shhh, it's OK.' I scrambled for words, trying to think. 'We'll figure something out. Just calm down. What else did Howard say?'

'Nothing. Just that I was to marry Christian.'

'What does Christian think?'

'He doesn't want to marry me either. It's an awful situation for both of us.'

I couldn't think straight, but Grace needed me and I tried to pull myself together. 'What are you going to do?' Oh no, what a stupid question. She'd have to marry him. It was the Lord's will. Or was it? Surely it couldn't be the Lord's will to force two unwilling people to marry, and if it was then God was playing jokes. I frowned.

'I don't know, but I refuse to marry him.' Grace straightened her back. Her defiance was back and while I rejoiced to see it, I was fearful.

'We'll make a plan,' I promised her, but I had no clue what that plan would be and I feared for her. 'Whatever you decide I'll back you a hundred per cent.'

Over the next few days, I wasn't able to talk privately with my friend. I'd never felt the distance between Gloriavale and Moana so acutely. Whenever I did catch sight of her, I thought she looked strained and defeated. My heart ached. There was nothing I could do to help her, not even take her away for a private talk.

However, one morning before chores began I was walking

through the main kitchen when she caught up with me. We hurried into an empty office before anyone caught us. She'd tried to run away—packed her bags and hidden them under a giant tree that stood by the Second Hostel. She'd used a secure phone line to ring an outside friend to come and rescue her, but a Standtrue girl had overheard the conversation and informed the leaders.

'They took me to a meeting and yelled at me. Then Fervent forced me to say that God has reformed me and I now believe Gloriavale is the one true church.'

'What did you do?' I asked.

'I said it was a lie and Christians shouldn't lie, but he told me that it's not considered a lie if you're doing it for the church.' She was crying. 'They've taken my job at Discoveries in Gardening away until I come to repentance. That job is the only good thing I have going in this wretched place.'

I'd never seen my friend so upset before. Uncontrollable sobs shook her body.

'I can't do it, Lil.' Grace stood in front of me, her shoulders heavy with defeat. 'They're adamant I have to marry Christian, but I just couldn't live with myself if I do.'

I went cold. Somehow I knew what she was going to say.

'I'm leaving Gloriavale for good. I can't bear to be dragged through yet another Leaders' Meeting, especially as it won't change the way I feel about the marriage.' Although she was visibly upset, her voice was clear and strong. She'd already been put through so many Leaders' Meetings for her nonconformity.

I was struck speechless. Her decision didn't surprise me but it cut my heart. Grace was my dearest friend. How could she leave me? The second I thought it I was outraged with myself. *How dare you be selfish right now, Lil. Look at her.*

Grace looked crushed. This was such a hard decision for her. My heart filled with compassion. In my mind I could clearly hear the voice of the leaders threatening eternal damnation for anyone who dared forsake the church, but at the same time, as I stared at my friend who had brought such depth of companionship and supportive encouragement into my life, I knew Gloriavale were wrong. If there was a God, he would willingly open his loving heart to receive my lovely friend. 'Have you told anyone? Oh Grace, you need to be careful! They'll haul you into a Leaders' Meeting the minute they suspect you're going to try to leave again!'

For some reason, all that did was make her give me a fleeting smile. 'It's OK. I snuck into the office and called your auntie in Christchurch. She got in touch with my parents and told them I wanted to leave. Mum wrote to the leaders telling them to let me go or they would involve the police.'

Oh my goodness, that was a bold move. They were using the same tactic of legal action to save their daughter from the fury of the leaders, like last time. But it still wasn't easy for Grace and I could see the weight of it pressed down on her.

She grew tense. 'Remember when Christian Helpful left the church?'

I nodded.

She frowned and said, 'A while back I visited Glenhopeful House. Have you seen the hut on the back of the property?'

A shiver crept up my spine. The old white hut on the bushline. I'd forgotten about it until now.

Grace leaned closer. 'I saw someone living there so I started asking questions about what it was used for. I found out that when someone leaves the church but wants to rejoin they are kept in the hut for a time of proving. Or if someone sins they are excommunicated to the hut.'

My eyes widened. A time of proving? I'd heard rumours. There'd been one couple, a boy and girl who'd become secret lovers. When the leaders discovered the sin, the couple were excommunicated and forced to legally marry without a wedding celebration. They'd been taken away and weren't allowed to see us, speak to us or eat with us until they confessed and repented of their sin.

'People should not be shunned or cast out,' Grace declared, 'It's inhumane. I accused the leaders of sinfulness and that is another reason I can't stay.'

The more she told me the more I knew she was right. 'Does Prayer know?'

She sighed. 'Yes. She says I'm in rebellion and obviously thinks I'm going to hell. Everybody's going to think so when the word gets round.'

I took her face in my hands and forced her to look at me. 'Listen to me, Grace. Don't you worry about what others think or say. The important thing is to do what you believe in your heart is right.'

She pulled my hands away but kept hold of them. 'Thanks, Lil. I couldn't do this without you. You've saved my sanity yet again. You're different from the others, more open-minded and accepting. Don't change, promise me.'

'I won't,' I vowed. 'Look, somehow we'll stay in touch. No matter what it takes, we'll find a way. I'll write to you, I promise.'

Grace nodded, but her face was full of sorrow. I wanted to let her know that she had my full blessing. I reached out and drew her into my arms hugging her tight. 'Dry your eyes, honey. Everything is going to be OK.'

Her body shook with sobs. God, I was going to miss her.

~

The next week Grace climbed into a van, waved and then she was gone. But I was determined that our separation wouldn't be the end of our friendship. She'd given me her email and I wrote as frequently as possible. I trawled the internet and set up an app called Skype so we could make toll-free calls. She moved with her family to Australia and they lived at Rocky Cape Christian Community. I worried that she'd been sucked into another institution just like Gloriavale, but she assured me it was much less strict. We missed each other so much that at night we'd leave the Skype call open so we could fall asleep together.

~

Grace's decision to leave set the alarm bells ringing in my head even louder. The questions about whether the Gloriavale authority was right plagued me. I felt it was more sinful to force a young woman to marry a man she didn't love, than it was for that young woman to refuse. Mum must have had the same thoughts when she was disturbed by Joanna's arranged marriage to Loyal.

This led to me thinking that surely forcing a marriage in this way couldn't be of God. Then if it wasn't from God where were the leaders receiving their guidance from? The only explanation that made sense was that they were making the decisions themselves. I realised that I was once again submitting to the authority of the men and not to God.

My eyes were opened even more.

Since I could no longer blindly trust the leaders' judgement, I decided to take matters into my own hands. I figured that the way in might also be the way out, so I went to the Bible for answers. If Gloriavale were interpreting it to manipulate us, then I would read it and decide for myself.

The only Bible we were permitted to use was the King James version, but I found a copy of the New International version at our Moana house. I knew that to read it was heresy. The leaders' interpretation of the Bible was clearly laid out in *What We Believe*, and by making my Commitment vow I had accepted their philosophy as my own faith, without question. But, if the leaders were lying, then I would have to deconstruct their teachings to discover the truth. I was desperate for answers.

I turned to the scripture I'd discovered in Colossians. *Don't let anyone capture you with empty philosophies and high sounding nonsense that comes from human thinking ... rather than from Christ.*

It read so much clearer and more simply than the same verse in the King James version.

Mum was washing dishes and I dragged her from the sink to sit with me. I knew she'd been questioning the authority of the church as well but felt sinful about doing so. 'Look, Gloriavale say their teachings are from God but they've been filling our minds with religious bigotry and pedantic practice. It's not the love of God.'

Her eyes widened and she looked stunned.

Words poured out of me. 'God doesn't care if we wear the wrong coloured underwear. God hasn't said we have to wear matching uniforms. God doesn't say we all have to live together in one geographical location.'

She put her hands to her heart. When she looked up at me her eyes were lighter. After several seconds she said, 'Lil, for months I've felt so condemned about what Dad and I are doing. This changes everything.'

'Me too. I kept fearing I'll be thrown to hell or lose my salvation if I follow my heart, but that's not right any more.' I couldn't believe what I was about to say. 'If you and Dad decide to leave, then I'm coming with you.'

Her shoulders relaxed and she sighed. I sensed a lightness in her, a release of a burden. I knew how heavily it had been weighing on her that she would have to leave me behind. She was choking with tears. 'It's been such a battle for me to think of life without you. When you told me you weren't coming with us it broke my heart.'

We hugged tightly and laughed—we'd just broken yet another of Gloriavale's man-made rules. Life was changing faster than either of us could keep up with but at least we were in it together.

∼

We continued breaking the rules. Twelfth Month—Sara and Sam now called it December—was nearly here. They told our parents they wanted to celebrate this day called Christmas.

Oh my gosh! All the Gloriavale teachings about how evil and

wrong that pagan festival was rose up to terrorise me. Grandad Hopeful preached that the Emperor Constantine had invented Christmas after he'd had a vision on the battlefield where God taught him about Christianity. When Constantine returned to his kingdom he ordered that the pagan feasts be changed to celebrate the birth of Christ and renamed Christmas. Grandad told us that the yearly celebration was sinful because of its origins and worldly parents lied to their children about a fake man called Santa. Lying was a sin.

I was relieved when my parents resisted, but Sara and Sam had their arguments well worked out. 'This is part of our life now and we'd like you to meet us halfway and be a part of our lifestyle choices. We accept that you wear headscarves. We go to town with you in your uniforms. We accept that you go back to Gloriavale every day. But we moved from Chrischurch to be with you. Can't you accept some of our choices?'

Vic piped up. 'It's not that different to celebrating a Young People's tea. You'll love it!'

Mum and Dad agreed and another rule bit the dust.

On Christmas Day we cooked a big meal of food we hardly ever ate in Gloriavale. We made proper pigs of ourselves and relished every mouthful.

The wonders of the day just kept on coming. Sara and the boys gave us all gifts, bought with money from the wages Gloriavale paid them for working in the swamps.

They gave me a book. I was over the moon although I was shocked too—it was a story about two women having a relationship. Holy moly! This was terrible, but also very interesting. It was my first exposure to relationships between people of the same sex. They hadn't known what it was about but, if they had, they'd have chosen it deliberately. They were always showing me wicked things, dragging me off to show me games, videos, music.

Christmas was so much fun and Vic was right: the celebration did remind me of celebrations at Gloriavale like the Young People's tea. There was lots of food, laughter and hugs. Why had the leaders told us this was evil?

Here was yet another realisation that Gloriavale had twisted the truth again. They'd put an evil spin on something that was essentially good.

I started to see that that it wasn't the world turning good things evil, like Grandad told us; in reality, it was the other way around.

THIRTY-TWO

Leaving

No husband ever has the right to ask his wife or children to leave the Church.

—*WHAT WE BELIEVE*, P. 62

During the weeks after I told Mum I'd leave with them if they decided to go, I had long discussions with her and Dad. I wanted to be sure I was making the right decision and I had so many questions.

Why did Gloriavale tear families apart?

Why did they force people to marry against their will?

Why did they twist scriptures to suit the leaders' whims and fancies?

Why did we have to renounce our earthly possessions and gift them to the church?

Why did everyone have to make a Commitment vow? Dad told me the leaders had only created the Commitment once people began leaving. It seemed now like they dreamed it up to guilt people into staying.

Each of the answers I was finding challenged everything I'd been taught since birth and exposed frightening truths about Gloriavale's leadership. I began to see the leaders through different eyes and their deceit and manipulation became apparent.

The way things were going, it didn't look like we'd be at Gloriavale for much longer. I began to collect my most precious belongings from our hostel room and transfer them to a box at Moana. When we went back each day there was tension in the air, a sense of anticipation that something was about to happen.

One First Day I was getting ready to return for the day in my long blue dress. I hated having to wear it because it felt like putting on all that pressure that came with it. As usual, I would leave putting the even more hated headscarf on until we arrived at the Gloriavale gates.

Mum came in. 'Lil, we want to talk to you.'

I followed her into the lounge. Dad was there. They both looked serious and I knew something important was about to happen.

Dad turned to me, 'I'm going to the leaders today. It's time for us to make a decision. I'm going to ask their blessing to leave Gloriavale and take care of our children. I believe they should release us from our Commitment vows.'

Mum turned to me. 'I don't want to put my soul in peril. I'm only going to leave if the leaders give us permission and release us from the vow.'

I could see how torn she was because Sara, Sam and Vic were adamant that they weren't ever going to live under the rule of Gloriavale again.

But leaving was a huge step. It had been a stumbling block for all of us as to how to reconcile our Christian belief and commitment to the church with leaving. It was like Dad would be asking for a divorce from the church and no family had ever done anything like this before, but if the leaders gave their permission it wouldn't be a sin.

'Are you with us, Lil?' Dad asked

'Yes. One hundred per cent.'

They both looked so relieved.

That First Day, Mum stayed at Moana with two-year-old Melodie to pack up the house for our anticipated departure.

Dad, me and the rest of the kids went back for First Day lunch with the community. Afterwards, Dad went to the Shepherds and Servants' meeting to ask for our release.

'Take the children to our family room and settle them,' he told me. 'I don't know how this meeting will go and you need to be ready to leave at a moment's notice.'

I felt uneasy.

He parked our van behind the kitchen in the loading zone where it would be easy and quick to get to.

Two hours later I'm getting nervous. The meeting is taking longer than usual. Dad should be back by now. The younger children are settled and playing quietly, but something feels off. I'm starting to fidget and pace around the room. What's wrong? Where is he? Why is it taking so long?

The stress is unbearable. I leave the hostel and start to walk across to the Main Building. I catch sight of Dad walking towards me. His head is bowed and as he draws closer I see him blowing his nose.

What! Dad is crying? I've never seen him cry in my whole life. The shock cuts my heart to pieces and I run to him. 'What happened?' I whisper.

'Get the kids in the van. Quickly!' he urges and his voice is heavy but firm. I move as quickly as I can into the hostel without drawing attention. My feet thump against the wooden bridge as I run. Thank God most of the community is bunkered down for the afternoon. Within seconds I'm in our room. 'Pack up kids, we're leaving. Hurry and be quiet.' My heart is pounding. Gloriana, Ash, Judah and Serena scurry about snatching up their toys and possessions. The kids are unusually obedient and quiet. Somehow they can sense the weight of what is about to happen. I glance around the room one last time to see if there is anything more that we need. I pause to take it in. The room is full of possessions that we can't take with us—the bedspreads I spent hours making for Mum, the lamp by my parents' bed, the toybox—so much of our life is here, but there is no time.

We bundle the children up, warning them to keep quiet as we creep through the lounge. Hurrying them to our van, I help them strap into their seats quickly. 'Dad, please wait. I need one minute.' There's one more thing I have to do before we go.

I run back to the hostel.

My cousins' room is just beside ours and I knock briefly then

what had happened. Then we drove to Christchurch and all eleven of us moved into a beat-up two-bedroom house. I opened the single cardboard box of my possessions and wanted to cry. This was all I owned in the world now, but I pushed the sorrow aside. I had my family and that was more important.

I shared a room with my little sisters—Gloriana and Serena. Melodie slept in Mum and Dad's bed. Vic, Judah and Ash slept in the lounge while Sara had a caravan at the back on the lawn. Sam was with us too and his partner and their son stayed with her family in town.

Dad didn't tell us kids much about the Leaders' Meeting because he wanted to protect us so that we only had good memories of Gloriavale. He'd suffered the blows of the leaders' wrath alone to spare us the agony.

However as the days passed, Mum told me a little about what had happened. 'It was horrific. They tore your father to shreds and cursed him with the Mark of the Beast.'

I hated them. 'Who were we kidding? They were never going to let us go nicely.'

No wonder my dad had wept. It only confirmed for me that we'd been right to leave.

THIRTY-THREE

Culture shock

Christians must come out from among the people
of this world and be separate.

—*WHAT WE BELIEVE*, P. 36

How did the world work? There was so much we didn't know.

The only money we had was a little Dad had earned from doing plumbing work at weekends and evenings for the Moana bach Frank and his family were building. But Mum had another plan.

In Gloriavale, government payments to support low-income families went first into the women's personal accounts. However the women all signed forms instructing the bank to transfer it into the Gloriavale sharing account.

Mum handled all the money in that account because she did the budgeting for the domestic realm including weddings, concerts and other events. In the weeks before we left she'd gone to the bank and arranged to stop our family money being transferred to the sharing account. She'd accumulated a few thousand dollars in her own account but when she went to check that account once we got to Akaroa, she was devastated to discover it had been emptied.

Mum was furious. How could Gloriavale be so petty? It was a nasty, calculated revenge. How could a family of twelve survive when they had nothing but the clothes on their backs? She'd worked so hard for nothing all her life and she wasn't going to submit to having what was rightly hers snatched away.

As a signatory to the sharing account she was able to get the bank to transfer the money back to her into a new account, one that had no connection with Gloriavale.

Word got out that an entire family had fled Gloriavale, and help began to arrive. We survived on gifts of food, second-hand clothing and homewares from my cousins' church friends. It wasn't a lot, but we were grateful.

~

For me, being in the outside world was a head spin. Who was I now? I knew I was no longer Lilia Just. I was Lilia Tarawa and I wanted to honour my Māori heritage. We changed our family name back to Tarawa and Mum said I could choose a middle name if I wanted to. We'd never been allowed to have middle names in Gloriavale.

I talked to Sacha about it. 'What'll I choose? I want something that feels authentic for me,' I said. The new love I'd discovered with my family and Taua played on my mind, 'What's the Māori word for love?'

'Aroha.'

I liked it. It sounded full and sensual and open but I needed to be sure it had the meaning I wanted. 'Does that mean deep love? A deep, expansive all-encompassing love?'

She said, 'In Māori we use a phrase "Te Aroha Maia". It means love that is great.'

I repeated it. 'Te Aroha Maia.' The words made my spirit feel restful. I knew that was my name.

The next week my birth certificate no longer read: Lilia Just. I was now Lilia Te Aroha Maia Tarawa.

~

I then needed to work out things like how I should dress. And, more importantly, what was I going to do with my life?

There were so many new experiences, so many things to learn how to do.

Dad took me to the bank, opened an account for me and I received my very first EFTPOS card. I had a lot of practical skills from Gloriavale as well as my self-taught design skills, but I'd never had a paid job before. I set about earning money by designing websites for friends and family.

Once I'd accumulated enough I wanted to spend it. Sacha took me shopping. Girls' day shopping—I'd never heard of such a concept.

She drove us to a huge building full of stores. The name on the outside was Westfield Riccarton Mall. Oh my goodness, I had no idea what to buy myself. Sacha took out a pen and paper. 'We'll make a list. This is what you need. We'll start with jeans, some tops, a warm jacket. Shoes. And you need a haircut.' I freaked out. A haircut! I couldn't possibly do that. But she was adamant, 'It will be OK. We don't have to cut off more than you want.'

And off we went to get the clothes. And make-up. If Grace were here she'd be stoked about that. We picked out a few garments for me to try on. It took ages. How do you decide what to get when nobody's telling you you've got to wear a long blue dress? Finally I settled on a pair of tight jeans and a cable knit sweater. I chose that because it reminded me of Grandad Hopeful's cable-knit cardigans and I was trying to cling to any tiny connection to my old world.

'OK, Lil,' Sacha said. 'Go up and pay for them now.'

I handed the clothes to the woman at the counter who added up the cost. She told me the total and I pulled out my EFTPOS card and just stood there, staring at it. I had no idea how to use it. I whispered to Sacha, 'What do I do?' I felt like such an idiot.

She talked me through the swiping and told me to put in the number. I'd made my first-ever purchase, with money I had been paid for work I'd done. And—I'd chosen my own clothes.

Awesome.

The make-up counter was like a candy store to a kid. Such a massive array, such variety. How were you meant to choose among all those products? Sacha was an expert, matching my complexion to the appropriate products. I was in a daze by now and simply let her get on with it. I said yes to everything.

When I got home I tipped the shopping out on my bed and put on all my new clothes. There was a long mirror in the room and I spun every which way in front of it. I looked great! There were curves where I hadn't known I had them. My ass looked so good! The tight jeans were horribly uncomfortable after seventeen years in a dress but I was determined to get used to them. They made my body look hot.

Applying make-up stumped me, so I jumped on the computer to consult YouTube and typed in: *how to put on make-up.*

It was fun practising and I got it wrong. Washed the whole lot off and started again. It made my skin look amazing and smooth and unblemished when I finally got it right. No pimples!

~

I spent quite a bit of time just looking at shops in town on days when I had a spare hour or two—and discovered the lingerie store. It was a fairy grotto filled with wonder. Lace, satin, red, black. Gloriavale decreed that black and red underwear were too sexy for single women to wear.

But I could do what I liked now. I picked out a red, lacy camisole and bra set to try on. It was a perfect fit. I felt attractive and sexy. The wickedest, most un-Gloriavale-ish thought popped into my head. *I'd like a man to see me in this.*

I paid for the outfit and left the store on a cloud of giddy excitement.

As I was leaving the mall I spotted a pharmacy displaying a large sign: 'Discount Perfumes'. At last! I was being gifted the opportunity to wear forbidden eau de parfum. I sniffed the perfumes until I was dizzy with happiness, then purchased a rich, alluring scent named Jimmy Choo. I proudly carried the box home and placed the fragrance next to my bed.

My next adventure in worldly clothing was buying a pair of high heels. Being me, I went to the extreme with the highest heels I could find and had to practise wearing them at home. I tottered back and forth across my bedroom. The heels felt tight and restrictive compared to the flat runners I'd lived in my whole life and I wobbled precariously. Oh my goodness, how did women walk in these things? And why would you have spikes coming out of your heels? But I was so determined to learn how to walk in them, and I loved the way they made my legs look. So vain, so un-Gloriavale. And I was loving it.

~

My cousin Bella was turning eighteen and booked out a bar in town for her party. She invited me, and with Sacha's help I bought a short dress, heels and blazer jacket for the occasion. Dad took one look at my dress and growled at me. 'Why are you wearing a low-cut dress? You know that's immodest.'

I ignored him. I knew he was trying to get used to this crazy new world as well. Also, I was full into being a rebellious teenager. I was done with being told what to do.

I'd never been to a bar and didn't know what to expect.

We walked into a dimly lit space. The people in the room were all leaning on high tables or walls. There was a man standing behind a long bench and handing out glasses of liquid that people seemed very eager to drink.

Bella introduced me to her friends. 'This is Emerald and this is Hanna.'

'Emerald! What a cool name.'

She looked at me and said, 'Gosh, you're so pretty.'

I blushed. No one had ever said anything like that to me ever before. She reminded me of my cousin Sweetness back at Gloriavale and I felt sad.

Bella towed me over to a sweet-faced Māori girl. 'Meet your cousin Ani.'

Another one? There was a whole bunch of them there that night—so many that I hadn't a hope of remembering names and faces.

Ani said, 'Let's get you a drink, Lil.' She gestured to the man behind the long bench. By this time I was certain the liquid he was pouring contained alcohol.

I'd never touched even a drop of evil alcohol in my life. I'd seen Sam drink it but what would it do to me? Would I get drunk and disgrace my family? I was so worried. Would it change me? But there'd been so many firsts in my life. What was one more? 'OK,' I said.

She helped me buy a lemon-flavoured drink that tasted bitter. After a few sips I told Ani I didn't feel very well.

'It's OK,' she said. 'You're just a bit tipsy. Just wait and it'll pass. And then you can have another drink.'

Bella and Ginnie came and grabbed my hands. 'We're going dancing.'

Really? What kind of dancing?

We jumped in a taxi which stopped outside a building with *Boogie Nights* written in lights above the door. We waited in line and a big, muscly guy wouldn't let me in the building until I showed him proof I was eighteen. I pulled out the 18+ card

Sacha had helped me get the week before.

Inside the club, music blasted my ears. I was confused. Why would you want to come to a place where you couldn't even hear your friends talk to you? Bella and Ani dragged me up to buy another drink.

There was a spinning globe hanging from the ceiling shooting coloured light around the room. People jostled about in the middle of the floor.

'Come on Lil, let's dance!' Ginnie headed for a section of the floor tiled with squares of flashing lights.

'Can I walk on these?' I'd never seen anything so bizarre but I soon did when Ginnie started rocking her hips and sashaying in time to the music. She and Bella were both doing it and singing along.

I felt so out of place—a total dork. But I wanted to see if I could dance too, so I began imitating them. It felt kind of cool but I didn't know any of the songs they were belting out. I hoped people didn't notice I wasn't singing because I didn't want to have to explain why I didn't know a single tune.

Later on we went to another club. This one was underground. So wicked and evil.

We met up with Sara and Sam, who bought me a drink in a bottle with a straw poking out the top. 'Try this. You'll like it.' Sam threw his arm around me. It felt great to be protected by my rebel big brother and let my hair down.

In the early hours of the morning we caught a cab back home. I tiptoed in, trying to be careful not to wake Mum and Dad. I wasn't feeling very well at all. I worried that I was getting the flu.

My stomach roiled and I only just made it to the sink in time to throw up. Oh, my goodness, I really was getting the flu.

In the morning Mum asked me if I'd vomited into the sink. 'Yeah, yeah. I was feeling really bad and I've got such a bad headache this morning. I must've caught a virus or something.'

I only found out later the truth of my 'flu'. For the first time in my life I'd got a hangover.

~

Even though I'd left Gloriavale behind me, in my heart I was still a Christian. My family searched for a church to join. I longed for the friends and community a church would give me. Erica and her husband took us to their church called Grace Vineyard.

It wasn't like Gloriavale. Here, they played music, which I loved. The worship was gentle with none of the strident preaching I'd been accustomed to. I went to my usual extreme by choosing to sit up the front where I could be a real Christian and take in every aspect of the service. It was the worst decision. For the whole hour I was certain the pastor was looking at me and judging me for wearing a short skirt, sheer tights and no head covering.

Mum wore a wide headband to church because she didn't feel she could worship with her head totally bare. I wished I'd done the same. The beliefs of Gloriavale still plagued us.

After the service, Emerald and Hanna came up to me. It was comforting to see familiar faces because everyone was a stranger these days. They invited me to attend Youth Group with them later in the week and I accepted immediately. It felt awesome to have girls of my own age who wanted to spend time with me. I missed Bethany and Serena a lot.

They said they'd pick me up and they'd be car-pooling. They had to explain what that meant.

At Youth Group there was some religious talk but there was lots of fun stuff as well. Towards the end of the night I joined a group of people, boys and girls all mixed up together.

I turned to a girl and said, 'Hi, my name's Lilia. What's your name?'

She was Meggy and she introduced me to a whole heap of other people as well, including a handsome guy who told me his name was Andy. I thought he was so good-looking.

The group of us, including Andy, started hanging out together. I was stunned. We were allowed to be in a mixed group without a church leader to act as chaperone? I was also horrified to see how some of the unmarried ones would greet each other with a hug, and some even kissed on the cheek. I found out that they were allowed to have boyfriends and girlfriends. They'd hold hands and cuddle each other in public. That wasn't Christian.

We went to the beach. Holy! They were so immodest and it couldn't be godly for guys to go around with bare chests, or for girls to wear bikinis. Surely they must be trying to make the boys lust after them . . .

But I decided if it was OK for them I was going to do it too. I bought myself a bikini, but I bought it one size too big for me because I hoped the extra fabric wouldn't be as immodest. I had to try to shut out the Gloriavale voices shouting that to expose any part of my body was vain like the wicked queen Jezebel of old.

The first time I wore it, I wanted to run and cover myself up. But I was determined to fit in. I gritted my teeth and lay on my towel on the sand.

Hanna took one look. 'Oh my gosh! You've got such a great body, Lil. You're so fit and so ripped.'

I was surprised somebody would say that to me, but I was so pleased. I'd been working on making my body look good by doing pilates from a YouTube tutorial—Gloriavale forbade us from doing anything to enhance the way our bodies looked. I was thrilled at my friend's compliment. It gave me the confidence to quit worrying about my exposed flesh.

I loved Emerald's blonde hair but I knew it wasn't her natural shade. 'Oh my goodness. It's awesome. How did you do it?' I was so hungry for new experiences. What if I could change my hair to a different colour?

'It's easy. I got hair dye from the supermarket.'

Next time I visited the supermarket I went straight to the cosmetics aisle. I chose a product where the woman on the carton looked great. This must be the right one for me.

It was a disaster. My hair turned orange. I was horrified. How could I go out in public like this? My uncle came to the rescue by giving me money to go to a good hair salon. The stylist coloured my orange hair a dark plum with highlights—and she cut a fringe straight across my forehead. 'You look great with bangs.'

Bangs? How cool to have bangs! I'd never heard of them before. I looked awesome. I loved my new hairstyle. The Church leaders at Gloriavale would damn me to hell if they saw me now.

I couldn't wait for my youth group to see me. I was thrilled when Andy said, 'Wow, Lil. You look hot.'

But there was so much about the world I didn't understand or know about. Our Youth Group would go on these excursions called 'road trips'. We'd stay overnight, pitch a tent at a campsite and sleep squashed up together like sardines. Boys and girls each wrapped in their own sleeping bag, lying side by side— TOGETHER.

The music they'd listen to—OMG! It wasn't music to my ears and I hated the swearing. They said it was rap and I realised it was the same music as on Frank's boat. When I listened carefully to the lyrics, I noticed it sounded like poetry. The artists told fascinating stories about their lives and addressed topics like racism and poverty, which I thought was good. I determined that rap was an artform, a creative outlet, and therefore it was OK for me to listen to.

I wondered how my new friends could be Christian while living such wordly lives. Although I'd realised that you didn't have to obey Gloriavale's rules to be a Christian, I was finding that hard to accept when I saw such blatant flouting of the Christian doctrines I'd been raised with. Gloriavale had taught me 'come out from the world and be separate', yet my new friends didn't look any different from others in the world. In fact, I couldn't actually tell the difference between a Christian and a non-believer these days.

My nineteenth birthday was coming up and by now I'd been to celebrations of my new friends' birthdays. I decided I wanted, for the first time in my life, to celebrate mine, too. A group of us went bowling. They gave me gifts! And one of my girlfriends and her boyfriend bought me a pair of neon pink, pointed toe, stilleto heels—wow! My girlfriend had seen me drooling over them in a shop window and purchased them in secret.

Oh, I was over the moon. What a birthday. I would so do this again. Stuff Gloriavale's rules.

It was the first time I'd been celebrated as an individual. In Gloriavale we weren't to put any man above another by standing out from the crowd. But this treatment was so different. I felt like I was coming out of my shell; I was a person in my own right.

I was starting to fit in but it was only on the outside. There were still so many worldly things I just didn't know. Some men talked about politics and I discovered we'd had two female prime ministers. Women as leaders? How could that be? I knew nothing about politics because the leaders decided who we had to vote for. Outsiders would bring booths into Gloriavale and we would enter them to tick whichever box the leaders had instructed us to tick.

We'd never been allowed to watch television news—it was most strictly forbidden. The only outside media reports we ever saw were articles that the leaders posted on the pinboard or sometimes if an earth-shattering world event occurred, we'd be shown footage of it. They showed us the terrorist attacks on the World Trade Center but to me it was so far away and too unreal. I couldn't believe the event had actually happened. It looked like a movie and I knew those weren't real. It was hard to believe that such a world existed outside Gloriavale, and it was even more unthinkable to dream of exploring that world. The leaders had told us the world outside Gloriavale's gates was full of sin and all men in the world would perish unless they came to repentance.

I kept thinking that if my new friends had any idea of how culturally unaware I was they'd judge me to be an idiot. That was confirmed for me when I didn't know who the singer John Legend was. My friend stared at me. 'What? You don't know who John Legend is? Have you been living under a shoebox or something?'

I didn't know what Chuck Taylors were, either. I'd never seen young women driving cars and I certainly hadn't seen women preach in churches—that was a whole other opening of my mind.

When Bella came to church one day dressed in a top with spaghetti straps I thought it was so immodest and disrespectful—we were in God's house. But I still thought she looked pretty.

Thank goodness Bella had shown me how to open a Facebook account because Andy had added me as a friend. This led to him inviting me to play tennis, after which we ate lunch and went swimming together. It was the first time I'd ever been permitted to spend time alone with a boy.

It felt incredible to receive positive attention and to have a relationship with a male. I was able, for the first time, to explore my feelings for a man.

I didn't know if he liked me or not. I was new to the dating scene. I'd been able to make friends with some other boys from church, so I confided in one of my male friends and asked if he thought Andy liked me. He said, 'Lil, does he text you as soon as he drops you off? He does? OK, he likes you.'

After that I felt more confident of my own feelings but I had never kissed a boy in my life so I wasn't sure how to cross that bridge. I didn't need to worry. It was what I'd always dreamed about when Andy kissed me. Totally amazing. I was so happy we didn't have five hundred eyes gawking at us.

But, oh my God, I was freaking out despite having all the new and wonderful sensations rushing around in my body. I didn't know how to kiss. Was I doing it right? Was he going to laugh at me? It took some practise before I felt I knew how to do it—he didn't seem to mind all the rehearsing though.

It didn't take long before I was head over heels in love with him. I hadn't realised how strong Gloriavale's teaching was, though; I simply accepted that, since we'd kissed, it meant that we would marry and live as man and wife forever.

But things began to get rocky when he changed to a different church and I wanted us to be in the same church community. I had also by now begun to question Christianity. If Gloriavale had lied about so many aspects of our lives, what else had they lied about? I wasn't willing to again allow my thoughts and way of life be determined by someone else.

The more I saw of the world, the more I felt that each of us makes sense of it based on what we know. Gloriavale had withheld so much knowledge from us and only fed us stories that upheld their belief system and way of life but now I wanted to explore.

After some months I became a Youth Leader in my new church. We'd go on camping trips, holidays and expeditions together. I loved being surrounded by a group of friends and was loving my role as a leader to younger girls.

However, more important than that was my longing to discover the truth about what was right and what was wrong. What did it mean to be a Christian? Did I have to be a Christian at all? If my world view was the result of Gloriavale's selective brainwashing, then the only way to break out of that was to deconstruct what they'd taught me, go back to a blank slate and figure out a way to follow my heart.

I struggled with the big questions. What was the meaning of life? What was the nature of God? Could it be something other than the wrathful God of judgement and vengeance Gloriavale thundered about? Did God even exist or was he entirely a fiction?

Andy and I weren't on the same page as I began pulling away from the church and avoiding Sunday meetings. We decided to separate and it broke my heart. It took a while to recover. He was my first love and I'd believed that we'd be married and be together forever.

The benefit was that our separation gave me the freedom I needed to start researching other religions—Catholicism, Islam, Agnosticism and Atheism. I felt blessed to have this amazing opportunity to explore the world, to make my own choices instead of being forced to follow Gloriavale's rule book. I felt a heady sense of freedom ditching the belief that disobedience would lead to an eternity in hell. It seemed to me that the essence of all the great faiths was the same. In some form or other they were founded on what I'd now come to believe that God was: *Love*. However, many of the adherents had twisted the essence of God to serve their own desires, which led to the creation of communities like Gloriavale. And too often people thought their way was the one right way to salvation.

I noticed that different belief systems had different names for God—they called God the Universe, Mother Nature, Vishnu, Allah, Buddha, the Source. The similarities between gods from different religions fascinated me and I began to wonder, *Is it all the same god?*

One day, when I was musing, a tree that grew near the back of my yard captured my attention. I realised that I referred to the plant as a tree, but Grace, who spoke Spanish, called it *árbol*. Suddenly I understood that, even though Grace and I used different labels to identify it, the tree itself didn't change. This helped me to understand how important it is to look at life through the eyes of others, instead of hastily judging what we don't understand.

Gloriavale had damned to hell anyone who didn't adhere to their doctrines, but the deeper I searched for truth, the more I understood Gloriavale's way of thinking to be ignorance.

I knew many of my Christian friends didn't yet have that awareness, so I had a heart-to-heart discussion with Hanna one night about my struggle with Christianity. I said to her, 'If I leave the church, I'll lose all my friends.'

Her response wasn't at all what I was expecting. She said, 'That's not true, Lil. There are so many of us who will love you regardless of how you choose to live your life.'

This comforted me. I knew I might lose some of my new friends, but those who truly loved me would still keep me in their lives.

THIRTY-FOUR

Breaking the seal

Once a man and a woman have become one flesh
in marriage they are bound to each other for life.

—*WHAT WE BELIEVE*, P. 57

I met my uncle Phil when he came to visit us. It was the first
time I'd seen him since I'd glimpsed him when he'd come to take
Cherish and Prayer away from Gloriavale. He offered me a job
at his digital signwriting company in Coffs Harbour, Australia.

I was thrilled. The chance to live in a different country! Australia
fascinated me. It was so different. I got used to seeing wallabies
and kangaroos hopping around. Snakes and spiders I could happily
have done without. The climate was hot and the scorched land
was nothing like the lush greenness of the West Coast.

It was exciting working for my maverick uncle. I loved the job and it was a novel experience to get a regular pay packet. Life was always exhilarating around Phil. You never knew what he was going to come up with next.

I met my cousins who Prayer had borne to Phil and it was strange to think I'd grown up like peas in a pod with their mother and sisters. *Cherish*. I missed her crazy ideas and freckles. I wondered if she was OK.

Towards the end of my time working for Phil he threw a massive party for his daughter Crystal's twenty-first. He flew her to the palatial venue in a helicopter! Mum and Dad and my whole family came over. I lost the plot when Grace walked through the door and we threw ourselves upon each other. Reunited at last!

What a night. We danced and sang. The villa had an infinity pool, a tennis court, its own theatre and gym. Bella and I acted like queens of the castle as we explored hallways hung with expensive tapestries and huge art works.

At the end of the celebration I flopped into bed. This was the life. At last I felt like I was living as my true self even though I still hadn't resolved the question of what to believe.

When I returned to New Zealand the party didn't stop.

Beyoncé was touring and she held a concert in Auckland. Finally I had the chance to attend the concert of this 'freedom fighter' whose music had made such an impact on me. Thousands of screams filled the auditorium while glitter and smoke shot up from the stage. I couldn't believe I was there, because I'd never thought this would ever be possible in Gloriavale. Beyoncé sashayed, sang, danced and lit up the stage.

When I flew back to Christchurch I went flatting with a

couple of girls from church and I still regularly hung out with the church crowd.

But I was also twenty-one years old and I was determined to live life to the full. I'd stopped attending most of the Sunday church services and I was determined to blaze my own path. If it took me to hell so be it. No way was I going to revert in any aspect of my life to that subservient, demure and obedient Gloriavale Lilia Just.

I was now Lilia Tarawa and I'd been let out of the box.

I went partying every weekend and would sneak home drunk and try not to wake my flatmates up. I made a ton of new friends and found that despite my peculiar background I fitted in quite nicely to this wicked world. When I put on heels and a tight dress, no one thought for a moment that I was an ex-cult girl. My secret was safe.

One night we were clubbing and a friend introduced me to a friend of his called Darrel. We danced and partied the night away. At the end of the night we exchanged numbers and he took me out to dinner. He was older than me and so respectful and caring. After that first dinner he kissed my cheek and said, 'I'll be in touch.'

We started dating. It was brilliant—a simple, straightforward friendship with intimacy but no heavy expectation. By this time I'd realised that a relationship didn't have to end in marriage.

I was twenty-two and although I'd come such a long way from the Gloriavale rules of no touching, no kissing and definitely no sex before marriage, I was still a virgin. I kept the fact that I was seeing him a secret from my Christian flatmates. He was not a church member and I was sure they'd disapprove. I loved his cool car and when the engine roared I feared my Christian friends would discover us. When he picked me up we'd scoot away really fast to avoid being caught.

I was attracted to Darrel. My body told me so, but I was scared that if I had sex with him there was no going back. All of my life, I'd believed that my virginity was something I must protect so that I could gift it to my husband. Grandad had told me so.

If I went against that teaching it would surely be enough to make my Christian friends disown me. What about my parents? They were still committed churchgoers and Mum would probably blame herself for my sin. Even though Darrel and I cared for each other I felt embarrassed because I guessed he was experienced sexually and I wasn't. One night when we were making out I awkwardly broached the subject and told him I was a virgin.

He smiled. 'Lil, I'd guessed as much.'

Such a relief. He didn't mock me or tease me and he hadn't tried to force himself on me. He'd waited patiently until I was ready.

The next time I stayed over the kissing went further. He was kind, loving and gentle. When he touched me I felt like a woman and I felt I could express myself sexually and take charge—something that was strongly discouraged in Gloriavale. A woman's body was for her husband to serve his needs regardless of her desires. It was such a huge step to go against the ingrained sexual rules of my lifetime. The act empowered me and it was the catalyst that gave me the strength to permanently step away from the church.

We saw each other for about ten months but when a job opportunity came up in Australia for him, I encouraged him to accept. I'd known in my heart that I wouldn't marry him so this was a perfect way for our relationship to evolve.

He left but we kept in touch and I still count him as a dear friend.

I'd kept my relationship with Darrel an absolute secret from my mother. Sex before marriage went utterly against her beliefs even though three of her children were by now living with partners out of wedlock. I was afraid that if I shared with her that I was no longer a virgin or a Christian it would upset her.

However we've always had such a close relationship and I knew I had to be open and honest. I told her I was no longer a Christian.

She burst into tears. 'This is all my fault. We never should have taken you kids away from Gloriavale.'

I was deeply saddened to make her so distressed. I wanted her to understand that things were different now from how we'd both been raised. 'Mum, I'm an adult now. The Gloriavale teaching that a parent is responsible for their child's sins is wrong. You have to get rid of the lies we were fed. I need you to respect my decisions and understand that I'm responsible for my life. You've got to realise that just because you believe something, it doesn't mean everyone else has to believe it too. That's Gloriavale's method and we're done with that. We're done with treating others or ourselves the way they do.'

Sharing honestly with her brought Mum and me together even though we now had different beliefs. I came to understand that people of different beliefs could live in harmony together, as long as they were empathetic and loving. It was such a different understanding from Grandad Hopeful's preaching that if you didn't agree with him then he wouldn't love you and you'd go to hell.

I knew it was hard for her. She'd had to come to terms with her children making decisions about life that were so foreign to her upbringing.

Mum had been pregnant when we fled Gloriavale and the birth of my youngest sister, Arielle, was difficult because Mum believed God had cursed her for leaving Gloriavale. She had the belief seared in her mind that she would be cursed with problematic childbearing because she had left Gloriavale.

The birth of my little sister brought the number of Tarawa children to ten. She would be the only one of us not born into Gloriavale and her worldly name was testament to the fresh start we'd been blessed with. It meant Lion of God. Arielle's loving kindness shed joy on each life she touched.

THIRTY-FIVE

An authority among men

Leadership in the Church is given only to men. No woman may teach or preach or usurp authority over any man.

—*WHAT WE BELIEVE,* P. 52

By now I'd studied design at polytech for two and half years but I dropped out before I finished the degree because I knew everything that they were teaching. I'd done it all at Gloriavale, where I'd figured it out for myself. The one class I loved was art history, because it gave me such an insight into other cultures.

After I left polytech I worked for my parents as an administrator in the office of their plumbing, drainage and electrical business. I learned all aspects of the business and involved myself fully in the day-to-day management. I threw myself into learning how each facet of the business functioned but once I had it figured out, I began to want something different, something more challenging to immerse myself in.

After two years, I took the hard step of telling my parents I wanted to leave—I needed to search for a career of my own, an aspiration forbidden to women in Gloriavale.

Before I left I went with my parents to visit their business mentor to finalise how the business would deal with my departure. I made suggestions about how the company could move forward and the mentor must have seen something in me because he turned to Mum and Dad. 'Why don't you make Lil your business manager? It looks like she's wanting more of a challenge seeing she's leaving.'

It was the first time a man had acknowledged my leadership abilities. His next words were even more shocking. 'Lil, how would you feel about owning 50 shares in the company? You'd have a vested interest and it'd give you something to work towards.'

What he didn't realise was that, for the three of us, he was suggesting something unheard of. I'd be in a position of authority and could even get into a situation where I'd have to advise my father. A woman usurping the authority of men? A woman in a position of authority over our group of qualified tradesmen, some of them much older than me?

Would they respect me? How would I lead as a woman, and a young one at that?

I loved my parents and wanted to help them build a future for the family so I accepted the position even though it went directly against the Gloriavale dictates. I was stunned, though, when Dad wholeheartedly agreed with the decision, although part of this didn't surprise me, because he'd been open-minded since the beginning. If he hadn't been, we'd never have been able to leave in the first place. I was so grateful for the opportunity and promised to make him proud.

Over the next few days I thought about how much Gloriavale had stunted my growth. Taking the leadership role was scary but if I wanted to break the cycle of suppression I had to trust myself.

What had Gloriavale qualified me for? Domestic duties and graphic design, not leadership. But I'd managed to find a creative niche for myself despite their determination to keep all women locked in the domestic sphere. And Patie had told me to ignore Grandad's terrible shaming of my school report. So perhaps there were leadership possibilities for me after all. I'd taught myself the design skills and computer expertise that already gave me wider scope than the Gloriavale women's world—that had to mean something.

Even when I'd lived in a church of oppression I hadn't let Gloriavale clip my wings or stifle my gifts. At the next company meeting my Dad announced to the staff my appointment as General Manager.

People told me my parents would never succeed at anything because they'd wasted their best years working for nothing in Gloriavale. I told them my parents had successfully defied a powerful church to bring our family to freedom. If that wasn't success then what was?

I was determined we would succeed and within a year we turned the company around. However, things became more difficult as time passed with Dad getting to the age where crawling under houses wasn't good for his knees and back.

Mum was also tired of running a business and wanted a nine-to-five job so we shut the company down.

I was devastated. I'd thought this business would be my career for the next ten years. Little did I know it was the best thing that could have happened to me in terms of career.

Where to now? In my heart I knew I had a gift for teaching and mentorship. My experience of being in charge of men allowed me to begin dismantling Gloriavale's teaching and gave me the courage to look for a career that was meaningful to me. I had no idea how to go about looking, nor where to begin.

THIRTY-SIX

Falling

When you face your demons head on, then you stand a chance.

—LILIA TARAWA

I still wasn't sure about heaven, hell and God. But if I was on the path to hell I was determined to blaze a bright trail along the way.

I was going out every weekend night. I adored being around lots of people because at Gloriavale I'd been surrounded with cousins and friends. Tired of the hangovers, I stopped drinking alcohol and would often go out to socialise then get my friends safely home. All this time I was learning about my personal style and working out what sort of clothes I wanted to wear.

By now I'd got rid of most of the clothes I'd bought with Sacha. I went to visit cousin Mike, who worked in the salon in

Melbourne. He called Melbourne the 'New York of Australia' because the shopping was so good. He was right. I bought a new wardrobe of clothes and I was obsessed with shoes and just kept buying them. The freedom from the flat shoes of Gloriavale was heady. Stilletos were my absolute favourite. I could hear them calling my name from the store window. I bought anything that took my eye and ended up with around 50 pairs. How wicked! How worldly! How utterly satisfying. I copied the style of movie stars, such as Audrey Hepburn and Emma Watson, and of Marilyn Monroe, who is quoted as saying, 'Give a girl the right pair of shoes and she'll conquer the world.' I could be anyone I wanted to be.

I loved the attention I got from men when I went out. It was the first time in my life I began to think I could perhaps be pretty. If we thought such things in Gloriavale it was regarded as vanity and we got slapped down for it. But my confidence was flourishing without the condemnation of Gloriavale to beat me down.

Now I wore stilletos with a figure-hugging dress that showed off my body. I kept thinking, *Oh my goodness, if my grandfather could see me now.* He would probably try to cast the demon of vanity out of me, but I wouldn't let him because that 'demon' and I were *very* good friends.

I was embracing my sexuality too. I explored the lingerie shop and spent up large on outfits that made me feel sexy—suspenders, thigh-high stockings, corsets—anything and everything forbidden by Gloriavale. The outfits made me feel womanly and I relished the right to choose clothing that accentuated my body.

One night at a bar in Christchurch, I was socialising with friends and became aware of a tall man standing next to me. I looked up to meet a pair of warm green eyes. For a moment we stared at each other before he motioned to my feet, 'I like your shoes.'

I was elated that he'd noticed. 'I love them, too. Aren't they the most amazing shoes you've ever seen?' I flicked up my heel so he could get a better view. They were pastel pink, high strappy heels from Miu Miu all embellished with flowers down the front. I adored the way my legs looked in them.

He smiled at me and I tried to remember to breathe because there was a warm tingling in my belly that meant something extraordinary was about to happen.

You know when you meet someone and introduce yourself, then chat about the weather and maybe comment on your work day or some other petty topic before bidding that person goodbye? Yeah, this was not that.

His name was Peter and when he spoke to me the world shook. Even more, when his green eyes focused on me, what I believed about men came crashing down around me. No man had ever given me the space to feel heard, respected and understood like Pete. For me, coming from a background where men used women as their servants it was so different to meet someone who was gentle, kind and thoughtful. He was so handsome and when his eyes gazed at me I could for once release my loathing of men.

We experienced the most amazing connection. We must have talked for two hours non-stop before he blinked and sat back in amazement. 'Lil, do you see what's happening around us?' I slowly came out of my reverie. Everyone had left and the bar was being packed up. We'd been so lost in each other we didn't even realise.

We kept running into each other at the same bar every week-end. Our conversations were stimulating and we had the same interests in psychology, personal development and human be-haviour. He stood behind me, slipped a hand around my waist and whispered in my ear, 'You're beautiful.'

His energy was so different from Grandad Hopeful's harsh, masculine vibe. Pete's was much more gentle and accepting. I was unused to being around a man who didn't feel the need to be brash and throw his weight around. Deep within, a wounded part of my soul began to heal.

I was falling in love.

∽

My family had been out of the community for almost six years by this time and things were happening on the Gloriavale front too. People were pouring out, including one whole family of my cousins. They informed me that the rebellion of our family had nearly torn the church at Gloriavale apart. My cousin Elijah found out about Hopeful's record of sexual abuse and began questioning our grandfather's ability to lead a church when he had such a record. He wanted to know why people hadn't been told.

Chris Cooke, the TV documentary maker who'd come to Gloriavale to film my Commitment, approached me to ask if I'd be willing to share my story. I thought it might be a good thing to do. It'd give me closure and I'd be able to have my say, which could help counter the uneducated opinions I often heard from people who'd never been to Gloriavale.

It was all arranged. The night before the interviewer Janet McIntyre was flying down to Christchurch, I met Pete at our usual bar. As we walked through the bar men turned their heads to gawk at me and Pete laughed. 'Doesn't the attention bother you?'

'Trust me. I've had people gape at me for much worse reasons than being beautiful,' I said. I hadn't told him that all my life people stared at me because of a strange blue uniform and headscarf. Pete knew nothing of Gloriavale because I was scared if he knew about my bizarre background then he wouldn't be interested in me any more and it would be over between us. I myself hadn't come to terms with it yet.

We had a glass of wine together and I shared with him that something intense was going on in my life.

'Tell me, Lil.'

All I could muster was, 'I'm not like other women that you know. My life has been very different from the norm.' When he urged me to open up to him I couldn't bear it and fled down the street. He caught up with me and took me in his arms.

For a long time that night we sat in silence and I felt comforted just being around him. I was so grateful for his moral support. The television interview the next morning was looming. I was scared.

I went home, got into bed and suddenly the reality of what was going to happen crashed down on me. I'd be telling my story to the nation, to people I didn't know and I was absolutely terrified. Memories flooded back. My heart began pounding. It felt like a weight had plummeted down on me. I couldn't move my legs. I began crying and crying. What was happening? I had no clue why I was such a mess.

I picked up the phone and called Mum. 'I can't breathe. What's wrong with me? I can't do this interview tomorrow.'

'Just tell me what's going on. It's all right. Calm down.'

I gasped out, 'Do you believe in evil spirits? Because there's one here with me. It's come from Gloriavale. It's the evil spirit of fear.' I could feel a black cloud in my room. I knew it wasn't of my own making. I knew it came from those horrific sermons that had been heaped on me. The ghost of Gloriavale was haunting me and I didn't know how I could overcome it. I didn't know what to do.

Mum called a friend who came over and cuddled me all night. I cried for hours and woke in the morning with a headache. I was nauseous and had no appetite.

I asked Mum if she could cancel the interview. 'Tell them I'm sick because I literally can't get out of bed.'

I got a text from the reporter saying they were in Christchurch.

I told her I didn't think it was the right time for me to do the story. I wasn't ready.

The experience was a wake-up call. I realised if I wanted to move forward with my life I had to take charge of what was happening in my mind. I needed to start sharing my history with people who cared about me and could support me.

I sat on the couch with Pete and poured my heart out, stumbling to explain about the place I'd been raised in. I said, 'It would take a book to explain even an ounce of what my life has been like.' When the tears flowed freely he didn't curse me for crying, like Grandad would. Instead he gathered me to his chest and rocked me as I wept in pain.

Finally he said, 'I want to show you something.'

He drove me out to Living Springs, over towards Diamond Harbour, and stopped the car on a hill overlooking the harbour. The view was so beautiful. The lights of Lyttelton Port twinkled in the distance. He said, 'You shared with me, and now I want to share something with you. This is my favourite place in the world.'

In that moment I realised I was deeply in love with him. I didn't know what do with the emotions and knew I was about to burst into another round of tears. 'I'm going back to the car.'

He was sitting on the park bench gazing across the bay. 'I'll be there soon.'

I climbed in the car and turned on my iPhone. The first song that came on was a piano piece that Grandad Hopeful used to play. It took me back to my life in Gloriavale and I realised that for the first time in six years this city of Christchurch felt like home. It was a sense of warmth and love.

The moment my heart opened, grief came crashing down on me. I desperately missed my family in Gloriavale. I hadn't seen them for seven years and I missed Mark and Lani's family so badly. I sobbed uncontrollably. This was the first time that I had been able to grieve for them and for the loss of them. It was the first time I'd truly acknowledged what had happened to me, of how I'd been cheated of them because of Gloriavale's rules forcing me to choose between my family here and my family in there.

For the past six years I'd buried the pain because I didn't have the strength to tackle it head on. The emotion had been too much to bear, but now I wanted healing and I knew unless I let go of Gloriavale and accepted my past then I wasn't going to be able to move into the future.

I set about extracting Gloriavale's claws from my soul. Even though I was no longer there, their teaching chained up my heart and prevented me from experiencing the freedom I wanted in my life. I began working with healing modalities and coaches to, piece by piece, begin stripping back the beliefs Gloriavale had beaten into me.

It meant expunging all the rubbish programmed into my mind about a woman's place, what she must do and what she couldn't, how she must dress, behave, think. I knew it'd be hard work to call a halt on the automatic responses hammered into me since before I could talk.

Dismantling the core inner beliefs was the worst and sent me into a tailspin. The panic attacks hit me hard and frequently. I'd curl in a ball on the floor of my room and sob for hours. I thought I was losing my mind.

When I thought about Gloriavale's brainwashing of us, I pictured my brain being thrown in the laundry machine to be beaten, rinsed and spun. That's what Gloriavale's sermons, rules and campaigns had done. My brain fought desperately to release harmful beliefs so I could be healed.

I was so traumatised because I'd lost control after a lifetime where everything had been so perfectly controlled. Extracting the lies was nightmarish.

I began to project my terror on to my relationship with Pete. The broken Commitment vow was the worst because I believed lifetime commitments were now a load of crap. I loved Pete but I was terrified to lose him. If I'd broken a commitment that I'd once been willing to die for then the only promise life held was the promise of uncertainty.

One day after I'd suffered a panic attack I dragged myself up to stand in front of the mirror. I barely recognised the woman I saw, her eyes were swollen almost shut and her hair was scraggled. Mascara blackened her puffy cheeks.

The voice of my Grandad screamed at me once again, 'You're not good enough,' but it was the fuel I needed. My rebel spirit blazed.

I would not let him defeat me. Ever.

'Enough, Lilia. This is not who you are,' I declared. I wiped my face, showered, brushed out my hair and dressed.

That day I vowed to never again let another person decide my worth, tell me what I could do, decide what I could believe or dictate my future.

I was making a new commitment and this time it was by me, to me and for me.

Grandad's voice hammered my mind and I saw I had to break the pattern if I wanted to end his control. I began creating new beliefs that empowered me.

I started with the teaching that for a woman to think she was beautiful was vanity.

Even though people gave me compliments I blushed and turned away not believing it myself. Now, instead, I thanked them for their kind words. I knew that feeling self-confident and acknowledging personal gifts of beauty and intelligence were key to well-being. I had to silence the critical voice in my head screaming at me: *You're not beautiful. You're not good enough. You can't be a leader. You're bossy. You're stroppy. You're stubborn. We don't want women like you.*

It was Grandad Hopeful's voice.

I set about undoing the damage. I inked on my mirror each morning: *I'm beautiful. I'm sexy. I'm talented. I'm intelligent. I am a leader. I am desirable.*

I read the affirmations aloud, looking at myself while I did so.

Self-love infused my spirit and spun a brand-new identity for Lilia Te Aroha Maia Tarawa. I was practising how to love myself and affirm my worthiness.

For the first time in my life I felt that I was a whole person.

I was becoming a leader, teacher and influencer. Not at all the submissive, subordinate drudge Gloriavale had tried to mould me into. This time I would be the author of my own story.

I broke through many limiting beliefs.

It wasn't easy. I chose to work on my fear of rejection that had been born from the way Gloriavale turned on people and disowned them in a barrage of hate if they didn't submit to church authority. I was terrified that Pete would turn on me in the same way if I didn't do what he said. And I'd been so fearful that my new church friends would cast me out if I no longer chose Christianity as my belief system. I learned to develop respect for my own choices.

Instead of suppressing my emotions as the voice of my grandfather commanded, I learned to listen to my inner self without judgement. I wept freely as the damage Gloriavale had inflicted surfaced. Once I'd built an understanding of the fear responses that drove me, I began allowing myself to feel emotion without having to react to it.

As the spiritual teacher and author Eckhart Tolle puts it, I 'became the observer of my mind'.

THIRTY-SEVEN

Finding myself

No matter my sexual preference, skin colour, gender or belief system, I am worthy of love.

—LILIA TARAWA

I moved in with Pete, but I didn't want him supporting me. Independence was mine now so I needed to find a career quick smart, so I could pay my bills.

All the positions I looked at asked for qualifications I didn't have so I took a job waiting tables in a bar in town.

Although my journey of healing had begun I still didn't feel well, wasn't sleeping properly and was lethargic.

My stomach was in severe pain but it didn't occur to me to get medical help because the Gloriavale teaching was that we just had to be tough and keep on working. To me it was a repeat of when I got terribly sick in Gloriavale with a virus. I'd had a fever and my body was aching. I was moaning and could barely walk. Grace had started to care for me, sitting up all night with me, fetching wheat packs and cooling face cloths until the fever passed.

The next morning Prayer ripped her to shreds, telling her I was just seeking attention. I was lazy and it was only because I was Miracle's daughter that I didn't have to get up and go to work.

So I believed I'd just have to go to bed and ride this one out but I needed help so I rang Mum and told her what was going on in my body. She ordered me to go to the hospital.

That admission resulted in emergency surgery to remove growths in my stomach. I developed an infection in my bowel and one night the pain was so unbearable that my friend Laura drove me to the hospital again. The doctors gave me antibiotics but the infection kept recurring.

In the end, I began thinking there must be another way. I was open-minded about natural ways of healing—no doubt thanks to my Gloriavale upbringing where prayer had been the main healing modality.

Pete's business was in alternative health and he put me on a pharmaceutical grade multi-mineral and antioxidant coupled with calcium, magnesium and fortified fish oil. I started taking a pro-biotic as well to counter the antibiotics killing my gut flora. Within two weeks I had the best sleep I'd ever had in my life. I woke up with so much energy. I'd slept for a full eight hours—so different from my usual four-hour stints of broken sleep.

Within three months my infection had disappeared, never to return. I noticed my endurance was much greater when I exercised and recovery much quicker.

My body was well again and my mind was on the mend. It was time to quit the hated bar job and look for a career. I asked for Pete's advice and he asked me some simple questions: What was important to me? What was I naturally gifted at? How did I want to make a difference? Why?

I realised that supporting people who desired independence and freedom was top of the list, especially women who lived in oppressive environments. I saw millions of people across the world still suffering discrimination in the name of 'God' or extremist belief systems. Sharing my experience of breaking the chains of Gloriavale could be a platform for helping others.

Life's painful lessons had taught me so much that could be valuable to others so I wrote down a goal of wanting to share my knowledge with more people. My regained health and extraordinary life experience had led to people asking me for help with their own mental struggles as well as exercise and nutrition advice.

This was so different from what Gloriavale had told me I could do and I loved it. But I wasn't making a living doing it and that bothered me.

One day my brother's girlfriend who ran her own business from home, a school for nail technicians, asked me why I wasn't running a business in the health and wellness industry. I remember staring at her, open-mouthed. Duh! That was exactly the right question at the right time. It ticked all the boxes. I hugged her and ran straight out the door.

I drove to town and interrupted Pete's business meeting. I wanted to meet his business partner, Michael Harris, who was a success coach and internationally recognised speaker and entrepreneur. Even though I'd scored a part-time role managing the office of a local car sales business, I had so many questions about how I might be able to pursue my goal of helping people break free from the confines of their minds and bodies and make a living doing it. I knew how it felt to be trapped and I wanted to help liberate others. It took many coffee meetings over the next three weeks but at the end of that time I launched my business as a holistic health consultant and business mentor. I began learning, training, teaching, mentoring—all these forbidden things—with other business owners. I began to study the science of the human body and was fascinated with how the mind–body connection so greatly impacted human well-being. I sought out ways to blend spiritual with scientific healing, and through my business I was able to share the knowledge I'd gained with other people. I started to travel, and met incredible people: men and women whose accomplishments blew my mind—but especially the women, because the difference they were making in the world directly opposed Gloriavale's doctrines. It was so enlightening to see women in positions of authority—and even more enlightening to realise I was one of those women.

The moment I started travelling, I fell in love with it. The freedom to explore suited my endless curiosity and my hunger for knowledge. When I was living in Gloriavale, I'd seen a map; I knew perfectly well there was a world wider than New Zealand, but I'd shut myself off from ever dreaming about it because travel away from the church was forbidden.

Now I was truly on the way to leaving Gloriavale behind me. Shockingly, I began to befriend people who were homosexual or bisexual. At first I had no idea what to think about that. It was so wicked according to Gloriavale's standards. They preached against homosexuality, calling it sodomy. They'd quote Leviticus, preaching how people in Old Testament times were put to death for homosexuality. They accused gay men of being effeminate, which was an abomination to God and the church.

They told the story of God destroying the wicked cities of Sodom and Gommorah with fire from heaven and they promised this would be the fate of any who strayed from the natural order of sexuality. People were only to couple with those of the opposite sex for pleasurable or reproductive purposes.

I was shocked to grasp the extent of discrimination rife in Gloriavale—women had been cast aside like dung and anyone who defied Hopeful was strung out to dry. Even my high-born blood granted me privileges that those lower in the pecking order longed for. But had the shade of my skin brought an evil curse upon me? Any religion not born of Hopeful had been cast out as a false church, especially the Roman Catholic church which was accused of being Babylon, the Mother of Harlots—a faithless, compromising whore. Gloriavale was uplifted as the pure virgin bride of Christ and preached an eternity of pain to those who broke away from their narrow and unkind rules. I saw now that Gloriavale, in their righteousness, had fallen into hateful pride and arrogance.

I'd come to the place where I disagreed with Gloriavale's teachings, but I was no longer hateful or resentful towards them. One day I searched the internet to find out what 'outside' people were saying about Gloriavale, and I was stunned by the hatred directed at the community and its members. Some of my friends and family who had left Gloriavale were sharing their stories with the world, and outsiders made comments like, 'These people deserve everything they get', 'They can go to hell at Gloriavale', 'Gloriavale should be burned to the ground' and 'They're murderers'.

I wondered if the people making these comments understood how their abusive barrage mirrored the very behaviour they were accusing Gloriavale of: abuse, discrimination, narrow-mindedness and lack of empathy or compassion. It was hypocrisy.

How would they feel if I cursed their loved ones in the same way? My cousins and childhood friends were still a part of Gloriavale. I had grown up in a loving church community; albeit a community fraught with religious control, but Gloriavale had still taught me useful life skills and had been a tobacco-, drug- and alcohol-free environment, with barely any crime.

I noticed certain media channels latched on to the sexual aspects of Gloriavale's history and wilfully ignored the positive things Gloriavale's lifestyle offered. Viewers and readers gobbled up messages fed to them without pausing to discern if the information was accurate or how it manipulated their perspective. It was the same way Gloriavale's leaders had brainwashed us into subjection by filling our vision with filtered propaganda, except this time it was being done by mainstream media.

I realised so much of humanity had become accustomed to discriminating that they'd forgotten how to love unconditionally.

I was angry and spoke out to my circles of influence: 'We're all products of our environment and culture. We shouldn't be so quick to judge others simply because they are different to us.'

The message struck home even harder when, on a holiday

with friends, I met Jeremy. He was huge fun but at the same time full of depth and wisdom. He was precious to me because he reminded me of my lost cousin, Christopher. His colourful personality often left me helpless with laughter and we shared a mutual love of living life to the fullest. We built a close friendship and travelled overseas together.

I'd known Jeremy for about a year when he came out to his parents and close friends that he was gay. His family was close, just as mine was, and they held strict religious beliefs similar to Gloriavale's regarding homosexuality. Some members of his family did not take the news well and told him they would never accept his homosexuality. Relationships were shattered or, at least, were severely damaged.

It was hard to watch someone I loved and respected go through so much pain when all he wanted was the freedom to be himself. It highlighted how inflexible religious beliefs tore families and friendships apart. I'd learned by now that acceptance and love were far more important than sticking to a rule supposedly decreed by an unknown and unseen God.

Their extremist attitudes reminded me of Grandad Hopeful and strengthened my new personal commitment. No matter my sexual preference, skin colour, gender or belief system—I was worthy of love as was every other creature on the face of the earth.

THIRTY-EIGHT

A new chapter

Transformation and healing don't happen
overnight. They take baby steps, a ton of love
and heaps of honest self-exploration.

—LILIA TARAWA

Sometimes I laugh when I look at the woman I've grown into.
Where I am now as a business-owning agnostic is light years away
from the strictly controlled world of arranged marriages, religious
control and spiritual abuse of Gloriavale.

After I'd been running my business for about a year and come
to terms with the life I'd lived, I wanted to share my story with
more people in the hope that it could inspire others in heart-
wrenching circumstances. The aim was to encourage them not to
be afraid to take risks and to stand up against aggressive authority.

I wanted to demonstrate that it was OK to ask big questions and live outside the box.

When Jenny Hellen from Allen & Unwin approached me about writing my story it felt like things were coming together. I was ready to open up and face my demons.

I started to write down my Gloriavale experiences during a flight to Los Angeles for a business conference. It was so painful to write about leaving my cousins I just wept. I didn't know how I'd be able to write it under such a weight of pain and loss.

I also struggled with the fact that certain members of my family would oppose my decision to share my story. I didn't want to hurt anyone, but I also believed that not talking about it was very damaging. An unattended wound will fester and rot, but if it's cleansed and bandaged then healing can take place. My past life held deep truths about the person I'd become, and for over six years I'd buried it because I lacked the strength to face it. The peculiar thing about Gloriavale was that, no matter how far I ran or how deep I buried my pain, it found a way to haunt me. The truth was incontrovertible and our family's future generations needed to know about their history and be told the courage of their ancestors Honore, Perry and Miracle.

When I got back home, Jeremy's sister-in-law Liberty asked me how work on the book was proceeding. She had a cousin who'd left Gloriavale so she understood more about it than the average person did.

I choked up as soon as I began talking. She took me aside and said, 'Lil, I consider you to be family and there are so many people who support you in this.'

The love of my lost cousins came back to me and filled my

heart. My body shook with sobs while she and her sister Sophia hugged me and rubbed my back as I mourned. 'It's OK, honey. You're so strong.' Their communion touched me and I felt I was receiving back a little of the intimate community Gloriavale had robbed me of. I could feel the love of Bethany, Serena and Chris with me.

'It's important that you write this book. There are so many people going through similar challenges. They need to know there's hope,' Liberty encouraged me.

After that I knew I had to write it but even so, the grief and pain of my loss was raw. For days, I sat at my laptop writing and crying. I'd clutch my chest to try to stop the pain and my night-time dreams were filled with the faces of those I'd lost.

The ghosts of Bethany and Serena haunted me. One night I tossed fitfully and dreamed of a great deep river that flowed through Gloriavale's pastureland. The men built a dam to curb the power of the river, but the sky blackened with rain clouds and I knew a flood was descending.

I tried to warn my cousins of the imminent danger and begged them to run away with me. Only Bethany heeded the plea, but when we fled Righteous chased us with a bloodied machete. We hid in the scrub then dived into the river to escape him, but the torrent swept us to the dam and there he stood, with his weapon raised, waiting to devour us.

I woke in a cold sweat and looked around my room in panic. I was in my home and morning birds sang outside the window. There was no cause to fear, but I knew my dreams exposed dark and hidden secrets.

I began to find solace in discovering that the more I put what had happened to me into words, the more I felt I could close that chapter of my life and open up a new one.

I began contacting family members to let each one know what I was doing. It was so important to have honesty and openness after all the lies and deception of Gloriavale.

I visited Vic at his home to talk to him. He, his partner and their four-year-old daughter, who'd been called Lily, opened their hearts and home to me. I'd been planning to get a dog and that day I crouched beside my little niece showing her pictures on my phone. She had her arm around my back and pressed her cheek against mine, giving a running commentary about each dog. In that moment, I realised there was an alternative reality in which I wouldn't have been allowed to know her or been able to have Vic in my life. My heart soared. I saw clearly that leaving Gloriavale had enabled me to be with my family and love them without guilt or judgement.

Vic had some reservations about the book, as did many others of my family, but he was supportive and appreciated that I'd come to tell him what I was doing. He liked that I wanted it to be about healing and overcoming challenge. Both of us wanted the truth to be told.

My grandfather's systematic brainwashing of me as a child was being undone. I'd overcome the fear of losing my salvation if I didn't submit my will to church leaders. The terror of being doomed to an eternity of hell because of unsanctioned choices was gone.

My only commitment now was to myself, my whole self, not the stunted self my grandfather demanded. I knew I'd now tapped into something far beyond Gloriavale's idea of God.

No longer could someone control me through the promise of heaven or the fear of hell. Any knowledge I sought or life experience I desired was available to me. I knew that Sara, my brothers and people on the outside of Gloriavale weren't the wicked sinners we'd been told. And I'd discovered it was possible to seek Christian faith outside of Gloriavale, should one so choose.

The bond of love and loyalty in our family had grown immensely through our reunion and mutual defiance of Gloriavale's control. I had so much respect for my parents' courage to wrestle with their ingrained religious beliefs and rescue us from Gloriavale's extreme rule.

The pressure to be a good Gloriavale Christian, or a Christian at all, was gone. Whatever path my life took I would now always trust my intuitive guidance, face my fears head on and remain open to new possibilities. My world view had been permanently altered.

By now, I also knew that fighting my past would only bring me grief.

I hadn't been back to Gloriavale since we'd left eight years before. But in January 2017, I felt strongly that it was time to return. We'd had to leave so abruptly and I still mourned not being able to farewell my cousins. I wanted to talk to Grandad Hopeful too. I had so many questions and I wanted him to understand how much he'd hurt me. Sometimes I even imagined him begging me to forgive him.

I got a call from Vic who was on holiday with his family at Moana. 'We're going up to Gloriavale tomorrow. I've called Grandad Hopeful and asked if we can come in peace. Little Lily needs to meet her great-grandfather and I want to reconcile with him. Want to come?'

'Yes. I'll be there.' It felt like things were falling into place.

All my siblings decided to go, but my parents had to stay behind at Moana because they weren't welcome at the Church. Gloriavale called my mother a witch. They said Dad was taken with the Devil. There was so much I needed to call my grandfather to account over.

We were careful to dress in modest clothing that wouldn't cause any trouble for us while we were there. I hated getting back into a long dress. It felt like a straitjacket.

When I arrived at Moana, Sara got in my face. 'Now, Lil, we're going in peace. This isn't the time for you to challenge Grandad's beliefs or start any philosophical or religious discussions.'

She knew me so well. I scowled and told her to mind her own business. Neville could do with an earful from someone. He had so much to answer for. Why go in peace to someone who'd torn your family apart for years? There were so many things that needed saying and I wasn't happy to pretend all was sweetness and light while he swept the hard stuff under the rug and ignored the past. I was open to forgiving and letting go of the past, but I wanted answers.

But I'd learned by now that just because I felt angry that didn't mean I had to react to it. The little kids were with us so I decided I'd be peaceful for their sake and not start an argument with my grandfather.

When our convoy drove on to the farmland property it was surreal. Eighteen years of my life—left behind here.

Sara and the boys tooted and hooted to announce our arrival.

What a crazy experience. The renegades ride again. We laughed so much, buoyed up by the fact that we'd even been granted permission to return on a visit. It was a massive triumph for us.

I had no idea, though, how it was going to go. I was so nervous.

The very moment we got out of the cars Hopeful was waiting for us at the front entrance. We all hugged him even though he didn't know who half of us were. He didn't give us the chance to run off and talk to anyone else, but ushered us into the Meeting Room where the leaders had shredded our father.

The girls brought us apple juice and chocolate chip cookies while Grandad launched into a tirade using the script I'd heard so many million times before. I'd learned a lot about social behaviours and good communication through my experience as a business owner, but Grandad didn't try to connect with us. He bragged about how many children Gloriavale had, how many businesses they owned, and why they chose to live in community. It was as if he didn't realise we were his family and that us older ones had grown up hearing this rubbish over and over.

He asked Vic one question about what industry he worked in. That was his single question and everything else was about Gloriavale. I realised he was so narcissistic that he'd forgotten how to connect and empathise with others.

We asked if we could walk around but he didn't want us to be able to talk to anyone and he himself took us on a tour of the buildings. They all looked shabbier and more run down than they had eight years before. He bragged about everything but I was now seeing the place of my childhood through the eyes of an adult woman who had travelled the world. It wasn't as glamorous as the picture I'd held in my memory.

The only building worth bragging about was the new school complex. It was massive. He told us it was a kitset building they'd imported and the men had whacked it all together in a really short time. He was proud that it was the biggest building of its type in the southern hemisphere and that it was valued at more than $10 million.

On our walk, we saw a couple of our cousins but weren't given the chance to do more than give them a wave and a quick hello. It was horrible. I wanted so much to see and talk with the people I'd grown up with.

When the tour ended, Hopeful took us to the front door and left us to get back in our cars. At that last minute, just as we were about to get in, we bumped into a group of our old friends. There was just time for a quick chat before one of the leaders would come out and we didn't want to get our friends in trouble. I could tell they'd have loved to have talked to us properly, it was easy to see their fascination at how we were dressed and how surprised they were to see us again. They were loving and receptive to us—a complete contrast to how Grandad Hopeful had treated us.

One of the girls said, 'Tell your Mum that we appreciate and love her so much for everything she did for our community.'

They hurried away but I ran over and called urgently to one of the girls, 'Can you tell Bethany that I love her and miss her?'

There was so much to process once we got back to Moana. My cousins came over and we sat talking for hours.

For me, the visit was a turning point. I knew now that the only way to move forward was to understand my history and look at it for what it honestly was. Hopeful's behaviour during our visit exposed so much about who he really was.

I began researching the sexual history of Gloriavale for the book. I needed to fully understand the subject that had never been talked about as I was growing up. I asked Mum to tell me honestly what had gone on and the causes of it. In the process, I was challenging again the lies Gloriavale had fed us all my life and again I was searching for the truth.

I'd known my grandfather had been sent to prison for sexual offending but I'd more or less accepted the leaders' spin on the reasons. I'd certainly never confronted my own opinions about it.

As I collected more information it shocked me how ignorant I'd been, but I was more shocked to realise how Grandad used Bible teachings to justify the things he'd done. He'd preached that people in the world take anything good and turn it into something bad. He said they took his good actions in 'helping' people who were getting married and turned it into sexual abuse. He'd used the same twisted logic in so many instances to justify his actions. He was the grandfather I had loved and committed my life to as a child and only now was I discovering the extent of his control over me.

Neville had exercised his position of authority to the point where nobody could refuse to obey him even if they wanted to. I was saddened for the vulnerable people whose lives had been destroyed by his actions. I was also deeply concerned about his teachings that children are ready for marriage the moment they sexually develop. Neville would have happily married off children of ten or twelve years of age if the law had permitted it. If the laws of New Zealand hadn't protected me as a child, then he most likely would have arranged my marriage as a twelve-year-old girl.

The realisation helped me come to terms with the fact that my grandfather was an extremist cult leader who abused the power he wielded over his community. I, too, had been a victim of his totalitarian, despotic rule. It wasn't going to define me any longer.

Now that I've more fully accepted where I've come from, I am able to embrace a future entirely different from my Gloriavale fate. There are now people in my life who won't disown me, who open-heartedly love me, no matter my life choices. My parents, Vic and his family, Grace, Pete, Liberty and Jeremy are such people.

I am very grateful to have been raised in Gloriavale, because the community way of living showed me how to build deep relationships with my friends and cousins there. Even though those relationships have been ripped from me and are not intact today, I appreciate the value they brought to my childhood.

There are also practical life skills that I have as a result of being raised in Gloriavale, and I have benefited hugely from having such an intelligent mother. Friends often compliment me on my cooking skills and tell me how awesome it is that I know how to sew, spin, knit and read music. I am surprised by how many women my age outside Gloriavale are ignorant in these realms, but that is the world we live in.

Above all, my past life in Gloriavale has been the catalyst for the work I am now so passionate about: liberating those trapped by their minds and bodies. Helping them fight for freedom. My past is the fuel to my fire and the reason I bound out of bed each day.

It's empowering to live according to the guiding intuition of my heart, which was always present but for so long was viciously suppressed. I no longer accept absolute truths; instead, I choose to live against the grain, adopt new beliefs and explore diverse philosophies.

Transformation and healing don't happen overnight. They take baby steps, a ton of love and heaps of honest self-exploration. You have to be willing to get uncomfortable, stay open-minded and speak up for what you believe in.

It is the best rebellion.

Acknowledgements

A big thank you to everyone who made this book possible.

To Jenny Hellen at Allen & Unwin, who oversaw the project from start to finish. Thank you for your professional guidance and encouragement.

An overwhelming thanks to Fleur Beale for your mentorship, prowess and compassionate sensibility during this process.

To my mother, Miracle Tarawa, my number-one supporter, friend and confidante. Thank you for standing by me. I love you.

Most especially, to Graciela Hoover, my most loyal and loving friend. Your contribution, both practical and emotional, has been priceless. This story would not have been possible without you.